Poptropica® English

TEACHER'S EDITION 3

Space Island

Aaron Jolly • Viv Lambert
Series advisor: David Nunan

Contents

Scope and sequence

Welcome

Vocabulary: **Numbers:** twenty-one to fifty
Days of the week: Sunday, Monday, Tuesday, Wednesday, Thursday, Friday, Saturday
Months of the year: January, February, March, April, May, June, July, August, September, October, November, December

Structures: What's your favorite day? My favorite day is Sunday.
When were you born? I was born in January.
Were you born in May? Yes, I was. / No, I wasn't. I was born in June.

1 Nature

Vocabulary: **Nature:** birds, sun, clouds, trees, animal, pond, mushrooms, rock, insects, flowers, butterflies, wind, ants, sky, worms, spiders, roses, rainbow

Structures: How many animals are there? There's one purple animal.
How many birds are there? There are two blue birds.
There are some spiders. / There aren't any spiders.
Is there a rainbow? Yes, there is. / No, there isn't.
Is there any wind? Yes, there's some wind. / No, there isn't any wind.
Are there any ants? Yes, there are. / No, there aren't.

Values: Play outside. Play safe!

Cross-curricular: **Math:** Plus, minus, equals

Phonics: air, ear
hair, year

2 Me

Vocabulary: **Physical characteristics:** blond hair, dark eyebrows, brown eyes, curly hair, gray hair, glasses, a black mustache, a short beard, blue eyes, red hair, black beard, white teeth, big chin, long eyelashes, pink lips, red nose, big mouth

Structures: I have glasses.
I don't have glasses.
He has dark eyebrows.
She doesn't have dark eyebrows.
Do you have long eyelashes? Yes, I do. / No, I don't.
Does he/she have curly hair? Yes, he/she does. / No, he/she doesn't.

Values: Have good habits. Keep clean and healthy.

Cross-curricular: **Science:** Wild animals

Phonics: ay, er
say, dinner

3 Pets

Vocabulary: **Animal body parts:** tail, beak, wings, feathers, claws, fins, paws, whiskers, skin, fur
Animal characteristics: soft fur, a hard shell, sharp claws
Adjectives: cute, scary, fast, slow

Structures: What does it look like? It has a tail. It doesn't have wings.
What do they look like? They have whiskers. They don't have fins.
Do you have a dog? Yes, I do. It's cute. / No, I don't.
Does it have soft fur? Yes, it does. / No, it doesn't.

Values: Take care of your pet.

Cross-curricular: **Science:** Animal life cycles

Phonics: ea, oi
tea, oil

4 Home

Vocabulary: **Furnishings:** picture, stove, sofa, shower, sink, mirror, trash can, TV, computer, plant, closet, window
Prepositions: next to, behind, above, below, in front of
Household items: toothbrush, towels, pots, blankets, comb, shelf, pans, plates

Structures: There's a plant in the living room.
There are two plants in the living room.
The plant is below the mirror. / It's below the mirror.
The plants are below the mirror. / They're below the mirror.
Is the computer in the bedroom? Yes, it is. / No, it isn't. It's in the living room.
Are the plates on the shelf? Yes, they are. / No, they aren't. They're in the sink.

Values: Help at home.

Cross-curricular: **Art:** Mosaics

Phonics: a_e, i_e, o_e
cake, time, home

5 Clothes

Vocabulary: **Clothing:** a baseball cap, a sweatsuit, a polo shirt, shirt, shorts, jeans, a belt, a uniform, a jacket, a sweatshirt, flip-flops, sneakers, sandals, beanie, hiking boots, scarf, tights, ski jacket, wool sweater
Material/style: plain, colorful, fancy

Structures:
What are you wearing? I'm wearing a baseball cap/sandals.
What's he/she wearing? He's/She's wearing a baseball cap/sandals.
Are you wearing a baseball cap/sandals? Yes, I am. / No, I'm not.
Is he/she wearing a baseball cap/sandals? Yes, he/she is. / No, he/she isn't.
This is my favorite scarf.
These are my favorite tights.
I love my scarf/tights.

Values: Be polite.

Cross-curricular:
Social science: Household chores

Phonics: **sc, sk, sm, sn, sp, squ, st, sw**
scarf, skate, smell, snip, spoon, squid, star, swim

6 Sports

Vocabulary: **Abilities:** do taekwondo, catch a ball, play tennis, run, play baseball, ride a bike, play basketball, play soccer
Sports facilities: gym, baseball field, basketball court, running track, stadium, ski slope, beach, swimming pool, tennis court, soccer field

Structures:
I/He/She can run and jump.
I/He/She can run, but I/he/she can't jump.
Can you/he/she play tennis? Yes, I/he/she can. / No, I/he/she can't.
I/He/She was at the gym.
I/He/She wasn't at the gym. I/He/She was at the baseball field.

Values: Be active.
Exercise every day.

Cross-curricular:
Health: Exercise

Phonics: **bl, fl, gl, pl, sl**
black, flag, glass, plate, sleep

7 Food

Vocabulary: **Fruit/vegetables:** peas, mangoes, carrots, cucumbers, plums, oranges, peaches, potatoes, tomatoes, strawberries, beans, broccoli, lettuce, spinach, cabbage, pears, apricots, avocadoes, cherries

Structures:
Do you like peas? Yes, I do. / No, I don't.
Does he/she like peas? Yes, he/she does. / No, he/she doesn't.
Is there any broccoli? Yes, there is. / No, there isn't.
Are there any pears? Yes, there are. / No, there aren't.

Values: Stay healthy. Eat more fruit and vegetables.

Cross-curricular:
Science: Healthy eating plate

Phonics: **br, cr, dr, fr, gr, pr, str, tr**
brown, crab, drop, frog, green, press, string, train

8 Things we do

Vocabulary: **Actions:** listening to music, walking, sleeping, reading, doing homework, drinking, eating, cleaning, dancing, playing the piano, playing the trumpet, playing the flute, playing the violin, singing
Adverbs of manner: quickly, quietly, terribly, loudly, slowly

Structures:
What are you doing? I'm sleeping.
What are they doing? They're sleeping.
What's he/she doing? He's/She's sleeping.
Are you singing? Yes, I am. / No, I'm not.
Is he/she singing? Yes, he/she is. / No, he/she isn't.
Is he/she singing quietly? Yes, he/she is. / No, he/she isn't. He's/She's singing loudly.

Values: Learn new things.
Develop your talents.

Cross-curricular:
Science: Flying machines

Phonics: **ft, mp, nd, nt, sk, sp, st**
left, bump, wind, paint, ask, wisp, nest

Introduction

Dear Teachers,

Welcome!

It is my pleasure to introduce you to *Poptropica English*. This is the most exciting and important series for teaching English to young learners on the market today. It is designed to educate learners for the twenty-first century. This involves more than teaching learners to communicate in English. It also involves helping learners to socialize and work cooperatively, to have a sense of responsibility to others, to develop their ability to reflect on their learning processes, and to begin learning and using English independently.

The series is based on some key educational principles. The most important of these is that of catering to the whole learner. This means that you are not just responsible for developing the ability of learners to communicate through English, you are also responsible for their emotional, social, and moral development. This is a very challenging task, but *Poptropica English* will provide you with resources to help you meet that challenge.

Through these materials, learners engage with English by using it in a wide range of interesting and fun situations that relate to their everyday lives. Yes, they have to learn vocabulary and master the pronunciation and grammar of the language, but they do so through engaging tasks that keep them motivated and show them the relevance of English to their lives beyond the language classroom.

The journey from infancy to adulthood is an amazing adventure, of which language learning is a part. I hope that you enjoy taking your students on the adventure with *Poptropica English*.

David Nunan
Series Advisor
Poptropica English

Poptropica English is a six-level course for children learning English at primary level. It offers best practice methodology in the classroom, while also offering teachers and students an innovative digital environment in the shape of the unique **Poptropica English World**.

Poptropica English is designed to provide teachers and students with a truly blended English language learning environment. It takes into account the current movement towards using an increased amount of technology in the classroom, and also at home, as more and more families use computers and want safe, effective, educational material for their children.

Poptropica English motivates children by introducing them to **Poptropica English World**, an online area which extends and enhances their learning. Students are introduced to a group of **Poptropicans** in an **Island Adventure Game** that echoes their books. Children follow the characters through their book, while listening to stories, singing songs, communicating, and playing games along the way. Most importantly, students will enjoy themselves, and make their own discoveries in English.

Methodology

Poptropica English assumes no previous knowledge of English and takes a "5Ps" approach to communication in order to provide support and encourage production from an early stage. The PPP (Presentation, Practice, and Production) method is a tried and tested approach which is favored by many teachers in the primary classroom. The lesson sequence is clear and easy to follow and works in a structured way. The **Poptropica English** "5Ps" approach adds also Personalization and Pronunciation.

Presentation is the first stage. The teacher demonstrates the key language, while providing a model (on audio or **Poptropica English World**) for students to hear the correct pronunciation.

Practice is provided in the form of controlled and more open activities, using the presented language.

Production activities encourage students to use the language either to speak or write something. These activities encourage students to become more autonomous, and to manipulate the language in order to communicate.

Personalization activities are also included in the lesson structure to engage students further with the unit language, and to help them with language recall.

Pronunciation is a key area in language teaching, and it is addressed in all units. Students practice it through fun and engaging songs and chants that help them acquire the stress, rhythm, and intonation of English.

Cross-Curricular Teaching

Children are naturally curious about the world around them. They want to know how nature works (natural science), how man's inventions function (technology), they are drawn to the exciting stories behind man's achievements and artistic creations (history/art), as well as the fascinating landscapes and customs of far-away places (geography/social science). Therefore, it seems natural and appropriate for their foreign language classroom to provide opportunities for them to explore this world, and to integrate the resulting knowledge and understanding with language learning.

Here are some other reasons for integrating content with language learning, and some tips for making the most of the cross-curricular pages in **Poptropica English**:

- Young students already bring an incredible amount of previous knowledge of the world to the language-learning classroom.

Tip 1: Start the lesson by inviting students to focus on the images on the page and ask a few warm-up questions, e.g., *What can you see on the page? What is the lesson about? What do you know about the topic? What else would you like to know?* Use the children's first language if necessary.

- What the students hear or read about a topic can later provide realistic reasons for speaking and writing about it.

Tip 2: As the students do the activities in the lesson, highlight any new vocabulary relating to the topic, and gather it in a simple diagram on the board. At the end of the lesson, invite the students to copy the diagram into their notebooks for later reference.

- Cross-curricular lessons can lead to very motivating individual or small group projects.

Tip 3: Invite students to read the instructions and help them visualize what the end product will be (a written list of physical exercises, possibly illustrated with drawings or photos, or a poster with pictures, captions, and a short text describing an animal from their country). Help students think about what to write, how to draft and edit and, finally, how to make it look nice (layout, design). Depending on the time available, allow students to do the project in class, or write a draft in class and complete the project at home.

- Mini projects can lead to research opportunities.

Tip 4: Help the students brainstorm sources of information for their mini project (the school library, the Internet, an "expert" from school, a relative or family friend). Teach them to gather – and check the relevance and reliability of – information.

Tip 5: You might like to give students feedback. You could give students two stars and one wish e.g., *Beautiful pictures!, Excellent coloring! Add one more picture label.* This could be given in L1.

Phonics

Poptropica English uses a systematic phonics approach adapted for EFL students. The phonemes of the English language are taught in a set sequence, which starts with the most frequent letter-sounds, and allows students to begin reading decodable words from the start. The approach builds on phonemic awareness to develop an understanding of the alphabetic code. Teaching and practice is focused on getting students to blend letter-sounds for reading, and to segment sounds for spelling, and to understand that these processes are reversible. Carefully selected words and added picture support adapt the approach for young EFL students.

Working Terminology

Phonemic awareness	The ability to hear the constituent sounds that make up a word. For example, students hear the word *shell* and can orally break it down into its three sounds: *sh-e-ll*.
Phoneme	The smallest unit of sound in a word. There are 44 phonemes in English. These phonemes can be represented in print in many different ways. For example, the sound f can be written as *f* in *fan*, or as *ph* in *dolphin*.
Grapheme	The representation of sound in print. Not only can a phoneme have many different graphemes to represent it, but one grapheme can represent different phonemes. For example, the grapheme *th* can be voiced as *this*, or unvoiced as *thin*.
Letter names	Written as words in the audio script, for example, *cee* for the letter *c*.
Letter-sound	Term to express that both the grapheme and phoneme are the teaching focus.
Blend / Decode / Sound out	The process of looking at the graphemes in a word and sounding out each phoneme to read out the word. For example, a student sees the word *cat* and then blends out loud c-a-t to read the word *cat*.
Segment / Encode	The process of hearing the phonemes in a word and being able to recall the graphemes to spell that word. For example, a student hears the word *cat* and recalls the graphemes *c a t* to write the word *cat*. Blending and segmenting are reversible processes.

Poptropica English phonics lessons take the following path:

Warm-up and review (optional)

Reviewing previously introduced letter-sounds is important as each unit builds on the next and all known letter-sounds are incorporated into each unit as they are taught. The suggested warm-up activities in the lesson plans provide the following review sequence:

1 Letter-recognition skills needed for reading.

2 Letter-recall skills needed for spelling.

3 Phonemic awareness — blending graphemes; segmenting phonemes.

Present new letter-sounds

Students hear the phoneme followed by the word, and can see the grapheme on the page. Alternatively, the teacher can teach this stage before opening the book, by writing the letters on the board, eliciting the letter names, and modeling the sounds.

Initial practice of new letter-sounds

Students identify the phoneme and try saying the letter-sound themselves.

Blending letter-sounds to read words

This is the main focus of the phonics lesson. Spend a lot of time on this stage. Give students as much time as they need to grasp the concept of blending the letter-sounds, so they can become successful at reading. Blending can be done using the book but there are many variations that you might like to try. For suggested activities, see the individual lesson plans.

Supported practice of reading

Students apply their knowledge to read a selection of words or sentences. The words or sentences are illustrated to support students' understanding of what they are reading.

Reading and spelling (optional)

Spelling is practiced through the Workbook, so it is a good idea to dedicate some time to segmenting for spelling in class. Each unit presents a different extension activity, which can be used like an activity bank with any of the phonics lessons.

What is Assessment for Learning?

Poptropica English includes elements of **Assessment for Learning** methodology, which help to enhance learning by supporting students in understanding what they know and what they need to do next, empowering them to move themselves forward, and making them active in their own learning, as well as helping teachers understand where their students are. **Assessment for Learning** is looking for ways to understand how students are doing, and using this information to help them improve, and to also help teachers make decisions about how to help students improve.

Assessment: isn't this testing?

It can be, but when we talk about **Assessment for Learning**, we're really talking about assessing students formatively, watching and listening to our students to see how far they understand, and using this to help decide what we need to do next. This can be during any activity in class, the kind of assessment you already do every day!

Why is Assessment for Learning important in Poptropica English?

Poptropica English provides fun and engaging material to help your students have an exciting and motivating early experience with English. A handful of **Assessment for Learning** techniques and activities have been integrated into each lesson, to build on this positive experience. These activities give students an awareness of what and how they are learning, and give you, the teacher, lots of opportunities to assess how each student is doing. Introducing the **learning adventure** in your classes to talk about students' learning, makes each step along their English language adventure visible and interactive, engaging and motivating students while also developing self-assessment skills.

What is the learning adventure?

The **learning adventure**, based on each of the **Poptropica English Islands**, is a path which represents how confident the student feels about a particular learning objective. Using this poster in class enables students to develop self-assessment skills, by reflecting on how well they can remember vocabulary, for example, from the lesson or unit. It can also help gather evidence for the teacher on who is confident about the lesson, and who needs more practice.

Where is the learning adventure used?

The **learning adventure** is used in *Vocabulary*, *Cross-curricular*, *I can do it!*, and *Wider World* lessons.

How do I introduce the learning adventure to my students?

It's a good idea to model with students how to use the **learning adventure** poster. The **learning adventure** poster can be put in the classroom, and the image is used in a sequence of activities, using both the Student Book and accompanying teacher's notes, and in **Poptropica English World** for class presentation.

There are four steps on the **learning adventure**:

1 ***Let's go!*** – This means that students have started a new learning objective and are at the beginning of their learning; maybe they know one or two words.

2 ***I'm on my way!*** – This means that students are moving along their journey with increasing understanding or knowledge; maybe they know five or six words.

3 ***I'm almost there!*** – This means that students are feeling increasingly confident about what they have learned, and have a good (though not necessarily 100%) knowledge or understanding.

4 ***I've arrived!*** – This means that students are very confident about what they have learned, and have a good (though not necessarily 100%) knowledge or understanding.

How do I use the poster with my class?

It's really useful if you can have the poster on the wall for every class. The poster is used in two different ways.

For Vocabulary, Cross-curricular, and Wider World lessons.

The poster works in the same sequence each time and the lesson plans show you exactly when and how. Every lesson begins with ***student-friendly objectives*** – these will appear in the teacher's notes for each lesson. You can write these on the board, or if you are using **Poptropica English World**, the objectives appear on screen at the start of each lesson sequence. The first activity in these classes is ***What do you know?*** – this is a Student Book activity asking students which words they know on this topic before the main class presentation. This will find out what students already know about a topic, engage them, and give students confidence that they know something already. Now, using the poster, ask the students, *Where are you on your learning adventure?* Ask students to think about how many words they know, and to say which stage on the poster they think they are at, e.g. if they know two or three words, they might say, *Let's go!* as they are at the beginning of their learning. You should respond positively, as they are already moving along their learning adventure! At the end of the lesson, ask the students again, *Where are you on your learning adventure?* Students think how many words they know now, and choose a stage on the poster, e.g. if they know eight words they might say, *I know teddy bear, car, kite, doll, boat, bike, ball, train*. It's a good idea to remind students of where they were at the beginning of the lesson, and where they are now, to really emphasize the progress they are making.

I can do it!

The poster is used to help students develop the skills needed to identify what they know and what they don't know, to help them focus and move themselves forward. With practice, this should make learning more efficient, produce confident students not afraid to ask for help from teachers and classmates, and underline that everyone can make progress. As with every lesson, we begin with ***Student-friendly objectives***. We ask students, *What can you remember?* This activity asks students to recall what topics/language they learned in the previous unit. Ask students, *Where are you on your learning adventure?* For each topic/language area, ask students to say where they are on their learning adventure. The students then complete a set of activities to help them review and consolidate the unit topic/language.

What other Assessment for Learning activities are there, and why should I use them?

What do you know? – Asks students if they know any words associated with the unit topic before the main class presentation.

Students will feel confident that they already know some words from the topic so they aren't at the beginning of their learning.

Pop Quiz – Gives you a quick end-of-lesson activity to help you check where who has "got it" and who needs more help.

Provides opportunities to see where students are in their learning, and helps you provide useful feedback and adjust your teaching in line with individual needs.

Extension questions – Asks students a question to help extend their thinking and learning.

Requires more than only remembering what they have learned, and illustrates that they have understood it.

I can do it! – Self-assessment lessons develop students' skills to assess where they are in their learning, and what they need to do next to achieve their learning goals, motivating them to continue learning.

Developing the skills to identify what you know and what you don't forms a huge part of learning. With practice, this should facilitate learning and produce confident students, not afraid to ask for help from teachers and their classmates.

When can I use the learning adventure?

You can use the **learning adventure** in any lesson with any learning objectives. For students new to this concept, it's good to begin with vocabulary, as it's easy to identify what you know and have learned.

What if my students do not use the learning adventure accurately?

It doesn't matter too much about accuracy. They aren't giving themselves grades, they are simply increasing their awareness about their own learning. What matters is helping your students to increase their awareness by modelling how to use the poster, using examples to show how many words you might know for each stage on the poster. Also, by encouraging students to think of their progress more positively if they underestimate on the **learning adventure**. Or, if students indicate too confidently where they are, ask students to think a little more carefully about how many words they can remember, for example. For strong students, keep them motivated by asking them to find out more about the topic or new words on the topic. Also, using the poster regularly in class will help students integrate this into their learning more easily.

What if my students are very shy?

If students don't want to say where they are, you can make cards that students can hold up in class. Each student can make a card for each stage, e.g., *Let's go.*

Components

For the student

- Four *Wider World* units;
- Four *Review* units;
- *Goodbye* unit to consolidate and wrap up;
- Festival pages in the back of the book;
- Picture dictionary;
- Activity stickers for further consolidation of language.

Poptropica English World is an online area where students can find a variety of resources which enhance their learning:

- the **Poptropica English Island Adventure Game**, which provides a safe, engaging, and highly-motivating environment where students meet the characters from the Student Book plus a host of other exciting characters, and follow them on an adventure. Students will engage in safe, "closed-chat" dialogs with the characters they meet, and will practice target language from the units. They will also follow instructions to help them solve puzzles, and learn supplementary language along the way. The **Poptropica English Island Adventure Game** is a great tool to make learning happen in an interactive way, and it further consolidates and extends the language learning process. Most of all, students will enjoy learning through play and will absorb English without realizing it!
- **homework** assigned by their teachers and automatically graded;
- **extra online games** to consolidate the language introduced in the classroom;
- **songs and chants** for the course;
- **videos** for the course, which contain four animated stories with **Poptropica English** characters.

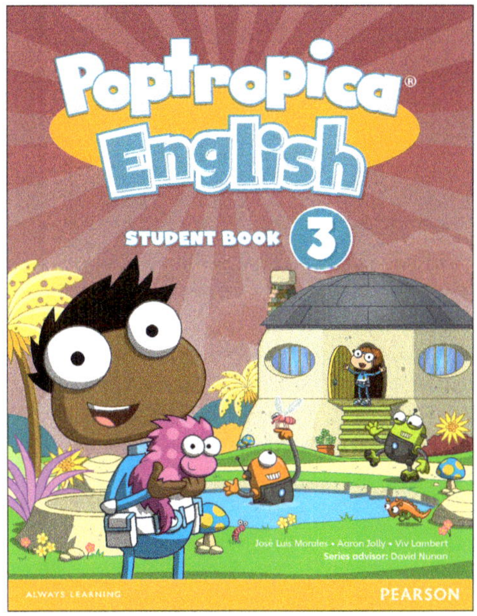

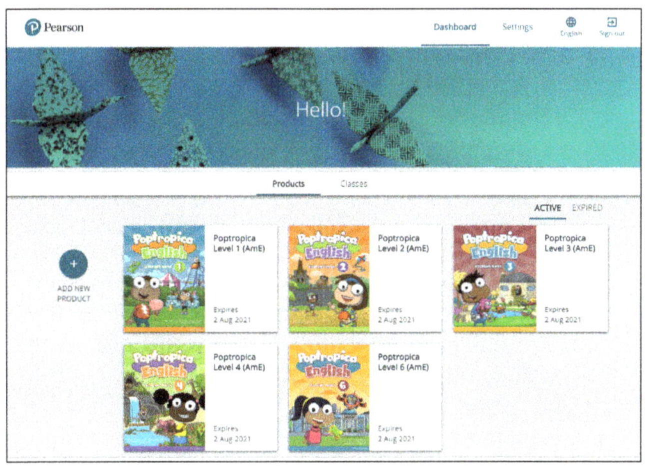

For the parent

Parents also have access to **Poptropica English World**, through their child's account and can track their children's achievements.

The **Workbook** provides reinforcement and consolidation of the language presented in the Student Book. It contains controlled and freer practice, plus personalization, further listening, and reading texts.

The accompanying **CD** contains all the audio for the listening activities in the Workbook.

For the teacher

The **Teacher's Edition** provides step-by-step lesson plans covering all the Student Book material.

Each lesson plan is clearly structured into stages:

- Warm-up activities;
- Step-by-step lesson plans;
- Pop Quiz.

The lesson notes are designed to be flexible support for all teachers, including those who may lack time for planning or who have limited access to resources. The Introduction includes recommended procedures for using games and stories effectively, and how **Poptropica English World** can be best exploited. For maximum flexibility and variety, the following **photocopiable materials** can be found in the Teacher's Edition:

- Story Cards;
- Activity Sheets;
- Tests.

Poptropica English World is one online location where teachers, students, and parents can find all the materials and tools which can be used inside and/or outside the classroom with **Poptropica English**. Teachers can use it for lesson preparation, for delivering lessons, to assign and track homework, to monitor students' performance, and to manage their classes. The resources available to teachers include:

- Online lessons which let you present the material using an interactive whiteboard or projector. The lessons contain activities mirroring the sequence of material introduced in the Student Book and in the Teacher's Edition but in an interactive format best suited to a digital experience. The lessons also contain all the audio for the course. An offline version of the lessons is also available.
- Assignable online **homework** with automatic grading;
- A tool for **tracking the performance** of both individual students and the whole class;
- Extra resources like **tests, worksheets, videos, posters,** and **Picture Cards**;
- Access to the **Poptropica English Island Adventure Game**, in which students can meet characters from the book in a safe, engaging, and motivating environment. The game consolidates and extends the material covered in the Student Book.
- **Poptropica English World** can also be used by parents and students at home. It will allow students to access extra activities and will give parents the opportunity to monitor their child's progress.

You will find more information on **Poptropica English World** on pages 13–15.

The **Class Audio CDs** contain all the songs (including karaoke versions), chants, stories, and listening activities which appear in the Student Book. They also contain audio for tests which are available in the Teacher's Edition. All the audio is also available online as part of **Poptropica English World**.

The **Picture Cards** present main target vocabulary in each unit. The teaching notes in the Teacher's Edition clearly explain how the Picture Cards can be used to present, practice, and consolidate language through games and activities. The Picture Cards are also available online as part of **Poptropica English World**.

The **posters** accompanying the course are of two types. **Learning adventure** posters help students and teachers gain awareness of what and how the students are learning. **Vocabulary** posters serve as another tool for teaching and consolidating vocabulary. All posters are also available online as part of **Poptropica English World**.

The **videos** are available in **Poptropica English World**. They give students a new context in which to recycle the language of the Student Book.

The **Tests** (Placement Test, Unit Tests, Review Tests, and End of Level Test) can be found at the back of the Teacher's Edition. The audio for these tests is on the Audio CD. These tests and the audio are also available online, as part of **Poptropica English World**.

Poptropica English World

Poptropica English has been designed as a course in which all the components are aligned to provide best practice methodology and an innovative digital environment, both inside and out of the classroom. The print components and the **Poptropica English World** environment allow teachers to choose varying degrees of blended learning approach in their lessons, depending on their situation.

What is Poptropica English World?

Poptropica English World is one online location where teachers, students, and parents can find materials and tools which can be used inside and/or outside the classroom with **Poptropica English**.

Poptropica English World consists of two main areas:

Teacher area

This is an area that teachers can use for lesson preparation, for delivering lessons, to assign and track homework, to monitor students' performance, and to manage their classes. It contains online lessons, which enable lessons to be delivered with an interactive whiteboard or projector. An offline version of the lessons is also available. It also contains **assignable online homework**. It has a tool for **tracking the performance** of both individual students and the whole class. It also has **extra resources** to use in the class, such as tests, videos, posters, and Picture Cards, and allows teachers download access to the **Poptropica English Island Adventure Game**.

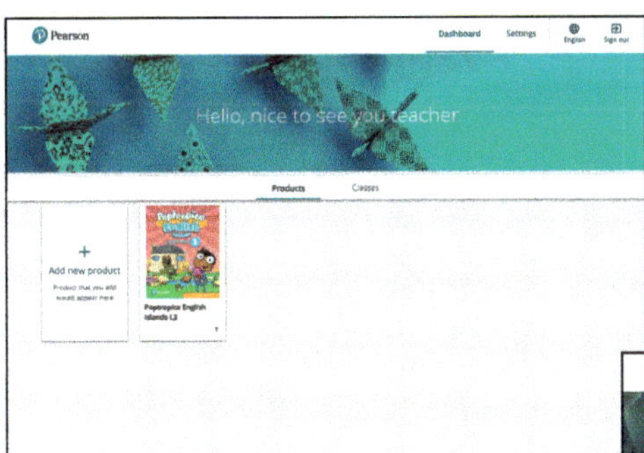

How can I use the print and digital components of Poptropica English?

Poptropica English can be used in all classrooms, whatever the level of technology. The lesson flow is the same irrespective of which medium you use, but you can use the components in different ways, depending on whether you have access to the Internet and/or to an interactive whiteboard.

Scenario 1

I have no Internet and no interactive whiteboard in my classroom. How can I benefit from Poptropica English World?

As long as you can get internet access somewhere (in the staffroom, at home), you can set online homework for students to do at home. Students' homework will be graded, and their achievements will be visible to you. You will be able to see how well the whole class and individual students are doing, and which structures or vocabulary still need further practice.

You can access extra resources such as tests to print and use with your class.

You can encourage your students to get more practice and/or use English outside of class, by asking them to explore other areas of **Poptropica English World**. They can do homework, play the **Poptropica English Island Adventure Game** or mini games at home in their free time, thus gaining extra exposure to the language covered in class. In the **Poptropica English Island Adventure Game**, they will meet characters from their coursebooks, and will be able to join them in their adventures. Students can also play extra games available for each unit of the book.

Finally, you can encourage students to return to the songs, chants, and videos covered in class, which are all available in **Poptropica English World**, to consolidate their learning.

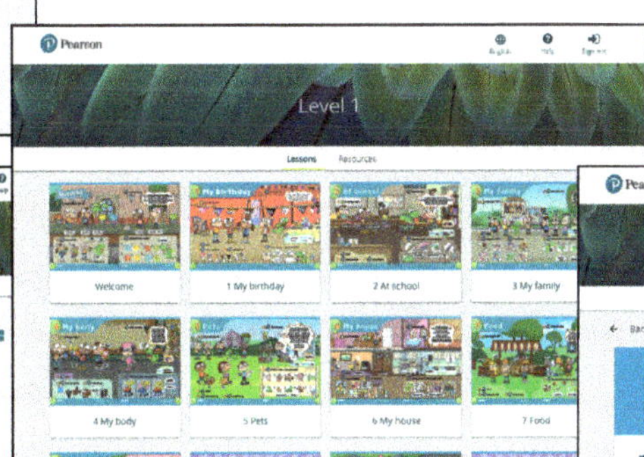

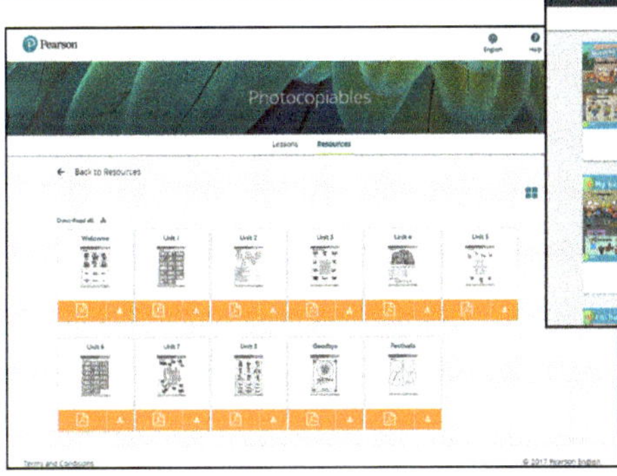

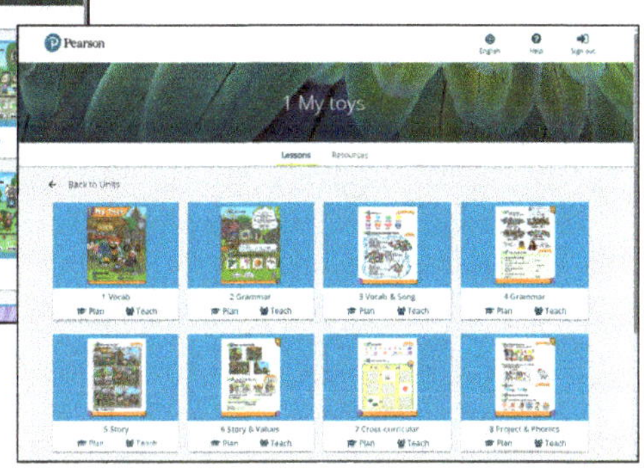

Scenario 2

I have an interactive whiteboard or projector but no Internet in the classroom. How can I benefit from Poptropica English World?

- You can do everything that teachers in scenario 1 can do.
- You can use the offline version of the lessons in the class via the interactive whiteboard. The lessons reflect the sequence of activities in the Teacher's Edition but using digital media. The activities themselves will sometimes have a slightly different format than in the book, in order to make them interactive and make the best of the digital medium. The parts of the lesson when children need to do individual practice can still be done in the Student Book or Workbook.

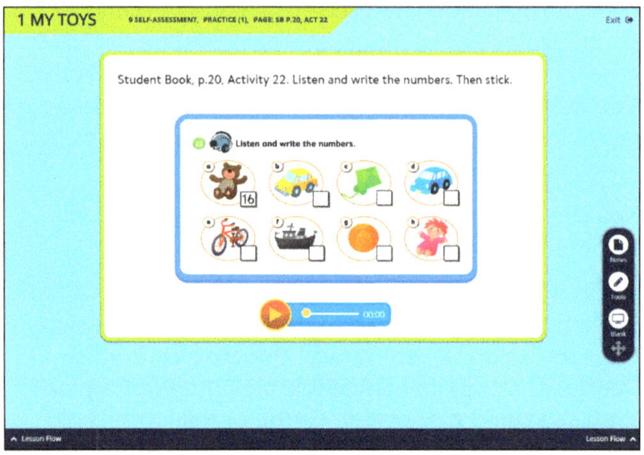

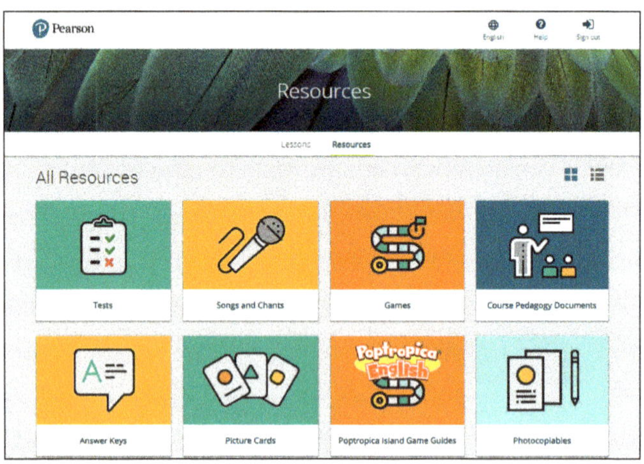

Scenario 3

I have a classroom with an interactive whiteboard and Internet. How can I benefit from Poptropica English World?

- You can do everything that teachers in scenario 2 can do.
- All the media that you need to deliver your lessons will be available in one location, and you can use them at any moment. In addition, you can preview and assign homework, access the additional resources, and student area content directly from the lesson.
- You can share in-class content with students.
- You can receive content updates.

Where can I find more information on how to use Poptropica English World?

There are help notes and help videos available in **Poptropica English World** to guide you through common questions.

What are the benefits of using both the print components and Poptropica English World?

- Your students will spend more time on their English exploring the student area outside of class, and reinforcing their in-class learning via a mixture of printed and interactive homework activities;
- Your students will get extra language practice via a different medium, which is attractive to them;
- Your students will be more engaged with their learning process as a result of a variety of media and fun activities, and will have some choice over how and what they learn;
- The use of **Poptropica English World** strengthens the link between home and school;
- As a result, your students will be more confident about their language skills;
- You will have broader information as to whether students have mastered course content and retained it after they have left the classroom.

Student area

This is an area where students can access resources applicable to them. They can do homework set by their teachers, which will be automatically graded, and reported to a performance area, where they can track their achievements. They can also play extra games, listen to songs, or watch videos linked to the units they are working on.

In addition, students can play the **Poptropica English Island Adventure Game** relevant to their level, in which they meet characters from the Student Book and follow them on an adventure. Students will engage in safe "closed-chat" with the characters they meet, and will practice and consolidate the language of the units. They will also follow instructions to help them solve puzzles, and learn supplementary language along the way. Within the game, they need to find cards like ones hidden in the opening pages of each Student Book unit. Clicking on them in the game will unlock additional games, which will give them extra rewards.

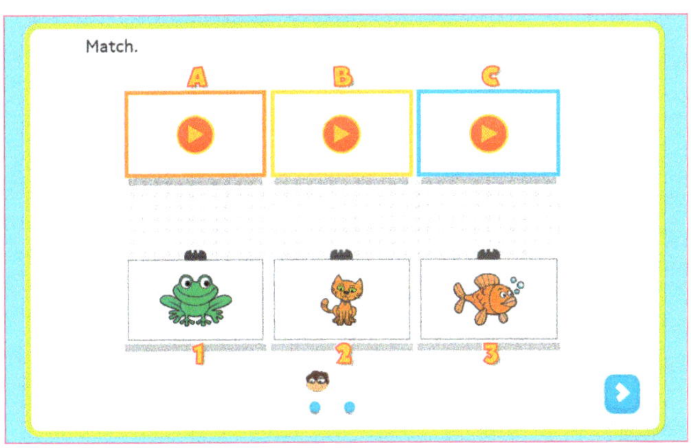

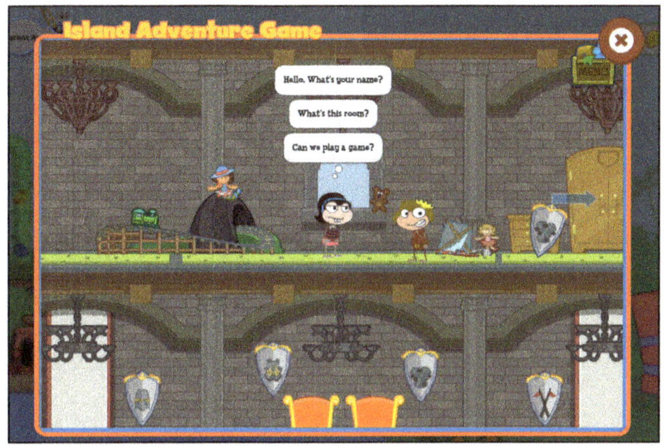

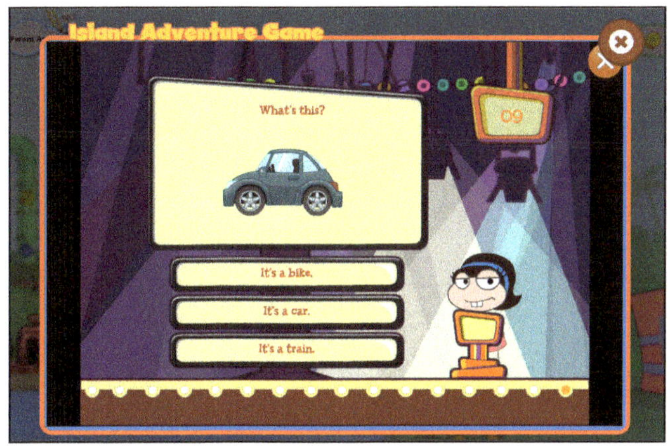

Unit Walkthrough

Lesson 1

Presentation and practice of vocabulary with audio support

Previous knowledge of the topic is activated through an **Assessment for Learning** activity.

Lesson 2

Presentation and practice of grammar with audio support

The new structure is presented in the unit chant and practiced in a listening activity.

The new grammar content is summarized in a *Look!* box on the Student Book page, and in the grammar presentation on the lessons in **Poptropica English World**.

Students listen to the key unit vocabulary in the context of a dialog between the characters. They then listen and repeat the vocabulary.

Target vocabulary is highlighted and labelled in the opening scene.

Further practice of the target language is provided in the Workbook for **all** lessons.

Clear and concise learning objectives help clarify the aim of the lesson for the teacher and parent.

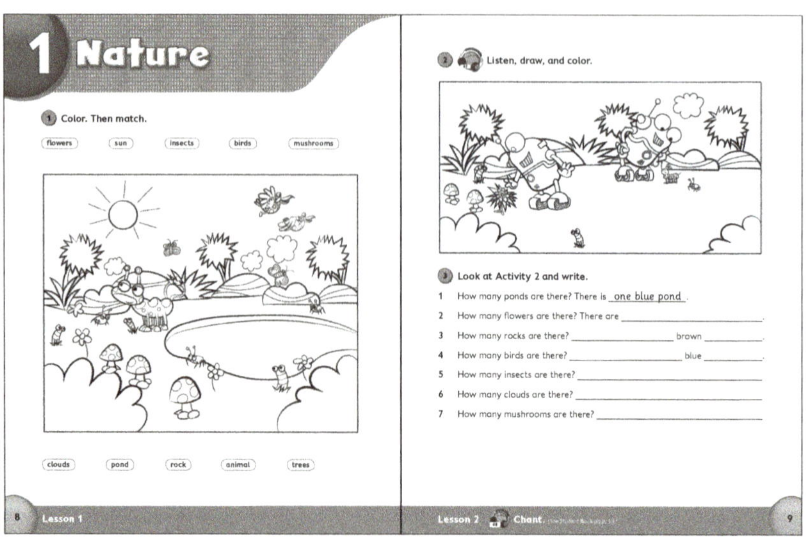

Lesson 3

Presentation and practice of vocabulary with audio support

Students learn a new set of vocabulary which is linked to the unit topic. This may be additional words or a separate vocabulary set. The language of the unit is then practiced in a song. Karaoke versions of the songs are included in the class audio and on **Poptropica English World**.

Extra individual practice of both vocabulary sets is provided via the **Poptropica English World** homework activity.

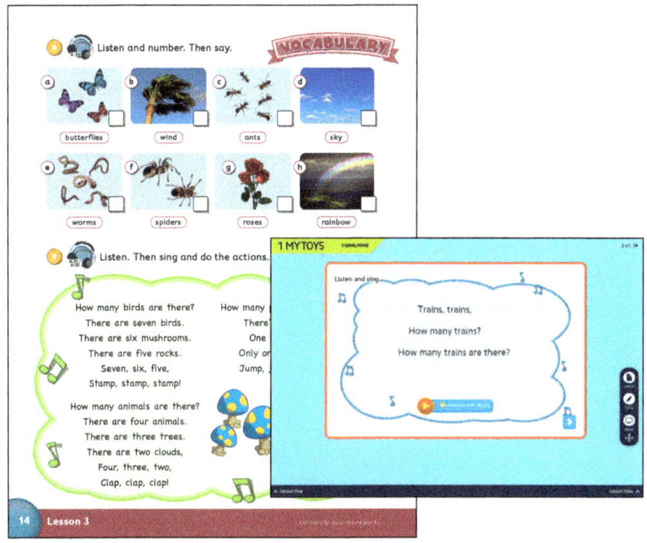

Lesson 4

Presentation and practice of grammar with audio support

The new structure is presented with a listening or speaking activity, and further consolidated with a skills activity. The new grammar content is summarized in a *Look!* box on the Student Book page, and in the grammar presentation on the lessons in **Poptropica English World**.

A skills activity helps to consolidate the grammar and vocabulary of the unit.

Extra individual practice of both grammar points is provided via the **Poptropica English World** homework activity.

Lesson 5

Story

The story is provided with speech bubbles and audio support. It consolidates vocabulary and structures from previous lessons, and introduces new functional language.

Lesson 6

Story comprehension and value

Students review the story before doing a comprehension activity to check understanding. The values topic for the unit is usually linked to the story, and is summarized in the **Values** box on the Student Book page.

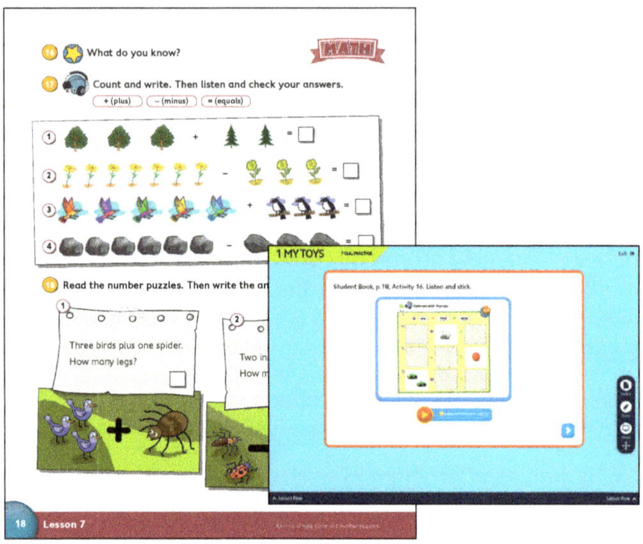

Lesson 7

Cross-curricular content

Target language is practiced and extended through a cross-curricular topic in English. The material may be related to math, science, social science, or health.

Lesson 8

Project and phonics

A project encourages further exploration of the topic and provides the opportunity for personalization of the unit language.

Two or three key letter-sounds are introduced in each unit. In Level 3, these include diphthongs and soft consonants. The phonics portion of the lesson is clearly structured, with repeated activities that students will quickly become familiar and comfortable with. Each sound is presented individually, then blended into words to develop reading and spelling skills.

Lesson 9

Self-assessment and review

Students complete a self-assessment in every unit. This involves students completing three activities – one vocabulary, one grammar, and one communicative. After completing each activity, students are invited to self-assess on what they can now do, by shading the **Assessment for Learning** bar next to the relevant statement in the "I Can" feature.

The **Poptropica English World** homework activity provides additional consolidation and practice of the unit language.

Lesson 10

Review and consolidation

Students consolidate and practice the unit language through a fun language game.

A final self-assessment is provided in **Poptropica English World** via a three-step activity. This activity involves students assessing the words they know or don't know, reviewing the words they don't know, and a final check activity to gauge the accuracy of their self-assessment.

Wider World

Culture lesson

After Units 1, 3, 5, and 7, students complete a Wider World lesson. Students read a text that explores an element of international culture linked to one of the unit topics. Each Wider World lesson includes a "Tell the Class" task, which encourages personalization and extension of the topic.

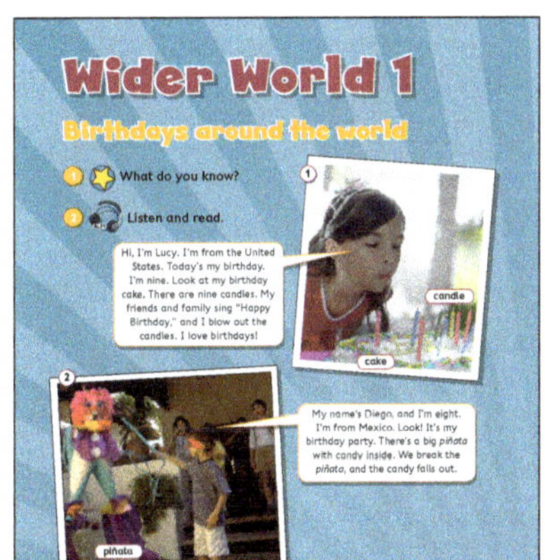

Review

After Units 2, 4, 6, and 8, students complete a Review lesson. This provides practice and consolidation of the language from the previous two units.

Course Planning

The following are suggested hour schedules, depending on the number of hours allocated to a course. We assume five basic scenarios of 52, 62, 80, 104, or 122 hours per level of a course. If more hours are available, the course can be extended further through the use of the variety activities found in **Poptropica English World** and other components.

	52 hours per level	62 hours per level	80 hours per level	104 hours per level	122 lessons per level
Welcome	3 hours	3 hours	4 hours	6 hours	6 hours
Unit 1	5 hours	6 hours	8 hours	10 hours	12 hours
Unit 2	5 hours	6 hours	8 hours	10 hours	12 hours
Review	1 hour	1 hour	1 hour	2 hours	2 hours
Unit 3	5 hours	6 hours	8 hours	10 hours	12 hours
Unit 4	5 hours	6 hours	8 hours	10 hours	12 hours
Review	1 hour	1 hour	1 hour	2 hours	2 hours
Unit 5	5 hours	6 hours	8 hours	10 hours	12 hours

Depending on the number of lessons you have to cover each unit, we suggest that you divide your time in the following way:

	5 lessons per unit/52 hours per level	6 lessons per unit/62 hours per level	8 lessons per unit/80 hours per level	10 lessons per unit/104 hours per level	12 lessons per unit/122 hours per level
Lesson 1 – Presentation	1	1	1	1	1
Lesson 2 – Presentation		2	2	2	2 3
Lesson 3 – Presentation/Song	2	3	3	3	4 5
Lesson 4 – Presentation/Skills			4	4	6
Lesson 5 – Consolidation (Story)	3	4	5	5	7
Lesson 6 – Comprehension/ Values				6	8
Lesson 7 – Cross-curricular	4	5	6	7	9
Lesson 8 – Project/ Phonics			7	8	10
Lesson 9 – Self-Assessment	5	6	8	9	11
Lesson 10 – Review				10	12

	52 hours per level	62 hours per level	80 hours per level	104 hours per level	122 lessons per level
Unit 6	5 hours	6 hours	8 hours	10 hours	12 hours
Review	1 hour	1 hour	1 hour	2 hours	2 hours
Unit 7	5 hours	6 hours	8 hours	10 hours	12 hours
Unit 8	5 hours	6 hours	8 hours	10 hours	12 hours
Review	1 hour	1 hour	1 hour	2 hours	2 hours
Goodbye	3 hours	3 hours	3 hours	5 hours	5 hours
Festivals	1 hour	2 hours	2 hours	2 hours	3 hours
Wider World	1 hour	2 hours	3 hours	3 hours	4 hours

Here is a suggestion of what components can be covered in various lessons of a unit, depending on the time available. The practice activities in the core material can be covered faster or in more detail depending on the students' capabilities, class size, and the length of the lesson.

The core material for each lesson is the same:

- **Poptropica English World** presentation and practice
- Student Book presentation and practice
- Workbook page practice

	Extension material
Lesson 1	Picture Cards Extra activities from games and extension banks Presentation of the **Poptropica English Island Adventure Game** in the class to set the scene for the unit
Lesson 2	Picture Cards Extra activities from games and extension banks
Lesson 3	Picture Cards Extra activities from games and extension banks Extra work on the song with karaoke versions
Lesson 4	Extra activities from games and extension banks
Lesson 5	Extra activities from games and extension banks Extra time devoted to role-playing the story
Lesson 6	Extra activities from games and extension banks
Lesson 7	Picture Cards Extra activities from games and extension banks
Lesson 8	Extra time devoted to phonics Extra time devoted to doing and presenting the project in the class
Lesson 9	**Learning adventure** poster Games and songs used in the unit
Lesson 10	Test Video available via **Poptropica English World**

How to Use Stories

Stories are an essential part of language learning because they allow students to absorb information in a fun and stimulating way. Learning outside the normal boundaries of a teacher-based classroom environment creates the opportunity for students to develop their creative and communicative skills. Using stories in the classroom greatly enhances students' ability to listen, and to actively respond to target language and structures in a fun and relaxed atmosphere. Stories increase motivation, and encourage less confident students to contribute with their ideas and opinions because they are not confined to the limits of a certain structure. They provide larger chunks of language in a context, and provide an opportunity for students to produce language.

There's a story in Lesson 5 of each unit, featuring the characters. These stories serve to review and reinforce the target language and structures of the unit. The artwork is visually stimulating, and the audio effects ensure students listen avidly from start to finish. Below is a four-step method for using stories in the classroom that starts with anticipation and ends with (assisted) performance.

Stage 1 – Anticipating the story

Before listening to the audio, ask students questions or carry out a simple discussion to get them thinking about the story. This can enable students to begin forming an idea of the theme of the story and how it might develop. It also provides an opportunity to introduce any new vocabulary or to review previously learned language, allowing teachers to assess how thoroughly students have absorbed the target language of the unit. Teachers should not provide any answers at this stage but rather allow students to think for themselves.

Stage 2 – Hearing and seeing the story

At this stage, students listen to the story and work through it to find answers to your questions. If access to technology is limited or if it fails during the lesson, teachers can simply read from the book.

Stage 3 – Checking the story

Some suggested questions to be asked after listening to the story are provided in the teaching notes. This gives teachers the possibility to further assess the depth of students' comprehension of the story and of the language used. It also sparks students' creativity and imagination by encouraging them to visualize how the story develops.

Stage 4 – Role-playing the story

After listening to the story several times, students are ready to role-play it in groups, providing them with the opportunity to say larger chunks of language. Props can be brought to class and used to make the experience even more stimulating. Teachers may play the audio, or read the audio script from the Teacher's Edition, while students role-play, or students may recite the story from memory. Try to ensure that, as far as possible, every student gets an opportunity to be involved in the role-play.

Below are some suggestions for extra work with the stories:

- While students listen to the story, they perform a specific action for target vocabulary (e.g. students clap when they hear the word purple, or stamp their feet when they hear the word blue).
- Students draw a new picture for any frame of the story.
- Students create a new ending for the story.
- Students draw or describe their favorite character.
- Students discuss real-life situations with connotations to the story.
- Students comment on how they would feel or how they would behave if they were in a similar situation to one of the story characters.
- You might like to give students feedback. You could give students two stars and one wish e.g., *Fantastic actions!*, *Great teamwork!*, *Speak a little louder next time.* This could be given in L1.

Classroom Management Tips

Poptropica English presents different classroom dynamics. It goes from individual work to pairwork, group work, and whole-class activities. When working in pairs, groups, or in a whole-class setting, students foster cooperative learning, where they learn with and from each other. The following suggestions focus on different ways of grouping or pairing students. All the activities presented here are suited to any group size, age, or interest.

Ideas on how to divide students into pairs and groups

Grouping by Order: Organize students in a specific order and then divide them up. Ask students to get in line in alphabetical order (according to their first or last name, or the number of letters in their name), order of birthdays (grouped either by month or by their day of birth), months of the year, days of the week, or height.

Animal Sounds: This is a loud but fun way to divide students up. Have names of animals on slips of paper. Distribute them and ask students not to show their slip to each other. When they are ready, ask them to start making the sound of that animal that they have on the slip of paper. They have to find the other members of their animal family.

Pick and Mix: Students can be divided into groups or pairs by having them pick objects from a bag. Then you will ask them to find their team mates. Some examples of objects you can use are:

Colored chips: (e.g. ask students to team with same colors together; different colors together; two same color chips and two different ones, etc.).

Colored pencils: (e.g. students who get the same colors are in the same group/pair, light and dark of the same color makes a pair, four different colors makes a group, etc.)

Numbered popsicle sticks: Prepare popsicle sticks by writing a number at the end of each stick and placing them number down in a small can or container. Each student picks one and finds their group/pair (e.g, same numbers, sequential numbers, odd numbers, etc).

Word jumble: Write vocabulary words from a topic on pieces of paper and put them in a bag or box. Ask students to pick one and find the rest of their group or pair. Students should look for others who have similar words or things (e.g. animals – all dogs together, all birds together, all cats together), others who group together (e.g. jungle animals, farm animals, sea animals) or others whose word starts with the same letter (e.g. roses, rainbow, rain, rock).

Strategic Grouping: Depending on the activity, you may want to group students using one of these combinations: stronger and weaker students together, stronger students together, weaker students together, talkers and listeners together. Whatever you choose, do not let students know what your strategy is.

Signaling that the activity has finished

When assigning speaking activities and playing games in large classes, it can often be hard to grab students' attention. With this in mind, here are some suggestions to help you deal with this situation.

Can You Hear Me? Start talking to them in a very low voice and say, *If you can hear me raise your hand.* Students who hear you raise their hand, which will call the other ones' attention and they will do the same.

Clapping: Clap your hands in different patterns and speed. Students have to join you in clapping. Say, *Clap once if you can hear me.* Some students join you. Then say, *Clap twice if you can hear me.* And finally, *Clap three times if you can hear me.* At this point, students will notice that the activity has finished.

Eyes on Me: Count to three saying, *One, two, three... eyes on me!* Students stop the activity and say, *One, two, three... eyes on you!* This way, if the other students have not heard you, they will hear the students and then notice that the activity is finished.

Give Me Five: Raise your hand and say, *Give me five.* Students put their hands up and say, *five.* Then they start to count from one to five. If that does not call everyone's attention, say, *Give me five again.* Students repeat the count.

Raising Hands: Raise your hands. Wait until students notice your hands up and gradually stop talking.

Ring a Bell: Set a timer for the amount of time you would like the activity to last, or ring a bell. When students hear the sound, they stop the activity.

Silent Request: Create a signal for silence. Then practice the signal with your students until they know that every time you make that signal it is time to stop the activity.

Singing: Play or sing a **Poptropica English** song or chant. Have students join you.

Stop Light: Make a stop light with removable color circles. When in green, students can talk in pairs or in groups. When in yellow, they must be ready to end the conversation. When in red, it is time to stop talking. If they are too loud, you can quickly go from green to red. If they are quieter again, go back to green.

Game Bank

Picture Card games

Guess the card: Cut out a small square in the center of a sheet of paper. Hold the sheet in front of a Picture Card, allowing students to see only a small part of the picture through the hole. Students guess the item.

Memory game: Stick Picture Cards on the board. After students memorize the cards, remove them and students list the items. To make the game more challenging, ask students to say the cards in the order they appeared on the board, or only remove one.

Picture Card mime: Invite a student to the front. Show him/her a card or a written word while hiding it from the rest of the class. He/She mimes the word silently. The student who correctly guesses the word is the next one to come forward. Alternatively, split the class into two teams, and ask a member of each team to mime the same word for their teams.

Sort the cards: Divide the class into small groups. Mix Picture Cards from different units, and divide them into piles according to the number of groups. Students arrange them back into categories. The first group to finish wins.

Tic-Tac-Toe: Divide the class into two teams. One is "O" and the other is "X". Draw a large grid on the board with nine spaces. Stick one Picture Card in each space, facing toward the board. Students select a card, turn it over, and say the word on the Picture Card. If it is correct, remove the Picture Card and write an "O" or an "X" accordingly.

Hot seat: A student sits with his/her back to the class. The teacher shows the class a Picture Card, e.g. lion. Students make sentences about the animal, e.g., *They live in Africa. They can run fast. They eat meat.* The student in the hot seat has to guess the animal as quickly as possible. Set a limit for the number of sentences students can make.

TPR games

Aye, aye, Captain! You are the Captain. Give orders to the class. This is a useful activity to review actions, parts of the body, colors, numbers, and classroom objects. For example, you say, *Jump three times. Touch your head. Turn around. Then* students say, *Aye, aye, Captain!* and carry out the action. Model a few times and then invite students to be the captain.

Basketball: Ask a question to a student. If he/she answers correctly, he/she has a shot at the basket. If the student gets the ball in the basket (or box), he/she wins two points. If he/she only hits the basket, he/she wins one point. The student with the most points is the winner.

Pass the ball: Students stand in a large circle. Make a paper ball (or use a soft ball), then call out a category, e.g., *family*, and throw the ball to a student. He/She must say a word in the category you mentioned. He/She then throws the ball to another student, who says another word in the same category. If a student drops the ball, he/she must sit down. Continue until one student remains. This game can also be used to have students ask and answer questions or practice vocabulary that follows a sequence, e.g. days of the week, months of the year, etc.

Teacher says: Give the students instructions but tell them to follow the instructions only if they are preceded by "Teacher says." If you say, *Pick up a pencil*, students should do nothing, but if you say, *Teacher says pick up a pencil*, students must pick up a pencil. They are out of the game if they do an action when they should not.

Team games

Category writing: Divide the class into groups. Each group chooses their "captain". Write the name of a vocabulary category on the board, e.g. sports, food, or animals. Each group helps their captain to write as many words as they can which belongs to that category in two minutes.

Drawing race: Divide the class into two teams and invite a student from each team to the front of the class. Whisper a word to the two students. Each student draws the item on the board. The first team to identify the picture correctly wins a point.

Parachute: Play a guessing game in teams. Draw a large parachute on the board with some strings leading to a stick figure hanging from the parachute. Think of a word students have learned, and draw a dash inside the parachute for each letter in the word. Students from one team try to guess the word. For each incorrect guess, erase one of the parachute's strings. Award points to the team when they guess the word correctly. If all the parachute's strings are erased before students guess the word, the other team can try.

Reading race: Write sets of sentences on strips of paper describing Picture Cards, e.g., *It's big. It's black and white. It has four legs.* Divide the class into teams and ask each team to stand in a line. Place a set of sentences face down at the front of each line. Stick the Picture Cards on the board. When you say, *Go!* one student from each team picks up a sentence, sticks it below the appropriate Picture Card on the board, and goes back to his/her team. The first team to stick all its sentences under the correct cards wins.

Phonics and spelling games

Spelling bee: Divide the class into two teams. The first player on Team A is given a word to spell. If correct, the team gets a point. This can also be done as a class competition, by having students line up to be given words one by one. When they make a mistake, they sit down. The last student standing is the winner.

Little books labeling: Do an activity to practice spelling words with the target sounds/graphemes. Give each student a sheet of paper and have them fold and tear it in half lengthways, and join the ends of the two strips with tape. Now fold the paper like a fan and stick some tape along the spine to make an eight-page book. Students write their name on the cover and then draw four simple illustrations on alternate pages. Next they swap books with a partner and label the illustrations in each other's books. Then check the books together.

Letter mess: Write a selection of letters on the board. Explain to the class that they have to make as many words as possible from the given letters. Model one or two examples on the board for them. Then give students a time limit to do the activity in pairs or small groups.

Speedy sounds: Make letter cards to review the key sounds from a unit. Show the cards in random order and have students chorus the letter sounds. Gradually increase the speed. Then show a card and elicit a word containing that sound. Repeat with the other cards.

Rhyming tennis: Play a game to practice spelling words with target sounds that rhyme, (e.g. *ou, ow, all, aw, ew*, or *y* graphemes). Put the class in two teams with a different set of letter cards. The first team must make a word using their first letter card, e.g. *y* and write it on the board, e.g., *try*. The second team must make a word that rhymes with *try* and write it on the board, e.g., *my*. The first team must hit back with another rhyming word, e.g., *fly*. The teams go back and forth until one team can't make a word. The game is over when all the cards are gone.

Spin the pencil: Play a game to practice spelling words with target sounds/graphemes. Put the students in pairs. Have them draw a large circle on a sheet of paper with graphemes around the edge of the circle (like a clock face). They take it in turns to spin a pencil in the circle and spell a word from the letter sound that the pencil is pointing to.

Spell check: Do an activity to practice spelling words with target sounds and to focus on punctuation. Write five sentences on the board, each with two errors, e.g. the sentence does not begin with a capital letter, the final punctuation is missing or wrong, sample words are misspelled. In pairs, students correct the mistakes.

Miscellaneous games

Bingo: Play bingo with any topic. Ask students to draw the bingo grids. Then they write or draw in the boxes the vocabulary items you wish to review. The winner is the first student to check off all the items on his/her grid.

Drawing game: Students draw pictures of target vocabulary on the board. They must do this slowly, line by line. The class tries to guess what he/she is drawing before he/she finishes the picture. The first student to guess draws the next item.

I spy: Choose something you can see and say, *I spy with my little eye something beginning with (g)*. Students guess the object. The student who guesses correctly has a turn at choosing an item.

Pass the secret: Have students sit in a circle. Start the secret by whispering a simple sentence to the student next to you, e.g., *I have a yellow hat*. The students whisper the secret around the circle. The last student says the secret out loud. Compare how close it is to your original secret sentence. If necessary, write the original secret sentence on the board.

Picture dictation: Divide the class into pairs. Student A describes a picture for Student B to draw. Then they switch roles. This game can be played with any lexical set.

Stop the bus: Write a letter on the board and shout, *Start the bus!* Students write as many words beginning with this letter as they can think of. When you shout, *Stop the bus!*, everyone stops writing. Students get one point for each word.

Song or Chant extension: Have students work in pairs or small groups. Prompt them to write a new verse for the song, using the lyrics on the Student Book pages. You can change just some words or all the lyrics depending on their level.

Extension Bank

Welcome

Touch It relay: Place Picture Cards 1–30 along the board. Have students line up in rows and face the front. Go to the back of the room. Ask the last student in each row to turn to you. Quietly say the number on one of the Cards. Have each student whisper the number, e.g. *twenty six,* to the student in front of him/her. The last student runs to the board and touches the correct Card. Repeat the game until every student has had a chance to run to the board.

Months jumble: Prepare sets of the months of the year, writing the name of each month on a different colored slip of paper. Divide the students into teams of 3 or 4. Give each team a complete set of months. Have students mix them up and spread them out on a table. Ask each student to pick a specific number of months and keep them. (e.g. in teams with three students, each student picks three papers, in a team with four students, each student picks two). Tell students you will give them five minutes to put the months in order. Check answers at the end.

Unit 1

Matching: Divide students into groups of four and give each group two copies of the activity sheet. Have the students complete and color the two sheets identically, then cut out the cards and spread them out face down. Have the students play a matching game, picking two cards and describing the people using the target language. If the cards match the student keeps the cards. Have the students continue until there are no cards left. The student with the most pairs at the end is the winner.

Counting game: Divide students into groups. Give each group fifty small objects (straws, toothpicks, beans, pasta, etc.). Teach the names of these items before you begin, so students can use the plural of the words. Call out numbers in various orders and have them count out that number of items. Alternatively have students count out a number of items and then ask their partner, *How many?* Their partner has to guess the correct number without counting them.

Unit 2

Guess who? Bring in magazine pictures of famous people or cartoon characters that the children will know and put them on the board. Tell students they will try to guess which one you are thinking about. Have students ask you questions, e.g., *Does he have a beard? Yes, he has. / No, he hasn't.* Ask students to raise their hands if they think they know who it is. If a student guesses correctly, they come to the front and choose a picture. Repeat until all students have had a turn at the front.

Mini project: Have students write about an animal. They can work in pairs or small groups. Ask students to draw or cut out pictures of their animal. Then they should label the pictures. Display the posters in the classroom or ask students to present them to the class.

Review 1–2

True or false: Working in pairs, students write four sentences to describe themselves. One of the sentences must be untrue. Remind them to write a mixture of positive and negative sentences (model this for students by telling four sentences about you). When students have finished, have them take turns to read their sentences to their partner. Their partner must identify the untrue sentence.

Unit 3

Imaginary pet poster: Ask students to imagine that they can have any pet that want. Ask a few students which animal they would have as a pet. Divide the class into pairs or small groups. Have students draw their pets and give them names. Then they should draw a few of the things they need to do to look after it. Display the posters in the classroom and do a museum walk, where the students go around looking at others posters.

Draw it fast: Divide the class into teams. Give each one some paper and pencils. Have a team member from each team come up to the board. Face the team members toward the class and show them a Picture Card (83–97). Make sure the rest of the class cannot see the Card. Have students run back to their team and begin to draw the body part or characteristic. They must not speak. The first team to guess the item correctly wins a prize.

Unit 4

My favorite room: Divide the class into small groups and give them a large sheet of paper and some old magazines they can cut up. Ask the groups to draw their favorite room and to furnish it. They can draw items of furniture or cut them from the magazines to make their ideal room. Display the pictures and ask each group to describe its picture.

Spot the mistakes: Retell one of the stories from the unit, making some deliberate mistakes. Every time they spot a mistake, students put up their hands and correct it. Alternatively this can be done with a picture or scene, which you show and describe to them.

Review 3–4

Category tennis: Divide the class into two teams. Call out a category such as days of the week, months, animal characteristics, animal body parts, furnishings, and household items. Team 1 says a word from the category, then Team 2 says another word. They go back and forth until they have run out of words to say. The team with the most words wins a point. Repeat with another category.

Unit 5

Dice game: Bring some clothing items and two die to class. Write on the items on the board with a number from 1–12, e.g. *belt 1, shirt 2, shoes 3, hat 4, scarf 4, tights,* etc. Organize the students in two teams, with the students lined up behind one another. Place the clothes a short distance away and roll the die. The first team identifies which item they need to find, runs to the clothes, and puts it on. The first one to arrive back with their team scores a point.

Unit 6

Things I can do: Give a copy of Activity Sheet 5 to each student. Have students cut out the pictures at the bottom the Activity Sheet. Have students glue four sports/activities they can do into the first box without telling their partner. Pair up students and have them sit so they cannot see their partners work. Then students have to guess what their partner can do, e.g., *Can you play basketball? (No, I can't. / Yes, I can).* When they guess correctly, they write that sport in the second column.

Exercise schedule: Display Picture Cards 142–159. Explain that they will plan their weekly exercise schedule. Divide the class into pairs and give each pair a large sheet of paper. Students divide it into seven columns and write the days of the week at the top. Then they should choose an activity or sport for each day and write it in their schedule. They can also write the sports facilities if they wish to. Then have each pair share their exercise schedule with another pair.

Review 5–6

Help draw an alien: Tell students you are going to draw an alien and they are going to help you. Ask students questions, e.g., *How many legs does it have? Does it have a hat? What can he do?* Draw as students answer and tell you what the alien looks like/can do.

Unit 7

Class survey: Divide the students into groups of three or four. Draw a chart on the board with one column for food and three or four columns for team member's names. Students copy the chart in their notebooks or on a sheet of paper. Ask students to write foods in the food column and names in the other columns. Students ask and answer questions about the food and check or put a cross for each food. Share the results in a class survey to find out the students favorite foods.

Supermarket shop: Divide the class into two teams. One team will be the "sales clerks" and the other the "shoppers". Give the "sales clerks" plastic toy foods or Picture Cards (160–177), and ask them to prepare their shops with the things they have. Ask them to write name sign for their shop and a list of the foods they don't have. The "shoppers" should work in pairs to write a list of the food they want to buy. Then they visit the shops and ask for their items. If the shops have the items they give the cards or the plastic food.

Unit 8

Touch it relay: Place the action Picture Cards (178–197) along the board. Have students line up facing the board. Whisper a sentence to the student at the beginning of the line using the vocabulary item from one of the cards, e.g., *He is dancing terribly.* Students whisper the sentence down the line and the last student runs to tap the correct Card. They then run to the beginning of the line. Repeat until all students have had a turn.

Review 7–8

Mini project: Ask student to create a poster about their favorite things. This should include their favorite things to eat or do. Give students a large sheet of paper, colors, and magazines to cut pictures out. Ask students to create their posters and describe them in writing. Students can share their posters at the end of the activity.

Goodbye

Topic tag: Choose a vocabulary category, e.g. family, face, animals, food. Have students run around while you pretend to chase them in order to tag them. When you tag a student, he/she must name a word from the category. If the student answers correctly, he/she takes your role. If he/she cannot answer or says a word that has already been used, they sit out until the next round. A great game to play in the school yard!

Team quizzes: Divide the class into eight small groups. Give each group one unit from the Student Book. Groups work together to write pop quiz questions for their classmates about the topic in the unit. They could include riddles, drawing/coloring instructions, or questions where students have to describe something. When teams are finished, photocopy the quizzes and hand them out to different teams for them to do.

Welcome

Unit Overview

Unit Objective

- I can talk about special days

Language

Target Vocabulary	Numbers: twenty-one to fifty Days of the week: Sunday, Monday, Tuesday, Wednesday, Thursday, Friday, Saturday Months of the year: January, February, March, April, May, June, July, August, September, October, November, December
Target Structures	What's your favorite day? My favorite day is Sunday. When were you born? I was born in January. Were you born in May? Yes, I was. / No, I wasn't. I was born in June.

Skills

Reading	• Can understand a story • Can identify characters in a story • Can count up to 50
Writing	• Can complete simple sentences about myself (*Workbook*) • Can complete simple sentences using numbers (*Workbook*) • Can write the days of the week and months of the year (*Workbook*) • Can complete simple sentences about when someone was born (*Workbook*)
Listening	• Can understand a story • Can identify characters in a story • Can count up to 50
Speaking	• Can count up to 50 • Can ask and answer What's your favorite day? • Can ask and answer about the month somebody was born

Lessons 1 and 2

SB pages 6–7 or Poptropica English World

Learning Objective
Can understand a story

- Play an ice-breaking game. When a student catches the ball/bean bag, they should call out, *I'm (name).* before throwing the ball/bag to the next person. The game continues around the class until all students have thrown the ball/bean bag.

Open books and ask students to look at the story. Ask, *What are we learning today?* Write the lesson objective on the board: *We're reading a story.*

1 Listen to the story. Read.

- Ask students what they think is happening in the opening scene. Ask, *Why are people sick? Why do they want a tifftiff plant? Where can they find a tifftiff plant? Where are they going?*
- Pre-teach the words *sick, medicine, plant, important,* and *problem* if necessary.
- Play the audio and have students look at the pictures. Then ask comprehension questions to make sure they understand the story.
- Have students close their books and play the audio again. Pause after each line and ask students to say who is speaking.
- Divide students into groups and have them practice reading the story and role-playing the scenes.
- Remind students of the treasure hunt in Student Books 1 and 2, and ask them what they think the characters are going to be looking for in this level.

Ask students, *Have you ever been sick? Did you take medicine? What do you think will happen in the story?*

Pop Quiz: Before the end of the lesson, ask students to look at the story again. Read out the first few words of a sentence from one of the speech bubbles. Have students find the speech bubble and read out the rest of the sentence, e.g., *Good. They... (can help us.) This is... (the problem).*

Materials
Ball/bean bag

Lesson 3 SB page 8 or Poptropica English World

Learning Objective
Can identify characters in a story

Warm-up

- Tell students they are going to meet the characters. from the story. Ask them what they say when they meet new friends. What information do they give about themselves?
- Put students into pairs. Have them introduce themselves to their partner. Invite confident students to come to the front to introduce themselves to the class.

Open books and ask students to look at the activities on the page. Ask, *What are we learning today?* Write the lesson objective on the board: *We're identifying the characters in a story.*

2 A:03 Listen, check (✓), and say.

- Ask students to look at the characters in the scene. Ask, *Who are they? Where are they?*. Point to the sign on the building and say, *Look! They're on Space Island.*
- Play the audio. Have students listen and check the speech bubbles as they hear them.
- Go through each speech bubble in turn. Model the text, or play the audio again for students to copy and repeat. Drill the pronunciation as a class. Encourage them to point to the correct character each time.
- When students have practiced the introductions chorally, pair them to practice the expressions together.

3 A:04 Listen and sing. Then find the tifftiff plant.

- Play the audio. Students listen and find the tifftiff plant in the picture.

Hey boys! Hey girls!
Come with us to Space Island.
Look up, down, here, there.
Look around everywhere.
Where's the tifftiff plant?
Come on, come on,
Let's find the tifftiff plant!

Pop Quiz: Make Picture Cards of the characters, stick them face down on the board, and have students guess who they show. Turn the Picture Cards over when students guess correctly.

Materials
Picture Cards of the story characters

Homework WB page 4

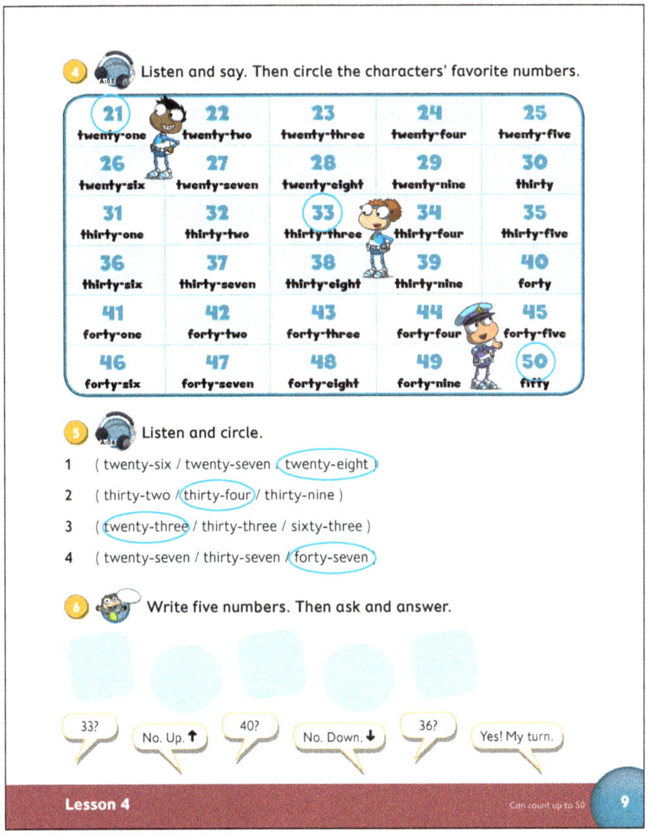
4 Listen and say. Then circle the characters' favorite numbers.

21 twenty-one	22 twenty-two	23 twenty-three	24 twenty-four	25 twenty-five
26 twenty-six	27 twenty-seven	28 twenty-eight	29 twenty-nine	30 thirty
31 thirty-one	32 thirty-two	33 thirty-three	34 thirty-four	35 thirty-five
36 thirty-six	37 thirty-seven	38 thirty-eight	39 thirty-nine	40 forty
41 forty-one	42 forty-two	43 forty-three	44 forty-four	45 forty-five
46 forty-six	47 forty-seven	48 forty-eight	49 forty-nine	50 fifty

5 Listen and circle.

1 (twenty-six / twenty-seven / twenty-eight)
2 (thirty-two / thirty-four / thirty-nine)
3 (twenty-three / thirty-three / sixty-three)
4 (twenty-seven / thirty-seven / forty-seven)

6 Write five numbers. Then ask and answer.

33? No. Up. 40? No. Down. 36? Yes! My turn.

Lesson 4 Can count up to 50 9

Lesson 4 SB page 9 or Poptropica English World

Learning Objective
Can count up to 50

Warm-up

- Write numbers 1–10 on the board in random order or put up Picture Cards 1–49 with the numbers written on them. Point at each number in turn and ask students to say them aloud. Then say, *Put the numbers in the correct order.* Mime to make the meaning clear.
- Repeat with numbers 11–20. Students say the numbers in the correct order.
- Put the number cards in a bag filled with shredded paper. Have students sit in a circle and pass the bag around while music is playing. Stop the music. The student who is holding the bag picks out a card and says, e.g., *nineteen*. If the answer is correct, he/she gets to keep the card. If not, he/she puts it back in the bag. Play until there are no cards left in the bag. The winner is the student with most cards.

Open books and ask students to look at the activities on the page. Ask, *What are we learning today?* Write the lesson objective on the board: *We're learning the numbers from 21 through 50.*

- Close books. Ask students what numbers they already know in English (numbers 1–20). Write or draw these on the board.

4 Listen and say. Then circle the characters' favorite numbers.

- Write number 20 and then show Picture Cards for numbers 21 through 50 in order. Repeat each number a few times.
- Play the audio. Have students listen, and point to the numbers, and repeat them. They circle the characters' favorite numbers.
- Stick the number Picture Cards on the board in random order. Play the audio again and pause after each number. Have individual students come to the front, identify the correct card, say the number, and put the cards in order.

Narrator: 21
Kim: Hey! 21! That's my favorite number.
Narrator: 22, 23, 24, 25, 26, 27, 28, 29, 30, 31, 32, 33
Katy: Thirty three is my favorite number.
Narrator: 34, 35, 36, 37, 38, 39, 40, 41, 42, 43, 44, 45, 46, 47, 48, 49, 50
Captain Conrad: My favorite number is 50!

5 Listen and circle.

- Play the audio and have students listen and circle the numbers they hear.

1 twenty-eight **3** twenty-three
2 thirty-four **4** forty-seven

6 Write five numbers. Then ask and answer.

- Point to the five shapes and ask students to secretly write a number from 21–50 in each one. Make sure they don't show their numbers to their classmates.
- Explain that students are going to play a guessing game – each student is going to try to guess his or her partner's numbers. Role-play the dialog with one student explaining that they should say *up* when the number is too low, and *down* when it is too high.
- Divide students into pairs and have them play the game.

Pop Quiz: As students are leaving the class, say three numbers to each student and have them say the next number. Start with consecutive numbers, (e.g., *21, 22, 23, ?*) then make it more difficult by going up in twos, fives or tens.

Materials
Picture Cards 1–49, bag, shredded paper, music CD

Homework WB page 5

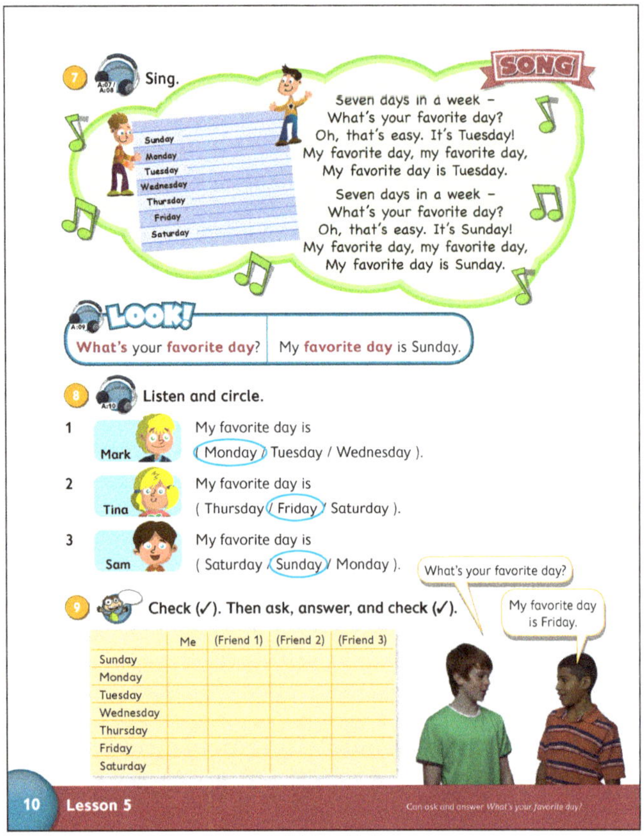

7 Sing.

SONG

Sunday
Monday
Tuesday
Wednesday
Thursday
Friday
Saturday

Seven days in a week –
What's your favorite day?
Oh, that's easy. It's Tuesday!
My favorite day, my favorite day,
My favorite day is Tuesday.

Seven days in a week –
What's your favorite day?
Oh, that's easy. It's Sunday!
My favorite day, my favorite day,
My favorite day is Sunday.

LOOK!

What's your favorite day?	My favorite day is Sunday.

8 Listen and circle.

1 Mark — My favorite day is (Monday / Tuesday / Wednesday).

2 Tina — My favorite day is (Thursday / Friday / Saturday).

3 Sam — My favorite day is (Saturday / Sunday / Monday).

9 Check (✓). Then ask, answer, and check (✓).

	Me	(Friend 1)	(Friend 2)	(Friend 3)
Sunday				
Monday				
Tuesday				
Wednesday				
Thursday				
Friday				
Saturday				

10 Lesson 5 Can ask and answer What's your favorite day?

Lesson 5 SB page 10 or Poptropica English World

Learning Objective
Can ask and answer *What's your favorite day?*

Target Language
What's your favorite day?
My favorite day is Sunday.

Open books and ask students to look at the book and the Look! box. Ask, *What are we learning today?* Write the lesson objective on the board: *We're learning the days of the week.*

Warm-up

- Show a calendar. Point at Monday and say the word a few times for students to repeat. Continue with the other days. Point at the days again and ask, *What day is it today?* Students answer.

7 Sing.

A:07 A:08

- Read through the Look! Box with the class and play the audio (track A:09). Say, e.g., *My favorite day is Saturday.* and explain why. Ask students if they have a favorite day.
- Play the song audio and have students listen and point to the day of the week when they hear the word.
- Play the audio again and have students sing along.

8 Listen and circle.

A:10

- Play the audio and have students listen and circle the favorite day of the week for each child.

Tina: What's your favorite day, Mark?
Mark: My favorite day is Monday. I'm always happy on Monday. What about you, Tina? What's your favorite day?
Tina: That's easy! My favorite day is Friday. I'm always excited on Friday. And you, Sam? What's your favorite day?
Sam: My favorite day is Sunday. I'm always tired on Sunday, but I can sleep.

9 Check (✓). Then ask, answer, and check (✓).

- Ask students to look at the table and explain the activity. Role-play the model conversation with one student. Then have them check their favorite day.
- Have students walk around the classroom and ask three classmates about their favorite days. Make sure they write their names as well.

Pop Quiz: Play *Bingo* with the days of the week.

Materials
Calendar

Homework WB page 6

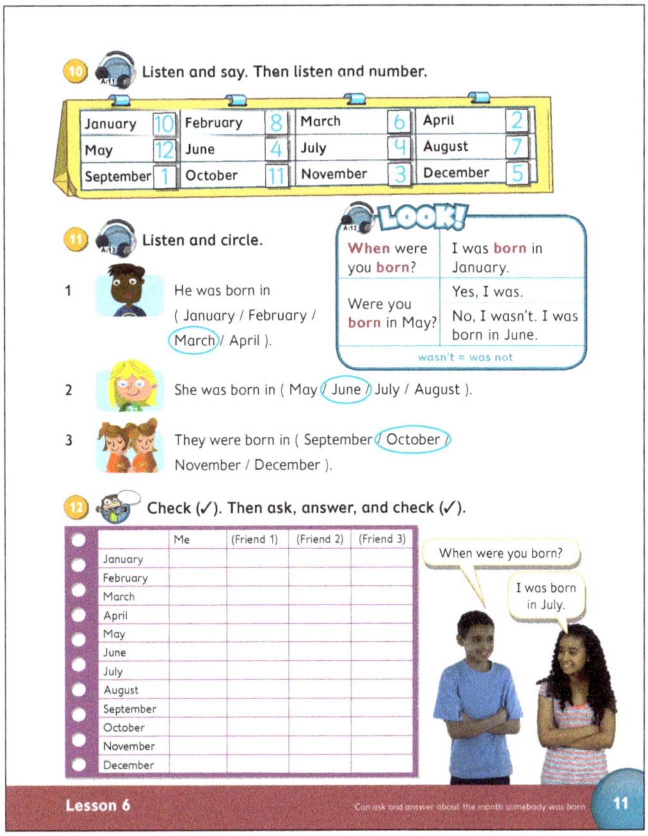
10 Listen and say. Then listen and number.

January	10	February	8	March	6	April	2
May	12	June	4	July	9	August	7
September	1	October	11	November	3	December	5

11 Listen and circle.

1 He was born in (January / February / March / April).

2 She was born in (May / June / July / August).

3 They were born in (September / October / November / December).

LOOK!

When were you born?	I was born in January.
Were you born in May?	Yes, I was. No, I wasn't. I was born in June.

wasn't = was not

12 Check (✓). Then ask, answer, and check (✓).

	Me	(Friend 1)	(Friend 2)	(Friend 3)
January				
February				
March				
April				
May				
June				
July				
August				
September				
October				
November				
December				

Lesson 6 Can ask and answer about the month somebody was born 11

Lesson 6 SB page 11 or Poptropica English World

Learning Objective
Can ask and answer about the month somebody was born

Warm-up

- Play a guessing game. Say the first two letters of a day of the week and have students guess the word, e.g., *S-a (Saturday)*. Divide students into pairs and have them play the game.

Open books and ask students to look at the book and the Look! box. Ask, *What are we learning today?* Write the lesson objective on the board: *We're learning the months of the year.*

- Close books. Ask students what months they already know in English. Write these on the board.

10 Listen and say. Then listen and number.

- Show Picture Cards 31–42 (months). Point at January and say the word a few times for students to repeat. Continue with the other months.
- Play the audio and have students listen and repeat.
- Play the audio again and have students find the correct month in the table and write the number next to it.

1 September	**7** August
2 April	**8** February
3 November	**9** July
4 June	**10** January
5 December	**11** October
6 March	**12** May

- Check answers by calling each month and having students call back the number. Play the audio again if necessary.

11 Listen and circle.

- Read through the Look! box with the class and play the audio (track A:12).
- Have students look at the children, and read each sentence with the four options. Then play the audio for the activity and have students listen and circle the correct month.

1 When were you born? I was born in March.
2 When were you born? I was born in June.
3 When were you born? We were born in October.

12 Check (✓). Then ask, answer, and check (✓).

- Ask students to look at the table and explain the activity. Role-play the model conversation with one student. Then have them each check the month they were born in.
- Have students walk around the classroom and ask three classmates when they were born. Make sure they write their names as well.

Pop Quiz: Before the end of the lesson, hand out Picture Cards of the months in random order and have students come to the front and stand in the correct order showing their cards.

Materials
Picture Cards 31–42

Homework WB page 7

Welcome Worksheet

Name ______________________ Class ______________

1 **Look and write.**

______! I'm ______.
I'm ______. How ______
are you?

Hello. My ______'s
Katy. What's your ______?

2 **Look and write.**

a	twenty-three	twenty-______	______-five	twenty-______
b	thirty-seven	______-eight	thirty-______	______
c	______-one	forty-______	forty-three	______

3 **Read and write.**

day favorite November Sunday Wednesday What's

1

Hello, I'm Jenny. My favorite day is ______.

2

Hi, my name's Joe. I was born in ______.

3

Hi, I'm Peter. My ______ day is Sunday. I'm always
happy on ______.

4

Hi, I'm Rose. My favorite ______ is Saturday.
______ your favorite day?

1 Nature

Unit Overview

Unit Objective

- I can talk about nature

Language

Target Vocabulary	Nature: birds, sun, clouds, trees, animal, pond, mushrooms, rock, insects, flowers, butterflies, wind, ants, sky, worms, spiders, roses, rainbow
Target Structures	How many animals are there? There's one purple animal. How many birds are there? There are two blue birds. There are some spiders. / There aren't any spiders. Is there a rainbow? Yes, there is. / No, there isn't. Is there any wind? Yes, there's some wind. / No, there isn't any wind. Are there any ants? Yes, there are. / No, there aren't.
Features	**Values:** Play outside. Play safe! **Cross-curricular:** Math: Plus, minus, equals **Phonics:** *air, ear* (hair, year)

Skills

Reading	• Can understand a simple story • Can understand details of a story • Can do simple sums and number puzzles
Writing	• Can do simple sums and number puzzles • Can complete simple sentences using numbers and colours (*Workbook*) • Can copy simple nature words (*Workbook*) • Can write simple answers (*Workbook*) • Can complete simple sentences about playing safe, nature, and my favorite place (*Workbook*)
Listening	• Can identify common nature words • Can understand a simple story
Speaking	• Can ask and answer about how many there are • Can ask and answer using *Is there a...? / Are there any...?* and *Where is he/are they?* • Can role-play a story • Can talk about playing outside and playing safe • Can pronounce the sounds *air* and *ear*

Lesson 1 SB page 12 or Poptropica English World

Learning Objective
Can identify common nature words

Target Language
birds, sun, clouds, trees, animal, pond, mushrooms, rock, insects, flowers

1 What do you know?

- Open books and ask students to look at the activities on the page. Ask, *What are we learning today?* Write the lesson objective on the board: *We're learning nature words.*
- Close books. Ask students what English words they know for nature, e.g., *tree, flower.* Write on board.
- Refer to the learning adventure poster and say, *Great! You are already moving along your learning adventure!*

2 A:14 Listen and find. What's missing?

- Use the Picture Cards of nature words (50–59) to teach the new vocabulary.
- Ask questions about the main illustration: *Who's this? Where are they?* Call out the nature words and have students find and point.
- Play the audio. Students listen to the dialog and circle the pictures when they hear the words. Ask, *What's missing? (an animal, mushrooms, clouds)*

Park keeper:	Hello! Welcome to the park. There are lots of things to see. Look! There's a pond here and there's a big rock.
PROD 1:	There are insects!
Katy:	Ooh, yes.
Park keeper:	There are trees.
Kim:	And there are blue birds. Look!
PROD 2:	The flowers are beautiful. Mmm...
Kim:	Ooh, the sun is hot. I like the park.

3 A:15 Listen and number.

- Ask students to look at the scene in their books and listen. Play the audio and ask them to find the items and number them.

1 There's a brown rock.
2 Look! Four pink insects, one, two, three, four.
3 There are two tall trees.
4 Look! Two birds! They're blue!

5 Can you see any mushrooms? There are four blue mushrooms.
6 There are two white clouds.
7 The sun is yellow. Ooh, it's hot!
8 The pond is blue.
9 The animal is funny. It has seven legs.
10 I can see five yellow flowers. One, two, three, four, five!

4 A:16 Listen and say.

- Ask students to look at the main scene again. Play the audio. Students point to the items as they listen.
- Play the audio again, pausing for students to repeat.

Ask students how many nature words they know now. Give students a minute to tell their partner the new words they know.

- Ask students to say where they are on their adventure now. Ask students which words they find easiest or most difficult to remember. Tell students, *Good job!* to reinforce the progress they are making.

Pop Quiz: Before the end of the lesson, show students a picture of something from nature and ask them to tell you what it is.

Materials
Poster, Picture Cards 50–59, a picture of something from nature

Homework WB page 8

Lesson 2 SB page 13 or Poptropica English World

Learning Objective
Can ask and answer about how many there are

Target Language
How many animals are there?
There's one purple animal.
How many birds are there?
There are two blue birds.

Warm-up

- Prepare some color cards and matching word cards. Divide the class into groups. Give each group a word card (colors) or color card. Say a color, e.g., *green*, then call out an action, e.g., *turn around*. Students in the group with the green card turn around. Continue with other colors and actions.

Open books and ask students to look at the chant and the Look! box. Ask, *What are we learning today?* Write the lesson objective on the board: *We're learning to ask and answer about how many things there are.*

5 Listen and chant.

- Play the chant about nature. Ask students to tell you what nature words they hear on the chant. Then ask them to point to the items in the main scene.
- Play the chant a few times and have students chant along. If students are confident, use the karaoke version.

6 Look at the scene. Count and say.

- Read through the Look! box with the class and play the audio (track A:19).
- Have students count the items in the scene and make sentences, e.g. *two birds. There are two birds. one pond. There's one pond.*

7 Play a memory game.

- Have students take turns to close their books and ask and answer questions about the picture, recalling from memory and using the new vocabulary and structure.
- Direct students' attention to the frog card on page 13. Tell students to go online to the Poptropica English Island Adventure Game and find the item. Once students click on it, they are taken to a supplementary language task.

Pop Quiz: Have students write *How many...?* questions about the classroom or things they can see from the window. Pair students and have them ask their partner the questions, e.g., *How many pencils are there? How many trees are there?*

Materials
Color cards, word cards

Homework WB page 9

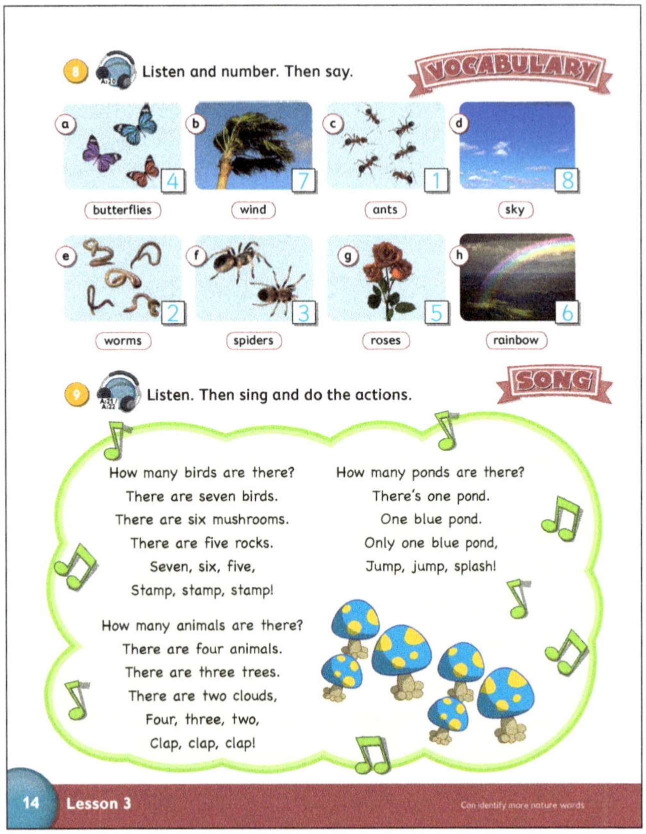

Lesson 3 SB page 14 or Poptropica English World

Learning Objective
Can identify more nature words

Target Language
butterflies, wind, ants, sky, worms, spiders, roses, rainbow

Warm-up

- Hold up Picture Cards 50–59 in turn and ask, *What's this?/What are these? What color is it?* Then ask individual students to come to the front and write the words on the board. Students say all the words.

Open books and ask students to look at the activities on the page. Ask, *What are we learning today?* Write the lesson objectives on the board: *We're learning more nature words, and we're following an action song.*

- Close books. Ask students what English words they know for nature, e.g., *sky, butterflies.* Write on board.
- Refer to the learning adventure poster and say, *Great! You are moving along your learning adventure!*

8 Listen and number. Then say.

A:20

- Introduce the new words with Picture Cards 60–67. Hold them up one by one and ask students to repeat the words after you. Then ask students to look in their books and point at the words as you say them.
- Play the audio and have students number the items as they hear them. Then play the audio again and have students repeat.
- Point to individual pictures and ask students to tell you the word.

9 Listen. Then sing and do the actions.

A:21 A:22

- Draw a bird on the board. Flap your arms up and down and ask, *What am I? (a bird)* Have children flap their arms and repeat, *flap, flap, flap!* Draw an insect on the board. Make a buzzing noise and ask, *What am I? (an insect)* Have children make the buzzing noise. Draw a pond on the board. Then jump and make a splashing noise. Ask students where you are *(in the pond).* Have them jump and splash. Then point to the different pictures on the board in random order and have them do the appropriate actions.
- Draw students' attention to the plural form of nouns. Draw a cloud on the board and ask, *How many clouds? (one cloud).* Now draw two more clouds and ask, *How many clouds? (three clouds).* Say, *three cloud**s**,* emphasizing the *s* sound.
- Ask students to look at the picture in their books and ask, *How many mushrooms?*
- Play the song audio and have students listen.
- Play the audio again and ask students to do the actions at the end of each verse.
- Play the song audio again and have students do the actions as they sing the song. If students are confident, use the karaoke version.

Ask students, *How many words for nature do you know now?* Give students a minute to tell their partner the new words they know.

- Ask students to say where they are on their adventure now. Ask students which words they find easiest or most difficult to remember. Tell students, *Good job!* to reinforce the progress they are making.

Pop Quiz: Play *Parachute* with the vocabulary items from this lesson, plus Lesson 1 combined. Put students into two teams and have them take turns to guess a letter. Teams win a point for each correct guess.

Materials
Picture Cards 50–59, 60–67, poster

Homework WB page 10

Look!

There are **some** spiders.	There aren't **any** spiders.
Is there **a** rainbow?	Yes, there is. / No, there isn't.
Is there **any** wind?	Yes, there's **some** wind. / No, there isn't **any** wind.
Are there **any** ants?	Yes, there are. / No, there aren't.

10 Listen and circle the correct screen. Then ask and answer.

11 Look, ask, and answer. SPEAKING

1 At the library
2 At the park
3 At the museum
4 At the playground

Look!

Where are they?	**At** the library.
Where is he?	**At** the museum.

Lesson 4 Can ask and answer using Is there a...? / Are there any...? and Where is he/are they? 15

Lesson 4 SB page 15 or Poptropica English World

Learning Objective
Can ask and answer using *Is there a...? / Are there any...?* and *Where is he/are they?*

Target Language
There are some spiders. There aren't any spiders.
Is there a rainbow? Yes, there is. / No, there isn't.
Is there any wind?
Yes, there's some wind. / No, there isn't any wind.
Are there any ants? Yes, there are. / No, there aren't.

Warm-up

- Stick five Picture Cards (from 60–67) on the board in a row. Call out four of the items. Have students name the card you didn't mention.

Open books and ask students to look at the book and the Look! box. Ask, *What are we learning today?* Write the lesson objective on the board: *We're learning to ask and answer using* Is there a...? / Are there any...? *and* Where is he / are they?

10 Listen and circle the correct screen. Then ask and answer.

- Direct students' attention to the four screens. Have them identify the objects using, *There is* or *There are...*
- Focus on the sentences in the Look! box and play the audio (track A:23). Ask students to read the text aloud.
- Explain that students are going to listen to a conversion between two aliens, one on Space Island, the other on the ground. Pre-teach *Ground Control* and the expression *over* (used to indicate end of communication).
- Play the audio and have students listen.

Space Island:	Space Island to Ground Control. There is rain and there is wind. Over.
Ground Control:	Are there any trees? Over.
Space Island:	Yes, there are. And there are some flowers. Over.
Ground Control:	Are there any birds? Over.
Space Island:	No, there aren't. And there aren't any insects. There are some mushrooms. Over.
Ground Control:	Thank you, Space Island. Over.
Space Island:	Goodbye, Ground Control. Over and out.

- Play the audio again. Have students look at the pictures and identify the correct screen. Ask them to circle the screen in their books.
- Pair students. Have one student choose a screen. The other student tries to guess the screen by asking questions. Partners can switch roles.

11 Look, ask, and answer.

- Focus on the sentences in the Look! box and play the audio (track A:25). Ask students to read the questions and answers. Check that they understand the meaning.
- Students work in pairs. They take turns to ask and answer the question, *Where are they?*, using the answers given. Check answers as a class.
- Ask a pair of students to read the example dialog for the class. Explain that the first sentence is a clue to the answer in the last sentence.
- Elicit more dialogs from the class, e.g., *There are some books. Where are they? In the library.*

Pop Quiz: Before the end of the lesson, ask volunteers to come to the front and act out being at the library, the park, the museum, or the playground, using appropriate actions. The class asks questions: *Are there any trees? No. Are there any books? Yes, there are lots of books. Are you at the library? Yes!*

Materials
Picture Cards 60–67

Homework WB page 11

Lesson 5 SB page 16 or Poptropica English World

Learning Objectives
Can understand a simple story
Can role-play a story

Functional Language
big, small, animal, pond
What color is it?
Is it big or small?
Is this...? I don't know. It's an...

Warm-up

- Ask students to look back at the main scene on the opening spread of Unit 1. Describe some items, but make deliberate mistakes, e.g., *There are ten yellow birds.* Have students say, *false* when they spot the mistake, and correct it, e.g., *There are two blue birds.*

Open books and ask students to look at the story. Ask, *What are we learning today?* Write the lesson objectives on the board. *We're reading a story and role-playing a story.*

12 A:26 Talk about the pictures. Then listen and read.

- Direct students' attention to the story and ask questions about the characters and the scene: *Who can you see? Where are they? What are they doing? Are there any flowers?*
- Play the audio and have students listen and follow. Check understanding, pointing at the pictures and asking questions: *What are they looking for? What does the tifftiff flower look like? Can you see a tifftiff flower? Who pushes PROD 1 in the water? Is PROD 1 happy?*
- Play the audio again, stopping after each line. Have students repeat.
- Play the audio again. Have students speak along to the audio and mime the action.

Ask the students: Is it safe in the park? Which things are dangerous? *(the pond, the trickster, some insects)* Students need to find the correct question for each of your answers.

- Give pairs two minutes to think of their answers. They might like to write their ideas in their notebooks. Write their suggestions on the board in two categories. Ask students to say why they chose their ideas.

13 Role-play the story.

- See the "How to use stories" section on page 22 for more ideas on how to build your students' confidence with role-plays.
- Divide students into groups of four. Give each group a set of cut-up Story Cards and have students place them in order.
- Have the groups role-play the story. When you say, *change*, they should change character and role-play a new character. Rotate through the characters, giving students the chance to play each one.

You might like to give the students feedback on their role-play.

Pop Quiz: Before the end of the lesson, make true and false statements about the story. Students say if they are *true* or *false*, e.g., *PROD 1 sees a tifftiff. (true) PROD 2 is in the pond. (false)*

Materials
Story Cards (Unit 1)

Homework WB page 12

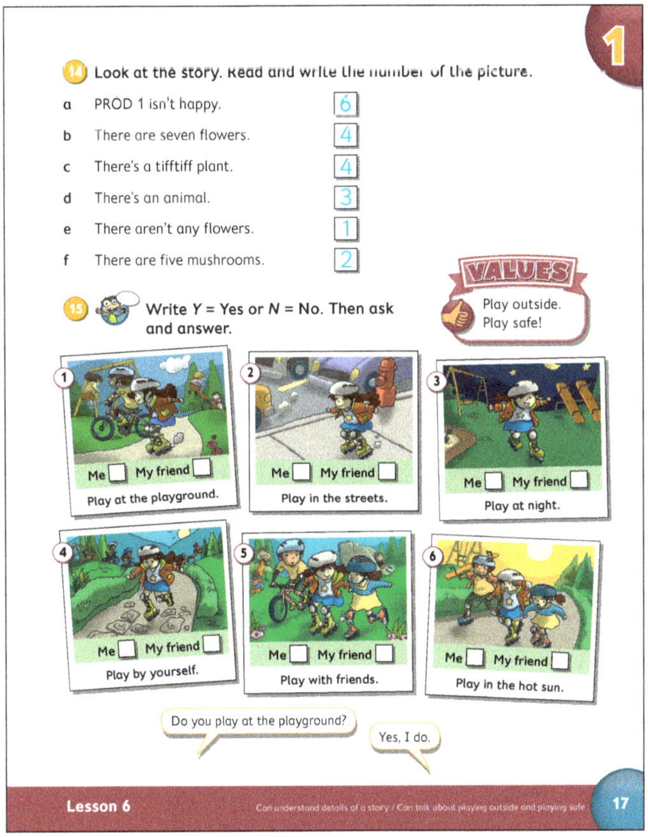

1

14 Look at the story. Read and write the number of the picture.

a PROD 1 isn't happy. 6
b There are seven flowers. 4
c There's a tifftiff plant. 4
d There's an animal. 3
e There aren't any flowers. 1
f There are five mushrooms. 2

VALUES
Play outside. Play safe!

15 Write *Y* = Yes or *N* = No. Then ask and answer.

1 Me My friend Play at the playground.
2 Me My friend Play in the streets.
3 Me My friend Play at night.
4 Me My friend Play by yourself.
5 Me My friend Play with friends.
6 Me My friend Play in the hot sun.

Lesson 6 17

Lesson 6 SB page 17 or Poptropica English World

Learning Objectives
Can understand details of a story
Can talk about playing outside and playing safe

Additional Language
play, playground, streets, at night, by yourself, with friends, hot

Value
Play outside. Play safe!

Open books and ask students to look at the activities on the page. Ask, *What are we learning today?* Write the lesson objectives on the board: *We're understanding details of a story and we're learning to play safely.*

Warm-up

- Play the story audio again (track A:26), and review the story with students. Review the characters' names and the objects.

14 Look at the story. Read and write the number of the picture.

- Have students work in pairs. They read the sentences and look carefully at the story frames to find which one they relate to. They write the number of the frame after each sentence.

15 Write Y = Yes or N = No. Then ask and answer.

- Read the value, *Play outside. Play safe!* Direct students' attention to the pictures of children playing. Point to each one, and ask, e.g., *Where are the children playing? (in the playground)* Then ask individual students questions, such as, *How about you? Do you play in the playground? Do you play in the streets? Is it safe to play in the streets?* Ask students to think about the dangers, e.g., *cars, dark.*
- Have students look at each picture and write *Y* or *N* depending on whether they do those things. Check their answers by asking questions, e.g., *Do you play at night?*
- Pair students and have them find out about their partners. Ask them to use the question in the model and write *Yes* or *No* for their partners.

Pop Quiz: Write on the board: *Playing outside is good.* Tell students to work with a partner and decide if playing outside is good or not, and to think of reasons why. Give pairs two minutes to think of their answers. They might like to write their ideas in their notebooks. Write their suggestions on the board. Ask students to say why they chose their ideas.

Homework WB page 13

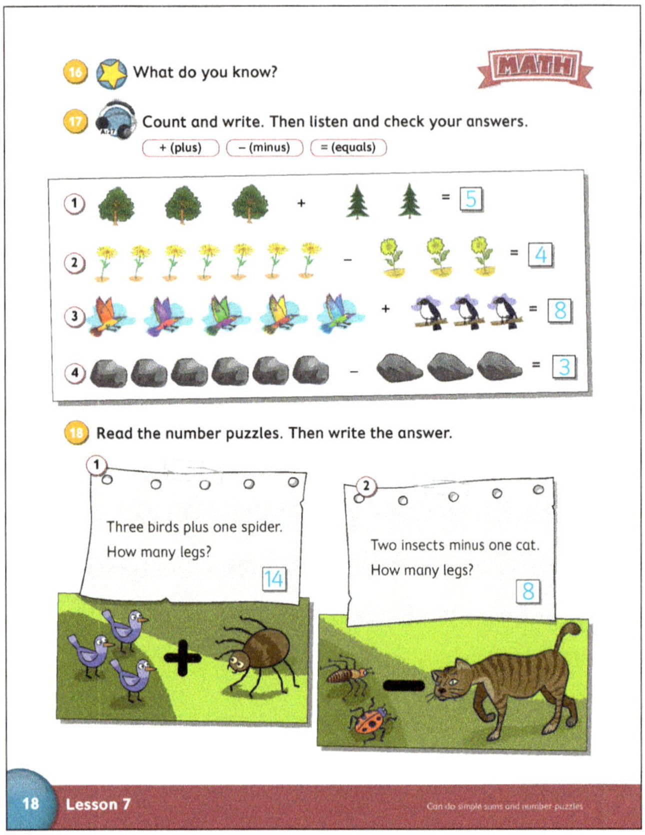
16 What do you know?

MATH

17 Count and write. Then listen and check your answers.

+ (plus) − (minus) = (equals)

1 = 5

2 = 4

3 = 8

4 = 3

18 Read the number puzzles. Then write the answer.

1 Three birds plus one spider. How many legs? 14

2 Two insects minus one cat. How many legs? 8

18 Lesson 7 Can do simple sums and number puzzles

Lesson 7 SB page 18 or Poptropica English World

Learning Objective
Can do simple sums and number puzzles

Additional Language
plus, minus, equals

Warm-up

- Divide the class into two teams. Call out random numbers and have students from each team walk to the front and write them on the board. Continue until students have written all numbers up to 50 on the board. The team with the most correct numbers wins.

16 What do you know?

- Open books and ask students to look at the activities on the page. Ask, *What are we learning today?* Write the lesson objective on the board: *We're learning to do simple sums and number puzzles.*
- Close books. Ask students what they know about adding and subtracting. Write their ideas on the board. Refer to the learning adventure poster and say, *Great! You are moving along your learning adventure!*

17 A:27 Count and write. Then listen and check your answers.

- Explain to the class that they are going to do some math exercises in English. Write the symbols +, −, and = on the board and ask, *What's this?* to elicit the words. Write the words (*plus, minus,* and *equals*) on the board as a reference for students. Say the words and have students repeat.
- Pair students to complete the activity. Students must count the items and write the correct sum. Encourage them to use English when counting.
- Play the audio and pause after each sum for students to check their answers.

1 Three trees plus two trees equals five trees.
2 Seven flowers minus three flowers equals four flowers.
3 Five birds plus three birds equals eight birds.
4 Six rocks minus three rocks equals three rocks.

18 Read the number puzzles. Then write the answer.

- Pair students and have them work out the numbers.
- Have students change partners and compare their answers.
- Check the answers as a class. Read each riddle, pausing after each animal(s) mentioned and writing the number of legs, e.g., *I'm the number of legs on three birds. (six)* Have students do the sums and compare their answers.

Ask students: *What else do you know about insects?* Tell students to work with a partner and say what they know about insects. Give pairs two minutes to think of ideas. Give students a minute to tell their partner the new ideas and words they can remember.

- Ask students: *Where are you on your learning adventure?* Tell students, *Good job!* to reinforce the progress they are making.

Pop Quiz: Before the end of the lesson, ask students some mental math problems: *What's 8 + 3? What's 22 minus 7? How many legs: two spiders plus one ant? Three butterflies minus one worm?*

Materials
Poster

Homework WB page 14

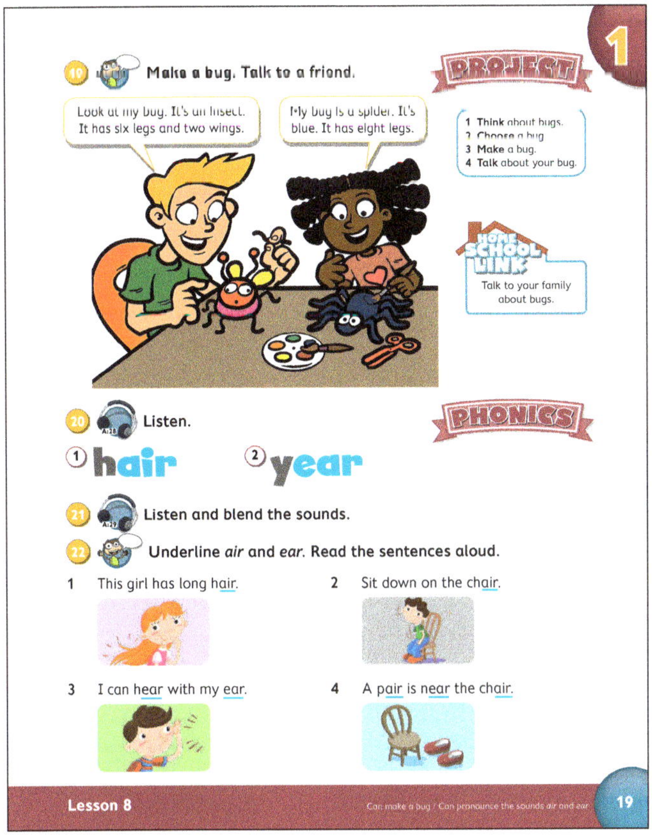

1

19 Make a bug. Talk to a friend.

PROJECT

1 **Think** about bugs.
2 **Choose** a bug.
3 **Make** a bug.
4 **Talk** about your bug.

HOME SCHOOL LINK
Talk to your family about bugs.

20 Listen.

PHONICS

① hair ② year

21 Listen and blend the sounds.

22 Underline *air* and *ear*. Read the sentences aloud.

1 This girl has long hair.
2 Sit down on the chair.
3 I can hear with my ear.
4 A pair is near the chair.

Lesson 8 Can make a bug / Can pronounce the sounds *air* and *ear* 19

Lesson 8 SB page 19 or Poptropica English World

Learning Objectives
Can make a bug
Can pronounce the sounds *air* and *ear*

Warm-up

- Draw simple pictures on the board of things with the grapheme *air* in them: *chair, air-plane*. Say, *ch-air chair, air air airplane*. Look around the room for anything else with *air*. All the time say, *air air air*. Encourage the group to join in saying, *air air air*.

Open books and ask students to look at the activities on the page. Ask, *What are we learning today?* Write the lesson objectives on the board: *We're learning to make a bug, and we're learning to pronounce* air *and* ear.

19 Make a bug. Talk to a friend.

- Show students the example models of bugs in their books. Explain that they are going to make their own bugs. Ask students to think about insects and bugs and to talk to a partner about what they know. Then have them choose a bug that they would like to make (real or imaginary).
- Provide the materials and give students time to make their bugs. Ask them to think about what materials they will use to make the body, legs, wings, etc.
- Display the bugs around the classroom and have the students talk to a partner, describing their bugs.
- Display the bugs in the classroom and ask students to choose their favorite.

You may also wish to give students feedback on their projects.

- **Home-School link:** Read the instruction with the class: *Talk to your family about bugs.* Ask students to do this at home.

20 Listen.

A:28

- Have students open their books and look at the two words, *hair* and *year*. Explain to students that they are going to read and pronounce the sounds *air* and *ear*. Play the audio.

1 air hair **2** ear year

21 Listen and blend the sounds.

A:29

- Introduce the concept of blending sounds. Make letter cards for *air* and *ear*. Start with the word *hair*. Put the *h* card on the board and sound out *h*. Have students repeat after you. Then add the *air* card, sound it out and have students repeat. Now sound out *h-air* while tapping your finger under each card and have the students repeat. Finally blend and say, *h-air hair*, a few times, eventually having the students join in with you. Now repeat with *year*.
- Turn to the book and do the activity on the page.

1 h air hair **2** y ear year

22 Underline *air* and *ear*. Read the sentences aloud.

- With books closed, write one of the sentences on the board, e.g., *This girl has long hair.*
- Ask students to scan the sentence to find the target grapheme *air*. Now run your finger under it as you sound out and read the words. Then have students open their books to find the same sentence on the page, then underline the target grapheme and read it aloud. Then they do the same with the other sentences.

Pop Quiz: Before the end of the lesson, write or show the sounds *air* and *ear* on the board. Say words containing one of the sounds, and have the students point to the right sound.

Materials
Letter cards (Unit 1), scissors, card/paper, colored pens or pencils, glue, string

Homework WB page 15

Lesson 9 SB page 20 or Poptropica English World

Learning Objective
Can assess what I have learned in Unit 1

Warm-up

- Write the following headings on the board: *Colors, Months, Numbers, Nature.* Say a color, month, number, or nature word, and have students say which category it belongs to.

Open books and ask students to look at the activities on the page. Explain to students that they are going to review what they have learned in this unit. Write the lesson objective on the board: *We're thinking about our learning adventure.*

- Ask students if they can remember the things they learned in this unit, e.g., *How many nature words can you remember?* Put their ideas on the board.
- For each example (e.g., *nature*), ask students, *Where are you on your learning adventure?*

23 A:30 Listen and number.

- Ask the students to look at the pictures and try to remember the name of each animal or object from nature.
- Play the audio and have the students point to the picture and write the number.
- Now ask students to work in pairs to help each other remember any of the words they couldn't remember.

24 Play a guessing game. Ask and answer.

- Ask students to work in pairs. They take turns to choose a picture from Activity 23. Their partner asks questions to find out which picture they have chosen. Then they switch roles.

25 Draw the view from your window. Ask and answer.

- Ask students to draw the view from their window. This can be the view from the class window, or from their bedroom window at home. In pairs, they ask and answer questions about their pictures.

Ask students how they feel about their learning in this unit. Ask students to tell you what they found easy and what they found the most difficult to learn in the unit.

- Students review the I Can statements at the bottom of the page and color each bar according to how confident they feel about the language point.
- Ask students, *Where are you on your learning adventure?* Students indicate where they think they are on the learning adventure poster. Tell students, *Good job!* to reinforce the progress they are making.

Pop Quiz: In groups of four, students tell the others the answers to the following questions: *Which is your favorite activity in the unit? Why? Which activity don't you like? Why? What is your favorite new word? Which word is the most difficult for you?*

Materials
Poster, colored pens or pencils

Homework WB page 16

Lesson 10 SB page 21 or Poptropica English World

Learning Objective
Can use what I have learned in Unit 1

Warm-up

- Stick Picture Cards 50–67 on the board. Write the words below each, but make some intentional mistakes. Teach the words *right* and *wrong*. Point to each in turn and ask, *Right or wrong?* Invite students to the board to correct your mistakes.

Open books and ask students to look at the activities on the page. Ask, *What are we learning today?* Write the lesson objective on the board: *We're learning about nature.*

Say, *I'm thinking of a question. The answer is: There are six.* Give students two minutes to think what the question might be. They might like to write their ideas in their notebooks. Write their suggestions on the board, e.g., *How many legs are there? How many flowers are there?* Ask students to say why they chose their ideas. With a confident class you might repeat this activity with a student giving the answer to a mystery question.

26 Spot the differences. Cover a picture. Ask a friend.

- Ask students to work in pairs. Each student chooses a picture and covers the other picture. Explain that they need to ask questions to find the differences between the two pictures. Have them circle the differences as they find them.
- When they have found several differences, have them uncover the pictures and look carefully at both pictures side-by-side to check that they have found all the differences. This activity helps build students' confidence as they are using the language they have learned in a different context.

I want to know more

- Ask students to choose anything they enjoyed from the unit and to go and find out more. You might like to set this activity as homework with a quick feedback session at the beginning of the next class, e.g. find out more words for nature, think of more ways to play safely, find out more information about bugs.

Are you ready for Unit 2?

- Ask students if they are ready to move onto the next unit. Tell students that it is fine if they do not remember everything as they will continue to practice throughout the level.
- Encourage students to ask if they have any questions about what they learned in Unit 1.

You may wish to give Unit 1 test (see page 188) at this time.

Materials
Picture Cards 50–67

Homework WB page 17

Unit 1 Story Cards

Wider World 1

SB pages 22–23 or Poptropica English World

Learning Objectives
Can understand texts about other children's birthdays.
Can talk about my birthday

Additional Language
I'm from (the United States/Mexico/Korea). I'm eight/nine (today).
birthday, cake, candles, party, candy, breakfast, seaweed soup, dishes

Wider World 1

Birthdays around the world

1 What do you know?

2 A:31 Listen and read.

1

Hi, I'm Lucy. I'm from the United States. Today's my birthday. I'm nine. Look at my birthday cake. There are nine candles. My friends and family sing "Happy Birthday," and I blow out the candles. I love birthdays!

candle

cake

2

My name's Diego, and I'm eight. I'm from Mexico. Look! It's my birthday party. There's a big *piñata* with candy inside. We break the *piñata*, and the candy falls out.

piñata

22 Wider World 1 Can understand texts about other children's birthdays

1 What do you know?

- Ask students when their birthday is. Ask if they celebrate birthdays in the family and if they have any special traditions.
- Bring a map of the world, or globe, and show it to the class. Locate your country on the map and say, *I'm from (Japan).*

Open books and ask students to look at the activities on the page. Ask, *What are we learning today?* Write the lesson objective on the board: *We're learning about birthdays.*

2 A:31 Listen and read.

- Tell students they are going to hear how the children celebrate their birthdays. Play the audio once and have students follow in their books. Then play each part separately, and ask questions to check comprehension, e.g., *What's his name? How old is he? What's the boy hitting?*

Materials
World map

3 Circle.

- Have students read the sentences, re-read the information about the children, and circle the correct words in the sentences.
- Check the answers with the whole class.

Tell the Class

4 Ask and answer.

- Have students work in pairs. They take turns to ask and answer about their partner's birthday parties using the questions on the page.
- Ask the children to think about how their birthdays are similar to those of the children from around the world, and how they are different.

Point at the learning objective on the board. Ask students, *How many words do you know for Nature now?* Give students a minute to tell their partner as many nature words as they can.

- Ask students, *Where are you on your learning adventure?* Ask students which words they find easiest or most difficult to remember. Tell students, *Good job!* to reinforce the progress they are making.

Pop Quiz: As students are leaving the class, ask them to tell the class one thing about their birthdays. Use the questions from Activity 4.

2 Me

Unit Overview

Unit Objective

- I can talk about physical characteristics

Language

Target Vocabulary	Physical characteristics: blond hair, dark eyebrows, brown eyes, curly hair, gray hair, glasses, a black mustache, a short beard, blue eyes, red hair, black beard, white teeth, big chin, long eyelashes, pink lips, red nose, big mouth
Target Structures	I have glasses. I don't have glasses. He has dark eyebrows. She doesn't have dark eyebrows. Do you have long eyelashes? Yes, I do. / No, I don't. Does he/she have curly hair? Yes, he/she does. / No, he/she doesn't.
Features	**Values:** Have good habits. Keep clean and healthy. **Cross-curricular:** Science: Wild animals **Phonics:** *ay, er* (say, dinner)

Skills

Reading	• Can understand a simple story • Can understand details of a story
Writing	• Can make a poster about animals • Can complete simple sentences about physical characteristics (*Workbook*) • Can write simple sentences about the physical characteristics people have or don't have (*Workbook*)
Listening	• Can identify physical characteristics • Can understand a simple story
Speaking	• Can describe people's physical characteristics • Can ask and answer about people's physical characteristics • Can role-play a story • Can talk about good habits and keeping clean and healthy • Can describe Australian animals • Can pronounce the sounds *ay* and *er*

Lesson 1 SB page 24 or Poptropica English World

Learning Objective
Can identify physical characteristics

Target Language
blond hair, dark eyebrows, brown eyes, curly hair, gray hair, glasses, a black mustache, a short beard, blue eyes, red hair

1 What do you know?

- Open books and ask students to look at the activities on the page. Ask, *What are we learning today?* Write the lesson objective on the board: *We're learning some physical characteristics.*
- Close books. Ask students what English words they know for appearance, e.g., *face, hair.* Write on board. Refer to the learning adventure poster and say, *Great! You are moving along your learning adventure!*

2 A:32 Listen and find. What's missing?

- Use the Picture Cards of physical characteristics (68–76) to teach the new vocabulary.
- Ask questions about the main scene: *Who's this? Where are they?* Call out the appearance words and have students find and point.
- Play the audio. Students listen and circle the pictures when they hear the words. Ask, *What's missing? (brown eyes)*

K: Look! Here's the space bus.
SH: Who is on the bus?
CC: There's a family from Earth. Look.
K: There are two children.
CC: They're Peter and Jane.
SH: Peter has short red hair and blue eyes.
CC: That's right.
SH: Jane has red hair too. Who's this?
CC: That's their mom. She has long blond hair and glasses.
K: And their dad has a black mustache and dark eyebrows.
SH: Yes, that's right. And who are they?
CC: They are their grandmother and grandfather.
SH: Oh, yes. Their grandfather has a short gray beard. He has glasses.
K: And their grandmother has brown curly hair. She doesn't have glasses.

3 A:33 Listen and number.

- Play the audio and ask students to find the items and number them.

1 Mum has long blond hair.
2 Dad has a black mustache.
3 Peter has blue eyes and short red hair.
4 Jane has red hair.
5 Grandfather has gray hair and small glasses.
6 Grandmother has curly hair and brown eyes. She doesn't have glasses.
7 Dad has dark eyebrows.
8 Grandfather has a short beard.

4 A:34 Listen and say.

- Play the audio. Students listen and repeat.

Ask students how many words for body parts they know now. Give students a minute to tell their partner the new words they know.

- Ask students to say where they are on their adventure now. Ask students which words they find easiest or most difficult to remember. Tell students, *Good job!* to reinforce the progress they are making.

Pop Quiz: As students are leaving the class, show them pictures of famous people. Point to facial features and have them say the words.

Materials
Poster, Picture Cards 68–76, pictures of famous people

Homework WB
page 18

Lesson 2 SB page 25 or Poptropica English World

Learning Objective
Can describe people's physical characteristics

Target Language
I have/don't have glasses.
He has dark eyebrows.
She doesn't have dark eyebrows.

Warm-up

- Review physical characteristics vocabulary by showing Picture Cards 68–76 one at a time. Reveal each picture slowly and have students say the words. Ask individual students to come to the front and write the words on the board.

Open books and ask students to look at the chant and at the Look! box. Ask, *What are we learning today?* Write the lesson objective on the board: *We're learning to describe people's physical characteristics.*

5 Listen and chant. A:33 A:36

- Read through the Look! box with the class, then play the chant (track A:37). Ask students to tell you what words for physical characteristics they hear on the chant. Then ask them to point to the items in the main scene.
- Play the chant a few times and have students chant along. If students are confident, use the karaoke version.

6 Play a guessing game.

- Model the dialog in the speech bubbles with a confident student.
- Have students take turns to describe a character from the main illustration, using the new vocabulary and structure. Their partner guesses who they are describing.
- Direct students' attention to the satellite dish card on page 25. Tell students to go online to the Poptropica English Island Adventure Game and find the item. Once students click on it, they are taken to a supplementary language task.

Pop Quiz: Have the students write descriptions of their classmates, e.g., *He has short brown hair. He has blue eyes and glasses.* They read out their descriptions and the class guesses who it is.

Materials
Picture Cards 68–76

Homework WB page 19

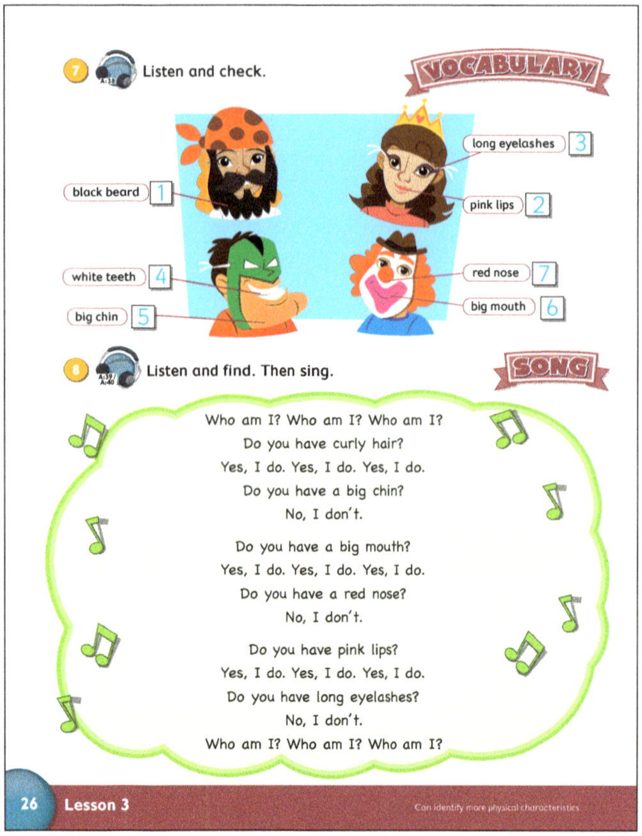

7 Listen and check. VOCABULARY

black beard 1
pink lips 2
long eyelashes 3
white teeth 4
big chin 5
big mouth 6
red nose 7

8 Listen and find. Then sing. SONG

Who am I? Who am I? Who am I?
Do you have curly hair?
Yes, I do. Yes, I do. Yes, I do.
Do you have a big chin?
No, I don't.

Do you have a big mouth?
Yes, I do. Yes, I do. Yes, I do.
Do you have a red nose?
No, I don't.

Do you have pink lips?
Yes, I do. Yes, I do. Yes, I do.
Do you have long eyelashes?
No, I don't.
Who am I? Who am I? Who am I?

26 Lesson 3 Can identify more physical characteristics

Lesson 3 SB page 26 or Poptropica English World

Learning Objective
Can identify more physical characteristics

Target Language
black beard, white teeth, big chin, long eyelashes, pink lips, red nose, big mouth

Additional Language
Who am I?

Warm-up

- Hand out Picture Cards 68–76 from Lesson 1 to students randomly around the class. Then stand at the front and ask students to hold their pictures up if they hear you call out their item.

Open books and ask students to look at the activities on the page. Ask, *What are we learning today?* Write the lesson objectives on the board: *We're learning more physical characteristics, and we're singing a simple song.*

- Close books. Ask students what English words they know for physical characteristics, e.g., *mouth, nose.* Write on board.
- Refer to the learning adventure poster and say, *Great! You are moving along your learning adventure!*

7 Listen and check.

A:38

- Introduce the new words with Picture Cards 77–82. Hold them up one by one and ask students to repeat the words after you. Then ask students to look in their books and point at the words as you say them.
- Play the audio and have students number the items as they are mentioned.

black beard	pink lips	long eyelashes	
white teeth	big chin	big mouth	red nose

- Play the audio again and have students repeat.

8 Listen and find. Then sing.

A:39 A:40

- Use pictures cut from magazines of *clown*, *pirate*, *princess*, and *superhero*. Take one and hold it behind your back and ask, *Who am I?* Have students ask you questions, e.g., *Do you have a big chin? Do you have a red nose? Are you a pirate?* When they guess correctly, repeat with a different picture.
- Play the audio and have students listen to find out who is being described (*the clown*). Ask them to point to the features that are mentioned as they hear them.
- Divide the class into two groups. Play the audio again and ask one group to sing along with the questions as they point to the features. Ask the other group to sing the answers and nod their heads for, *Yes*, or shake their heads for, *No*. Groups switch and repeat. If students are confident, use the karaoke version.
- For further practice divide students into groups of four. Give each group a copy of Activity Sheet 1 (see page 155). Have students cut it up into cards. Each student completes and colors in two identical faces. Have students mix up the cards and spread them face down on the table. They take turns flipping over two cards and describing the people, e.g., *He has a mustache and thick eyebrows.* If the cards match, the student says, e.g., *They are twins. They have a mustache and thick eyebrows.* and keeps the cards. If they are different, the cards remain face down. The student with the most pairs at the end is the winner.

Pop Quiz: Play *Parachute* with the vocabulary items from this lesson, plus Lesson 1 combined.

Materials
Picture Cards 68–76, 77–82, poster, pictures of clown, pirate, princess and superhero (cut from magazines), Activity Sheet 1, colored pens or pencils, scissors

Homework WB page 20

Lesson 4 SB page 27 or Poptropica English World

Learning Objective
Can ask and answer about people's physical characteristics

Target Language
Do you have long eyelashes? Yes, I do. / No, I don't. Does he/she have curly hair? Yes, he/she does. / No, he/she doesn't.

Warm-up

- Divide the class into two teams and have them stand in two lines facing each other. Assign each team member a number from one to four. Place a few Picture Cards (from 68–82) in the middle of the two teams. Call a number and a card, e.g., *Student three – curly hair.* The student assigned that number must go into the center, touch the card, and shout the phrase. The student who touched and called first can take the card.

Open books and ask students to look at the book and the Look! box. Ask, *What are we learning today?* Write the lesson objective on the board: *We're learning to ask about physical characteristics.*

9 Listen and number.

- Ask students to look at the three children in the pictures. Call a name, e.g., *Arisu*, and have students describe her, e.g., *She has curly hair and long eyelashes.*
- Focus on the sentences in the Look! box and play the audio (track A:41). Ask students to read the text aloud.
- Play the audio and have students listen. They should match each description to the correct picture.
- Play the audio again, pausing for students to write the correct number in the box.

1 She has long eyelashes and curly hair. She has pink lips.
2 He has a red nose and a big mouth.
3 She has a black beard and a mustache.

10 Look at Activity 9. Ask and answer.

- Ask students to look at the three children in the pictures in Activity 9 again. In pairs, have them ask and answer questions about the three children.

Pop Quiz: Before the end of the lesson, ask volunteers to come to the front and play a guessing game. They choose somebody in the class and write the name of that student on a sheet of paper. The rest of the class guesses who it is by asking questions, e.g., *Does he/she have long hair?*

Materials
Picture Cards 68–82, a sheet of paper

Homework WB page 21

Lesson 5 SB page 28 or Poptropica English World

Learning Objectives
Can understand a simple story
Can role-play a story

Additional Language
bus, let's go, spots

Functional Language
Hooray! What!?!! Uh, oh.

Warm-up

- Ask students what they can remember about the story from the previous episode. Use the Unit 1 Story Cards as prompts. Ask what they saw in the park, and what happened to PROD 1. Remind students that the characters are looking for a tifftiff plant.

Open books and ask students to look at the story. Ask, *What are we learning today?* Write the lesson objective on the board: *We're reading a story and we're role-playing a story.*

11 Talk about the pictures. Then listen and read.

A:43

- Direct students' attention to the story and ask questions about the characters and the scene: *Who can you see? Where are they? What are they doing? What does she look like?*
- Play the audio and have students listen and follow. Check understanding by pointing at the pictures and asking questions: *What are they waiting for? Who is on the bus? What is PROD 2 doing? Does Dr Bones have a beard?*
- Play the audio again, pausing after each line. Have students repeat.
- Play the audio again. Have students speak along to the audio and mime the actions.

Write the following question on the board: *What is tickilitis?* Tell students to work with a partner and think about what tickilitis might be. Ask, *Have they ever had spots/been sick? How did they feel?* Give pairs two minutes to think of their answers. They might like to write their ideas in their notebooks. Write their suggestions on the board. Ask students to say why they chose their ideas.

12 Role-play the story.

- See the "How to use stories" section on page 22 for more ideas on how to build your students' confidence with role-plays.
- Divide students into groups of seven. Give each group a set of cut-up Story Cards and have students place them in order.
- Have the groups role-play the story. When you say, *change*, they should change character and role-play a new character. Rotate through the characters, giving students the chance to play each one.

You might like to give the students feedback on their role-play.

Pop Quiz: Before the end of the lesson, make true and false statements about the story. Students say if they are *true* or *false*, e.g., *Dr. Bones has blond hair. (true) Dr Bones has a mustache. (false)*

Materials
Story Cards (Units 1 and 2)

Homework WB page 22

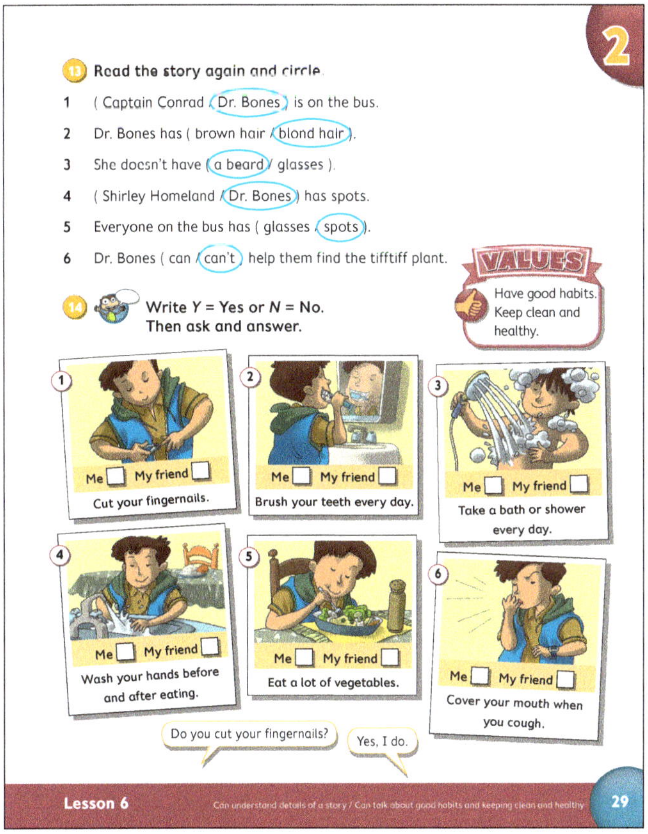
2

13 Read the story again and circle.

1 (Captain Conrad / Dr. Bones) is on the bus.
2 Dr. Bones has (brown hair / blond hair).
3 She doesn't have (a beard / glasses).
4 (Shirley Homeland / Dr. Bones) has spots.
5 Everyone on the bus has (glasses / spots).
6 Dr. Bones (can / can't) help them find the tifftiff plant.

VALUES
Have good habits. Keep clean and healthy.

14 Write *Y* = Yes or *N* = No. Then ask and answer.

Lesson 6 Can understand details of a story / Can talk about good habits and keeping clean and healthy 29

Lesson 6 SB page 29 or Poptropica English World

Learning Objectives
Can understand details of a story
Can talk about good habits and keeping clean and healthy

Additional Language
fingernails, cough

Value
Have good habits. Keep clean and healthy.

Open books and ask students to look at the activities on the page. Ask, *What are we learning today?* Write the lesson objective on the board: *We're understanding details of a story, and we're learning to have good habits and to keep clean and healthy.*

Warm-up

- Divide students into small teams. Each team forms a circle and the students hold hands. Give each team a balloon. As a team, they have to keep the balloon in the air, but when it touches a part of someone's body, that student has to shout out a physical characteristics phrase, or a sentence containing one, e.g., *I have brown eyes.* Continue until all the characteristics they know have been used. Then change the topic, e.g., days of the week, months, nature, or numbers.

13 Read the story again and circle.

- Have students work in pairs. They look at the story frames and read the sentences, circling the word that makes a true statement.
- Have students read the true statements aloud to check that they are correct.

14 Write Y = Yes or N = No. Then ask and answer.

- Read the value, *Have good habits. Keep clean and healthy.* Direct students' attention to the six pictures and read the captions. Have students repeat until they are familiar with language and pronunciation. Have students ask and answer the questions for themselves and write *Y* or *N* in the boxes.
- Pair students and have them ask each other the questions, and complete the boxes for their partner.

Write the following questions on the board: *Why is it good to be clean. (It helps us to stay healthy.) What other things can we do to stay clean? (wash our hands after playing outside, change your clothes regularly)*

- Tell students to work with a partner. Give pairs two minutes to discuss and note down their answers. Ask students to share their answers with the class.

Pop Quiz: Before the end of the lesson, play a *Guess who?* game, using characters from the story. Choose a character without telling the class. They ask questions to guess who it is, e.g., *Does he/she have brown hair? Does he/she have glasses?*

Materials
Balloons

Homework WB page 23

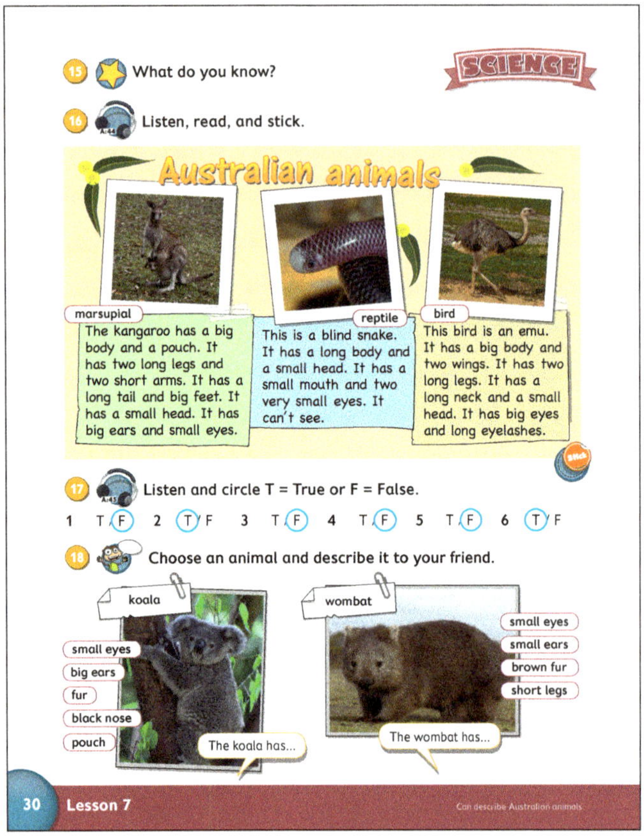

15 What do you know?

SCIENCE

16 Listen, read, and stick.

Australian animals

marsupial
The kangaroo has a big body and a pouch. It has two long legs and two short arms. It has a long tail and big feet. It has a small head. It has big ears and small eyes.

reptile
This is a blind snake. It has a long body and a small head. It has a small mouth and two very small eyes. It can't see.

bird
This bird is an emu. It has a big body and two wings. It has two long legs. It has a long neck and a small head. It has big eyes and long eyelashes.

17 Listen and circle T = True or F = False.

1 T (F) 2 (T) F 3 T (F) 4 T (F) 5 T (F) 6 (T) F

18 Choose an animal and describe it to your friend.

koala

small eyes
big ears
fur
black nose
pouch

The koala has...

wombat

small eyes
small ears
brown fur
short legs

The wombat has...

30 Lesson 7 Can describe Australian animals

Lesson 7 SB page 30 or Poptropica English World

Learning Objective
Can describe Australian animals

Additional Language
marsupial, pouch, reptile, blind, snake, emu, feathers

Warm-up

- Brainstorm animals that students have learned. Write the words on the board and classify them into *pets*, *wild animals* and *farm animals*. Ask, *Is it long/short/big/small?* for each animal.
- Display pictures of animals on the board and ask students to describe them.

15 What do you know?

- Open books and ask students to look at the activities on the page. Ask, *What are we learning today?* Write the lesson objective on the board: *We're learning about Australian animals.*
- Close books. Ask students what they know about Australian animals. Write their ideas on the board. Refer to the learning adventure poster and say, *Great! You are moving along your learning adventure!*

16 A:44 Listen, read and stick.

- Pair students and have them read the paragraphs and underline any words they don't understand. You can also play the audio while they read.
- Have students find the three stickers at the back of the book and stick them on the correct spaces. Have them go through the paragraphs again and see if they can work out the meaning of the unknown words from the pictures and context.

17 A:45 Listen and circle T = True or F = False.

- Play the audio and have students listen.

1 The kangaroo doesn't have a pouch.
2 The emu has feathers.
3 The blind snake has a round head.
4 The kangaroo has small ears.
5 The blind snake has big eyes.
6 The emu has two long legs.

- Pair students. Play the audio again, pausing after each sentence for students to think, decide, and circle the correct letter, *T* or *F*.
- Play the audio again and check answers as a class.

18 Choose an animal and describe it to your friend.

- Introduce the two animals in the pictures, the koala and the wombat. Ask students if they know where they live, and if they have seen them. Describe an animal, e.g., *It has brown fur and small eyes. (wombat)*, and have students guess the animal.
- Pair students and have them take turns describing each of the animals to their partners.

Ask students: *What do you know about Australia? Where is it? What language do they speak? Which other animals live there?* Accept any answers and promote discussion.

- Tell students to work with a partner and say what they know about Australia. Give pairs two minutes to think of ideas. Give students a minute to tell their partner the new ideas and words they can remember.
- Ask students, *Where are you on your learning adventure?* Tell students, *Good job!* to reinforce the progress they are making.

Pop Quiz: Before the end of the lesson, play a drawing game on the board. Think of an Australian animal. Have students ask questions to guess the animal, e.g., *Does it have a long tail?* When they answer is *yes*, draw that part of the animal's body. If the answer is *no*, have students ask another question.

Materials
Pictures of animals, poster, stickers

Homework WB page 24

Lesson 8 SB page 31 or Poptropica English World

Learning Objectives
Can make a poster about animals
Can pronounce the sounds *ay* and *er*.

Warm-up

- Prepare large letter cards to review the sounds and letters. Show the cards in random order and have students chorus the letter-sounds. Start slowly and then increase the speed.
- Put the letter cards on the board. Say a letter-sound and choose a student to come to the front and touch the correct letter. Repeat until everyone has had a go.

Open books and ask students to look at the activities on the page. Ask, *What are we learning today?* Write the lesson objectives on the board: *We're making a poster about animals, and we're learning to pronounce* ay *and* er.

19 Make a poster. Talk to a friend.

- Explain that students are going to make animal posters. Ask them to think about animals from their country and to talk to a partner about what they know about them. Then have them draw or find pictures of animals they would like to use.
- Have students work in small groups. Show them a map of your country. Have them copy the map onto a large sheet of paper – one per group. Provide the materials, and give students time to draw or cut out animal pictures and place them on the map.
- Display the posters around the classroom and have students describe their posters.
- Display the posters in the classroom and ask students to choose their favorite.

You may also wish to give students feedback on their projects.

- **Home-School link:** Read the instruction with the class: *Show your poster to your family.* Ask students to do this at home.

20 A:46 Listen.

- Have students open their books and look at the two words, *say* and *dinner.* Explain to students that they are going to read and pronounce the sounds *ay* and *er.* Play the audio.

1 ay say **2** er dinner

21 A:47 Listen and blend the sounds.

- Play the audio, pausing after each letter-sound to allow students to do the activity. Repeat several times.

1 s ay say **2** d i nn er dinner

22 Underline *ay* and *er*. Read the sentences aloud.

- Blend the sample words one by one in a different order from the book, by writing them up on the board. Model the blending yourself. Now have students turn to their books and do the same blending activity in pairs. Then play the audio for students to check.
- You may wish to spend some time on the two-syllable words. Clap your hands to show the two syllables, and have the students join in. Explain that the middle letters are doubled to *nn*, *mm* and *tt*, but the sound does not change.

Pop Quiz: Before the end of the lesson, ask the students to write *ay* in blue on one sheet of paper, and *er* in red on another. Say words containing the sounds, and have students hold up the right sheet of paper, e.g., say, *supper* (they hold up the red *er*); say, *day* (they hold up the blue *ay*).

Materials
Letter cards (Units 1 and 2), a map of the teacher's country, sheets of paper, scissors, glue, colored pens or pencils

Homework WB page 25

Lesson 9 SB page 32 or Poptropica English World

Learning Objective
Can assess what I have learned in Unit 2

Warm-up

- Display the physical characteristics Picture Cards (68–82) to review the vocabulary. Ask, e.g., *Does he/she have a small nose? (Yes, he/she does. / No, he/she doesn't.)*

Open books and ask students to look at the activities on the page. Explain to students that they are going to review what they have learned in this unit. Write the lesson objective on the board: *We're thinking about our learning adventure.*

- Ask students if they can remember the things they learned in this unit, e.g., *How many physical characteristic words can you remember?* Put their ideas on the board.
- For each example (e.g., *characteristics*), ask students, *Where are you on your learning adventure?*

23 Read and check (✓).

- Ask the students to look at the pictures and try to remember the name of each feature.
- Have the students read the words under each picture and check those that are in the picture.
- Now ask students to work in pairs to help each other remember any of the words they couldn't remember.

24 Listen and check (✓). Then check with a friend.

A:48

- Play the audio. Ask students to listen and check the picture of the person that is described. Have them check their answers in pairs.

1
Boy: My grandfather has a beard. He doesn't have a mustache.
Girl: Does he have glasses?
Boy: Yes. He has big glasses.
2
Boy: My sister has big eyes and long eyelashes.
Girl: Does she have long hair?
Boy: No, she has short, blond hair.
3
Boy: My dad has short black hair and glasses.
Girl: Does he have dark eyebrows?
Boy: Yes, he does.
4
Boy: My mom has short brown hair.
Girl: Does she have glasses?
Boy: No, she doesn't.

Ask students how they feel about their learning in this unit. Ask students to tell you what they found easy and what they found the most difficult to learn in the unit.

- Students review the I Can statements at the bottom of the page and color each bar according to how confident they feel about the language point.
- Ask students, *Where are you on your learning adventure?* Students indicate where they think they are on the learning adventure poster. Tell students, *Good job!* to reinforce the progress they are making.

Pop Quiz: In groups of four, students tell the others the answers to the following questions: *Which is your favorite activity in the unit? Why? Which activity don't you like? Why? What is your favorite new word? Which word is the most difficult for you?*

Materials
Picture Cards 68–82, poster

Homework WB page 26

Lesson 10 SB page 33 or Poptropica English World

Learning Objective
Can use what I have learned in Unit 2

Warm-up

- Ask students to recall all the new words they've learned in this unit. Ask which activity or lesson they found most interesting. Ask what they found easy and what was difficult.
- Flip through Picture Cards 1–82. Have students call out the words as quickly as possible.

Open books and ask students to look at the activities on the page. Ask, *What are we learning today?* Write the lesson objective on the board: *We're learning about physical characteristics.*

Ask volunteers to flick through the unit and choose a character from any picture (a story character, a masked character, or even an animal) and come to the front. Students ask questions to find out who the character is, e.g., *Do you have big ears? Do you have a mustache?* etc. Give pairs two minutes to think of their questions. They might like to write their ideas in their notebooks. Write their suggestions on the board. When they have guessed correctly, ask the volunteer in the hot seat to say why they chose that character.

25 Choose. Then play.

- Direct students' attention to the pictures. Point to random pictures and say, e.g., *This is Jonas. He has blond hair and blue eyes.* Make sure students are familiar with the names. Say the numbers and have students call out the person's name.
- Pair students then explain the game to the class. Students choose a person without telling his/her partner, who has to guess the name by asking questions about physical characteristics. Students take turns. Decide on the number of people each student can choose (five or six) depending on the class time available. The winner is the one who makes the most correct guesses.
- Model the language with a student if necessary.
- Pair students again and have them play the game with new partners.
- This activity helps build students' confidence as they are using the language they have learned in a different context.

I want to know more

- Ask students to choose anything they enjoyed from the unit and to go and find out more. You might like to set this activity as homework with a quick feedback session at the beginning of the next class e.g. find out more words for physical characteristics, think of more ways to stay clean and healthy, find out some more information about where different animals come from.

Are you ready for Unit 3?

- Ask students if they are ready to move onto the next unit. Tell students that it is fine if they do not remember everything as they will continue to practice throughout the level.
- Encourage students to ask if they have any questions about what they learned in Units 1 and 2.

You may wish to give Unit 2 test (see page 190) at this time.

Materials
Picture Cards 1–82

Homework WB page 27

Unit 2 Story Cards

Review Units 1 and 2

SB pages 34–35 or Poptropica English World

Learning Objective
Can talk about nature and physical characteristics

Warm-up

- Put a selection of Picture Cards (1–82) on the floor and spread them out, some with pictures facing up, some with words facing up. Students line up and take turns throwing a small bean bag onto the Cards. They should be at some distance from the Cards. When the bean bag successfully lands on a Card, the student reads the word or identifies the picture. If the student is correct, he/she takes the Card. The game continues until there are no more Cards on the floor.

Open books and ask students to look at the activities on the page. Ask, *What are we learning today?* Write the lesson objectives on the board: *We're talking about nature and physical characteristics.*

1 Play a guessing game.

- Explain the game. Students take turns choosing a picture and describing it. They use all the words they have learned for nature and for physical characteristics. Their partner should try to guess the picture by identifying its number. Decide on the time limit for the game. The winner could be the student with the most correct guesses or the pair with the highest number of chosen cards.
- Have students play the game in pairs.

Watch the video story *Changing colors* on Poptropica English World. Ask students what happened in the story. Watch again, stopping at key points, and ask them about the language, the images, or the story. Ask the students to role-play the story. Assign the roles of two of the characters to confident speakers and let other students play the other parts. Encourage them to say as much of the dialog as they can and prompt them where necessary.

Materials
Picture Cards 1–82, small bean bag

Point to the learning objective on the board. Ask students, *How many words do you know for physical characteristics now?* Give students a minute to tell their partner as many words for physical characteristics as they can.

- Ask students, *Where are you on your learning adventure?* Ask students which words they find easiest or most difficult to remember. Tell students, *Good job!* to reinforce the progress they are making.

Pop Quiz: As students are leaving the class, say the number of a picture from the game in the Student Book to each student. Students describe the relevant picture, e.g., say, *Picture 11.* The student says, *It's big and gray. It's a rock.*

You may wish to give Review Test 1 (see page 204) at this time.

3 Pets

Unit Overview

Unit Objective

- I can talk about pets

Language

Target Vocabulary	Animal body parts: tail, beak, wings, feathers, claws, fins, paws, whiskers, skin, fur Animal characteristics: soft fur, a hard shell, sharp claws Adjectives: cute, scary, fast, slow
Target Structures	What does it look like? It has a tail. It doesn't have wings. What do they look like? They have whiskers. They don't have fins. Do you have a dog? Yes, I do. It's cute. / No, I don't. Does it have soft fur? Yes, it does. / No, it doesn't.
Features	**Values:** Take care of your pet. **Cross-curricular:** Science: Animal life cycles **Phonics:** *ea, oi* (tea, oil)

Skills

Reading	• Can understand a simple story • Can understand details of a story	• Can understand short texts about animal life cycles
Writing	• Can complete simple sentences about my pet • Can make a butterfly life cycle wheel • Can complete simple sentences about pets and animal life cycles (*Workbook*) • Can write simple sentences about animal characteristics (*Workbook*)	
Listening	• Can identify animal body parts • Can identify animal characteristics	• Can understand a simple story • Can understand short texts about animal life cycles
Speaking	• Can ask and answer about what an animal looks like • Can talk about pets and their characteristics	• Can role-play a story • Can talk about taking care of my pet • Can pronounce the sounds *ea* and *oi*

Lesson 1 SB page 36 or Poptropica English World

Learning Objective
Can identify animal body parts

Target Language
tail, beak, wings, feathers, claws, fins, paws, whiskers, skin, fur

1 What do you know?

- Open books and ask students to look at the activities on the page. Ask, *What are we learning today?* Write the lesson objective on the board: *We're learning about animal body parts.*
- Close books. Ask students what English words they know for parts of their bodies, e.g., *ears, legs.* Write on board.
- Refer to the learning adventure poster and say, *Great! You are already moving along your learning adventure!*

2 A:49 Listen and find. What's missing?

- Use the Picture Cards of pets (83–92) to teach the new vocabulary. Say the words and have students repeat.
- Ask questions about the main scene: *Who's this? Where are they?*
- Play the audio. Students listen to the dialog and find the pictures when they hear the words. Ask, *What's missing?* (*tail, fins, skin*)

ZK:	Hello! Welcome to the zoo. There are some amazing animals here on Space Island. But tell me about your animals.
K:	OK. PROD 1. Let's show the zookeeper some animals.
P:	This is a mouse. It has a long tail. It has four pink paws and a pink nose.
ZK:	Ha, ha! It's funny!
K:	Look! This is a parrot. It has two legs, and two wings. It doesn't have fur, it has feathers. They're blue and yellow.
K:	It has a beak. Can you see it?
ZK:	Oh, yes, it's beautiful. Can it fly?
K:	Yes, it can.
P:	This animal is a rabbit.
ZK:	What does it look like?
K:	It has white fur and pink eyes. It has two long ears. It has a pink nose and a lot of white whiskers.
ZK:	Your animals are great! Now come with me and see my animals.

3 A:50 Listen and number.

- Play the audio again and ask them to find and number the items.

1 The snake's skin is green.	**6** The fish has orange fins.
2 The parrot's beak is yellow.	**7** The rabbit has long white whiskers on its face.
3 The feathers are blue and yellow.	**8** The mouse has a long tail.
4 It has two wings.	**9** The dog has brown fur.
5 The rabbit has four white paws.	**10** It has long claws.

4 A:51 Listen and say.

- Play the audio. Students listen and repeat.

Ask students how many words for animals and their bodies they know now. Give students a minute to tell their partner the new words they know.

- Ask students to say where they are on their adventure now. Ask students which words they find easiest or most difficult to remember. Tell students, *Good job!* to reinforce the progress they are making.

Pop Quiz: Before the end of the lesson, draw an animal on the board very slowly. Students call out the parts of the body as they see them, and guess the animal.

Materials
Poster, Picture Cards 83–92

Homework WB page 28

5 Listen and chant.

A:52/A:53

Does it have two eyes?
Yes, it does.
Does it have four legs?
No, it doesn't.
Does it have a tail?
Yes, it does.
Does it have two hands?
No, it doesn't.
Splish, splash, splish.
It's a fish.

LOOK! A:54

What	**does** it / **do** they	look like?
It	**has** / **doesn't have**	a tail. / wings.
They	**have** / **don't have**	whiskers. / fins.

6 Look at the animals in the chant. Ask and answer.

Lesson 2 Can ask and answer about what an animal looks like 37

Lesson 2 SB page 37 or Poptropica English World

Learning Objective
Can ask and answer about what an animal looks like

Warm-up

- Use Picture Cards 83–92 to review the target vocabulary. Hold up the Cards in turn for students to say the words. Ask individual students to come to the front and write the words on the board.
- Pair students and have them play the game with partners.

Open books and ask students to look at the chant and the Look! box. Ask, *What are we learning today?* Write the lesson objective on the board: *We're learning to ask and answer about what animals look like.*

5 Listen and chant.

A:52 A:53

- Play the chant. Ask students to tell you what new words they hear. Then ask them to point to the items in the main scene.
- Play the chant a few times and have students chant along. If students are confident, use the karaoke version.

6 Look at the animals in the chant. Ask and answer.

- Read through the Look! box with the class and play the audio (track A:54).
- Ask students to look at each picture and identify the animal. Read aloud the speech bubbles with a volunteer. Model one or two more examples.
- Pair students and have them ask and answer.
- Direct students' attention to the bird house card on page 37. Tell students to go online to the Poptropica English Island Adventure Game and find the item. Once students click on it, they are taken to a supplementary language task.

Pop Quiz: Use Picture Cards of animals from Level 1. Invite volunteers to come to the front. They choose a picture without showing the class. The class asks, *What does it look like?* The volunteer describes the animal, one feature at a time: *It has... / It doesn't have....* The class guesses the animal.

Materials
Picture Cards 83–92, Picture Cards of animals (Level 1)

Homework WB page 29

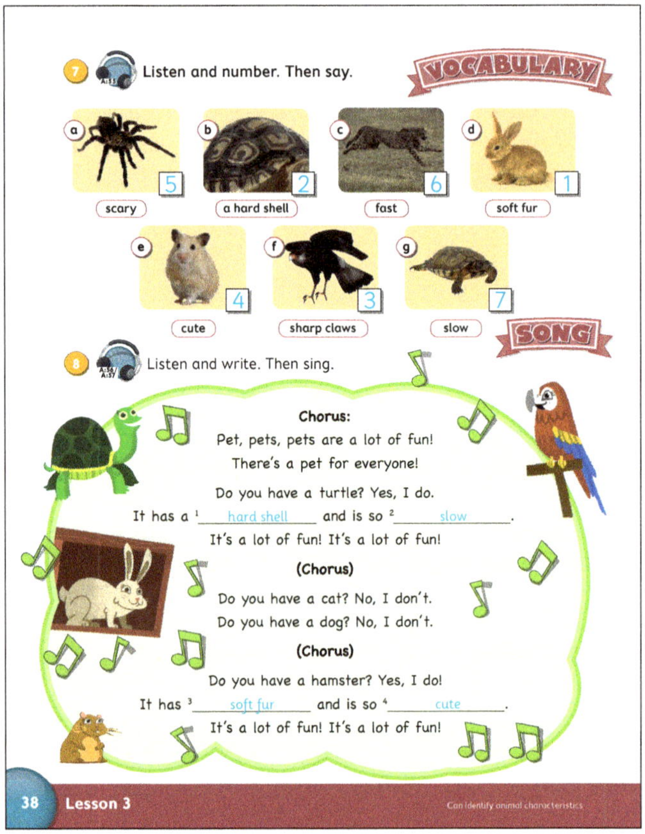
7 Listen and number. Then say. VOCABULARY

a scary 5 · b a hard shell 2 · c fast 6 · d soft fur 1 · e cute 4 · f sharp claws 3 · g slow 7

SONG

8 Listen and write. Then sing.

Chorus:
Pet, pets, pets are a lot of fun!
There's a pet for everyone!

Do you have a turtle? Yes, I do.
It has a 1 hard shell and is so 2 slow.
It's a lot of fun! It's a lot of fun!

(Chorus)

Do you have a cat? No, I don't.
Do you have a dog? No, I don't.

(Chorus)

Do you have a hamster? Yes, I do!
It has 3 soft fur and is so 4 cute.
It's a lot of fun! It's a lot of fun!

38 Lesson 3 Can identify animal characteristics

Lesson 3 SB page 38 or Poptropica English World

Learning Objective
Can identify animal characteristics

Target Language
soft fur, a hard shell, sharp claws, cute, scary, fast, slow

Warm-up

- Ask students to vote on which song/chant from the previous units is their favorite. Choose a class favorite and play it once or twice to get students moving.

Open books and ask students to look at the activities on the page. Ask, *What are we learning today?* Write the lesson objective on the board: *We're learning more animal characteristics.*

- Close books. Ask students what English words they know for animal characteristics, e.g. *fur, slow, etc.* Write on board.
- Refer to the learning adventure poster and say, *Great! You are moving along your learning adventure!*

7 Listen and number. Then say.

A:55

- Introduce the new words with Picture Cards 93–99. Hold them up one by one and ask students to repeat after you. Then ask students to look in their books and point at the words as you say them.
- Play the audio and have students number the items as they hear them. Then play it again for students to say the words.
- Point to individual pictures and ask students to tell you the word.

1 soft fur	**5** scary
2 a hard shell	**6** fast
3 sharp claws	**7** slow
4 cute	

8 Listen and write. Then sing.

A:56 A:57

- Have students look at the pictures. Students identify and name the animals.
- Play the song and have students listen and follow. Play the audio again and have students write the words.
- Have students check their answers in pairs.
- Divide the class into two groups. Group A sings the questions, and Group B sings the answers. Everyone sings the chorus together. Play the song with each group singing their lines.
- If students are confident, use the karaoke version.

Ask students, *How many words for animal characteristics do you know now?* Give students a minute to tell their partner the new words they know.

- Ask students to say where they are on their adventure now. Ask students which words they find easiest or most difficult to remember. Tell students, *Good job!* to reinforce the progress they are making.

Pop Quiz: Play a game with the vocabulary items from this lesson, plus Lesson 1 combined. Put students into two teams. Put a picture of an animal on the board. Teams take turns to provide a word that relates to the animal – this can be nouns or adjectives, e.g., *four legs, cute, brown fur, fast,* etc. Teams win a point for each word they provide. When they run out of words, put different animal picture on the board, and play again.

Materials
Poster, Picture Cards 93–99, pictures of animals

Homework WB page 30

LOOK!

Do you have a dog?	Yes, I do. It's cute. No, I don't.	Does it have soft fur?	Yes, it does. No, it doesn't.

9 Choose a pet. Ask and answer.

1 paws, tail, claws, soft fur
2 hard shell, slow, fun
3 beak, feathers, wings, fast
4 soft fur, short tail, cute, fast
5 fins, tail, small
6 no legs, long, scary

My pet has wings. It's fast.
Do you have a bird?
Yes, I do.

10 Write.

WRITING

My pet
Animal: tarantula
Name: Boris
Home: Arizona
Age: three years old
Color: brown
Legs: eight
Food: insects

Hi, I'm Alex, and I have a pet. It's a [1] tarantula, and it's from Arizona. Its name is Boris. It's [2] three years old. It's brown. It doesn't have a tail. It has eight [3] legs. It likes to eat [4] insects. Some people say it's scary. I say it's cute and very smart. I love my pet tarantula.

Lesson 4 Can talk about pets and their characteristics 39

Lesson 4 SB page 39 or Poptropica English World

Learning Objective
Can talk about pets and their characteristics

Target Language
Do you have a dog?
Yes, I do. It's cute. / No, I don't.
Does it have soft fur?
Yes, it does. / No, it doesn't.

Warm-up

- Divide students into small teams. Give each team a balloon. As a team they have to keep the balloon in the air, but when it touches a part of someone's body they have to shout out an animal body part or characteristics phrase.

Open books and ask students to look at the book and the Look! box. Ask, *What are we learning today?* Write the lesson objective on the board: *We're learning to talk about pets and their characteristics, with* Do you have... *and* Does it have....

9 Choose a pet. Ask and answer.

- Read through the Look! box with the class and play the audio (track A:58). Have students look at picture 3. Read the model dialog with a student.
- Choose another pet and describe it. Have the class guess the pet.
- Pair students and have them play the guessing game until they have asked and answered questions about each picture.

10 Write.

- Have students close their books. Describe Alex's pet, e.g., *It's brown. It has eight legs.*, and have students make guesses.
- Ask students to open their books, and read the descriptions. Then ask questions to check comprehension, e.g., *What's its name? (Boris) Where's its home? (Arizona)*
- Have students complete the text in the speech bubble.
- Pair students and have them read each other the complete sentences to compare answers. Write the correct answers on the board.
- For further practice pair students. Give each pair a copy of Activity Sheet 2 (see page 156), and a dice. Students play a game using erasers or coins as counters. They take turns throwing the dice and moving along the board game. When a student lands on a space, his/her partner asks as many questions as possible about the picture. Students write down the number of questions and the correct answers for each player. When they both reach the "Finish" space, they count them. The winner is the student with the most questions asked and the most correct answers.

Pop Quiz: Before the end of the lesson, ask students to write notes about their own pets (or an imaginary pet) on a card. They should use the headings in SB Activity 10 as a template: *Animal: Name: Home:*, etc. Take all the cards in and redistribute them, making sure students do not get their own animal. The aim is to find their own pet cards, by moving around the class asking questions. Students refer to their 'new' cards to respond. e.g., *Do you have a dog? Yes. Does it have brown fur? Yes. Is its name Boris? Yes. That's my dog!*

Materials
Two balloons, cards, Activity Sheet 2

Homework WB page 31

Lesson 5 SB page 40 or Poptropica English World

Learning Objectives
Can understand a simple story
Can role-play a story

Additional Language
teeth, beautiful

Functional Language
Please help me! Ow! Ow! Ow! Ooooh!
It's beautiful!

Warm-up

- Ask students to remember what has happened in the story so far. Use Unit 1 and 2 Story Cards as prompts.

Open books and ask students to look at the story. Ask, *What are we learning today?* Write the lesson objective on the board: *We're reading a story and we're role-playing a story.*

11 Talk about the pictures. Then listen and read.

A:39

- Direct students' attention to the story and ask questions about the characters and the scene. Ask, *Who can you see? Where are they? What are they doing? What does it look like?*
- Play the audio and have students listen and follow. Check understanding by pointing at the pictures and asking questions: *Who has the wabberjock? What does it look like? Does it have sharp teeth? Who has the wabberjock at the end?*
- Play the audio again, stopping after each line. Have students repeat.
- Play the audio again. Have students speak along and mime the actions.

Write the following question on the board: *What is a wabberjock?* Tell students to work with a partner and think about what a wabberjock might be. *What does it look like? Can it swim? Is it cute? Is it scary?* Give pairs two minutes to think of their answers. They might like to write their ideas in their notebooks. Write their suggestions on the board.

12 Role-play the story.

- See the "How to use stories" section on page 22 for more ideas on how to build your students' confidence with role-plays.
- Divide students into groups of five. Give each group a set of cut-up Story Cards and have students place them in order.
- Divide students into groups and have them role-play the story. When you say, *change,* they should change character and role-play a new character. Rotate through the characters giving students the chance to play each one.

You might like to give the students feedback on their role-play.

Pop Quiz: Before the end of the lesson, read individual speech bubbles from the story. Students say which character said those words, e.g., *Oooh! It's beautiful.* (PROD 2)

Materials
Story Cards (Units 1, 2, and 3)

Homework WB page 32

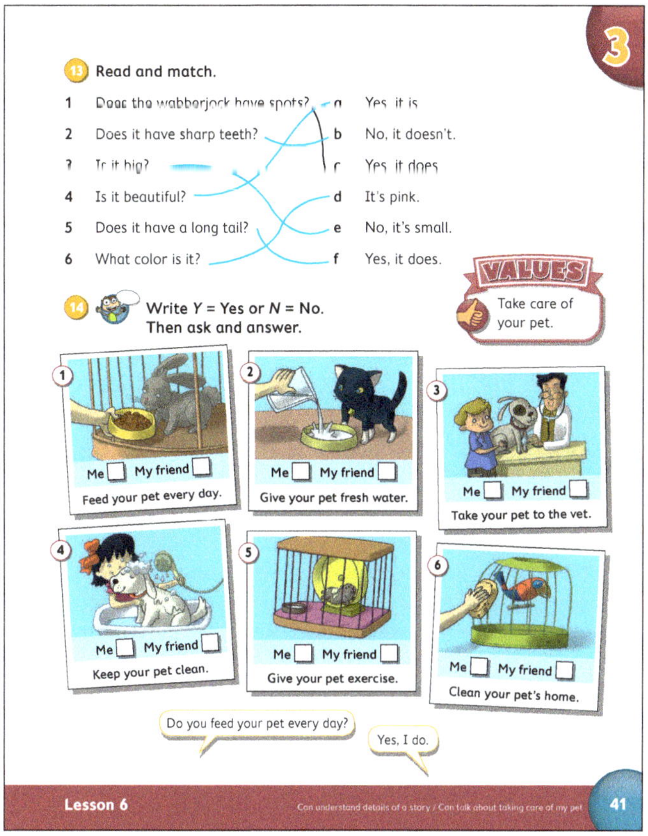
13 Read and match.

1 Does the wabberjock have spots? a Yes, it is.
2 Does it have sharp teeth? b No, it doesn't.
3 Is it big? c Yes, it does.
4 Is it beautiful? d It's pink.
5 Does it have a long tail? e No, it's small.
6 What color is it? f Yes, it does.

VALUES
Take care of your pet.

14 Write Y = Yes or N = No. Then ask and answer.

1 Me My friend Feed your pet every day.
2 Me My friend Give your pet fresh water.
3 Me My friend Take your pet to the vet.
4 Me My friend Keep your pet clean.
5 Me My friend Give your pet exercise.
6 Me My friend Clean your pet's home.

Do you feed your pet every day?
Yes, I do.

Lesson 6 Can understand details of a story / Can talk about taking care of my pet 41

Lesson 6 SB page 41 or Poptropica English World

Learning Objectives
Can understand details of a story
Can talk about taking care of my pet

Additional Language
feed, give fresh water, take to the vet, keep clean, clean, every day

Value
Take care of your pet.

Open books and ask students to look at the activities on the page. Ask, *What are we learning today?* Write the lesson objectives on the board: *We're understanding details of a story, and we're learning how to take care of pets.*

Warm-up

- Have a dance party in the classroom. Play some music, and create some interesting moves to teach the class. Call out actions while you're dancing (e.g., *move your arms, shake your body).*

13 Read and match.

- Have students work in pairs. They look carefully at the story frames and match the questions to the answers.
- Have students work in pairs to read the questions and answers and check that they are correct.

14 Write Y = Yes or N = No. Then ask and answer.

- Read the value, *Take care of your pet.* Direct students' attention to the pictures and elicit the phrases, e.g., *Feed your pet every day. Give your pet fresh water.*, etc. Then invite students who have pets to come to the front and have the rest of the class ask questions, e.g., *Do you feed your pet every day? Do you give your pet exercise?*, etc. The class tries to guess the pet.
- Have students complete the *Me* box for their pets. Students who don't have a pet can use an imaginary pet.
- Pair students. Have them ask and answer the questions, and complete the *My friend* box.
- Ask students to look at the six pictures again and to consider whether these tips apply to all animals, e.g., if they have a fish, perhaps they only feed them once a week. If they have cats, they may not bathe them. There is no correct answer, but this will extend thinking on the value.

Write the following questions on the board: *Why is it good to take care of your pets? (It helps them stay healthy.) What other things can you do to take care of your pet? (Play with them every day. Talk nicely to them.)*

- Tell students to work with a partner. Give pairs two minutes to discuss and note down their answers. Ask students to share their answers with the class.

Pop Quiz: Before the end of the lesson, play an acting game. Students role-play one of the six activities from Activity 14 in front of the class, e.g. they role-play taking a dog for a walk (*give your pet exercise*), or scattering a pinch of food into a fish bowl (*feed your pet*). Their classmates say which value is being mimed.

Materials
Music CD

Homework WB page 33

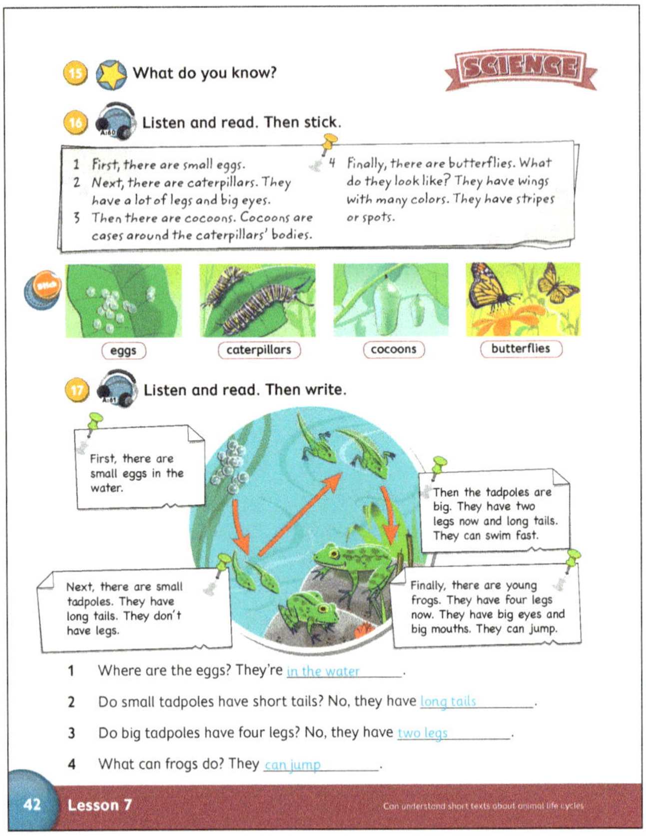

15 What do you know?

SCIENCE

16 A:60 Listen and read. Then stick.

1 First, there are small eggs.
2 Next, there are caterpillars. They have a lot of legs and big eyes.
3 Then there are cocoons. Cocoons are cases around the caterpillars' bodies.
4 Finally, there are butterflies. What do they look like? They have wings with many colors. They have stripes or spots.

eggs | caterpillars | cocoons | butterflies

17 A:61 Listen and read. Then write.

First, there are small eggs in the water.

Then the tadpoles are big. They have two legs now and long tails. They can swim fast.

Next, there are small tadpoles. They have long tails. They don't have legs.

Finally, there are young frogs. They have four legs now. They have big eyes and big mouths. They can jump.

1 Where are the eggs? They're in the water.
2 Do small tadpoles have short tails? No, they have long tails.
3 Do big tadpoles have four legs? No, they have two legs.
4 What can frogs do? They can jump.

42 Lesson 7 Can understand short texts about animal life cycles

Lesson 7 SB page 42 or Poptropica English World

Learning Objective
Can understand short texts about animal life cycles

Additional Language
first, next, then, finally caterpillars, cocoons, cases

Warm-up

- Make up cards with the target words on them. Make one card for each one. Fold each card. Have students sit or stand in a circle. Give the cards to different students and motion to start passing the cards when you start playing the music. Stop the music. The students holding cards open them, show them to the class, say the words, and make a sentence, e.g., *My pet is fast.* Students who make a mistake are out of the game. Then fold up their cards. Start the music again and have students pass the cards.

15 What do you know?

- Open books and ask students, to look at the activities on the page. Ask, *What are we learning today?* Write the lesson objective on the board: *We're learning about the life-cycles of butterflies and frogs.*
- Close books. Ask students what they know about the life-cycles of butterflies and frogs. Write their ideas on the board.
- Refer to the learning adventure poster and say, *Great! You are moving along your learning adventure!*

16 A:60 Listen and read. Then stick.

- Pair students and have them read through the sentences. Ask them to underline any words they don't know.
- Play the audio and have students follow. Have students find the stickers and decide on the order. Read each stage and have students stick the sticker onto the correct spaces.
- Call out numbers one to four, and have students respond with the correct word *(eggs, caterpillars, cocoons, butterflies)*.
- Put students into pairs and have them read the stages again to see if they can work out, from the pictures/context, the meaning of the words they underlined.

17 A:61 Listen and read. Then write.

- Read or play each of the four texts with the class, stopping after each one so students can find the appropriate stage of the frog's life cycle in the picture. Then have students re-read the texts to the class, with individual students reading a sentence each.
- Ask questions about the picture. Explain that they have to read the texts to find the answers, e.g., *Where are the eggs? Do small tadpoles have legs?*, etc.
- Put students into pairs. Have them read and answer the four questions, and write the answers. Check answers with the whole class.

Ask students: *What do you know about butterflies and frogs? Have you seen tadpoles? Are there many butterflies in your country? Do you see more butterflies in summer/winter?*

- Ask students: *Where are you on your learning adventure?* Tell students, *Good job!* to reinforce the progress they are making.

Pop Quiz: Before the end of the lesson, give each student a word card (cards should consist of sets of four words, as follows. Set 1: *eggs, caterpillars, cocoons, butterflies*; Set 2: *eggs, small tadpoles, tadpoles with legs, frogs.*) Students say or show their words to each other, and form groups of four. They stand in a circle in order, and describe the life cycle, e.g., *First there are eggs. Next there are caterpillars. Then there are cocoons, Finally, there are butterflies.*

Materials
Word cards, cards, music CD, poster, stickers, word cards prepared by the teacher

Homework WB page 34

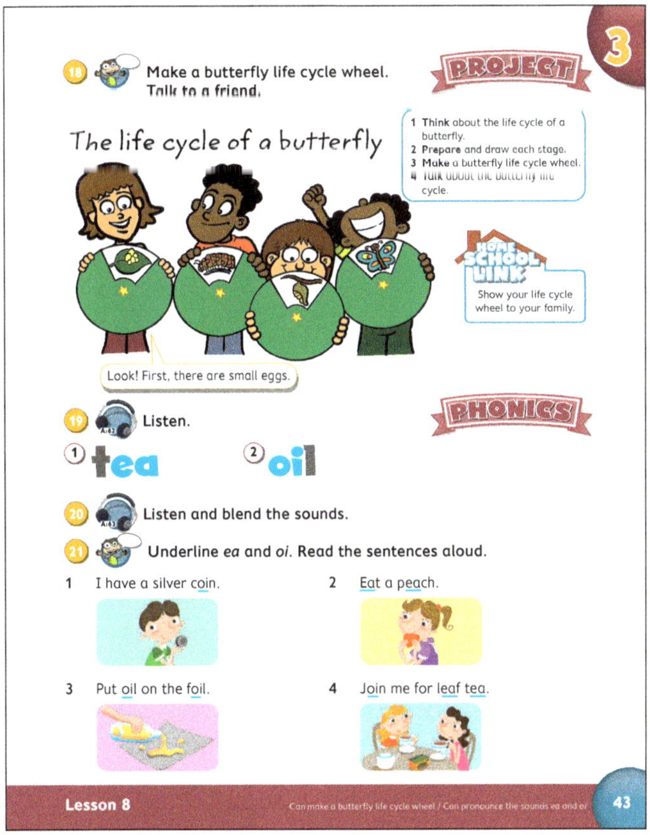
3

PROJECT

18 Make a butterfly life cycle wheel. Talk to a friend.

The life cycle of a butterfly

1 Think about the life cycle of a butterfly.
2 Prepare and draw each stage.
3 Make a butterfly life cycle wheel.
4 Talk about the butterfly life cycle.

Look! First, there are small eggs.

HOME SCHOOL LINK
Show your life cycle wheel to your family.

PHONICS

19 Listen.

1 tea 2 oil

20 Listen and blend the sounds.

21 Underline *ea* and *oi*. Read the sentences aloud.

1 I have a silver coin.
2 Eat a peach.
3 Put oil on the foil.
4 Join me for leaf tea.

Lesson 8 43

Lesson 8 SB page 43 or Poptropica English World

Learning Objectives
Can make a butterfly life cycle wheel
Can pronounce the sounds *ea* and *oi*

Warm-up

- Use large letter cards to review the sounds and letters. Show the cards in random order and have students chorus the letter-sounds. Start slowly and then increase the speed.
- Put a sample word on the board, e.g., *summer*, and choose a student to come to the front and underline the phonemes *s u mm er*, and read out the word. Do this with a few words.

Open books and ask students to look at the activities on the page. Ask *What are we learning today?* Write the lesson objectives on the board: *We're making a butterfly life cycle wheel, and we're learning to pronounce the sounds* ea *and* oi.

18 Make a butterfly life cycle wheel. Talk to a friend.

- Explain that students are going to make their own butterfly life cycle wheels. Ask students to think about the different stages in the life cycle of a butterfly to talk to a partner about what they know about them. Then have them draw or find pictures of the different stages.
- Provide the materials students need and give them time to draw or cut out two circles. Show them how to cut a window from the second circle and pin them together using a split pin.
- Have the students talk to a partner about the life cycle of a butterfly, using their wheels.
- Display the butterfly life cycle wheels in the classroom and ask students to choose their favorite.

You may also wish to give students feedback on their projects.

- **Home-School link:** Read the instruction with the class: *Show your life cycle wheel to your family.* Ask students to do this at home.

19 Listen.

A:62

- Have students open their books and look at the two words, *hair* and *year*. Explain to students that they are going to read and pronounce the sounds *air* and *ear*. Play the audio.

1 ea tea **2** oi oil

20 Listen and blend the sounds.

A:63

- Stay silent. Show the group the first letter card for a word, e.g., *tea*, and elicit the phoneme *t*. Place it on the board. Now repeat this for *ea*. Now tap your finger under each card to prompt the students to blend the letter-sounds. Finally make a 'What is it?' gesture to elicit the word and then look delighted when they get it. Now repeat with *oi-l*.
- Turn to the book and do the activity on the page.

1 t ea tea **2** oi l oil

21 Underline *ea* and *oi*. Read the sentences aloud.

- With books closed, write one of the sentences on the board, e.g., *Join me for leaf tea*. Run your finger under the sentence as you sound out and read the words. Ask students which picture relates to the sentence. Then they do the same with the other sentences.
- Have students do the activity individually. Check answers as a class.

Pop Quiz: Before the end of the lesson, say a mixture of different words with *ea* (*eat, tea, leaf*, etc) and *oi* (*coin, join*, etc) in them. Ask students to call out the correct letter sound each time.

Materials
Letter cards (Units 1 & 2), sheets of thick paper, scissors, split pins

Homework WB page 35

Lesson 9 SB page 44 or Poptropica English World

Learning Objective
Can assess what I have learned in Unit 3

Warm-up

- Review the song on page 38. Play the audio (track A:56) and have students sing along.
- Divide the class into groups, and have them replace the animals, and the body parts and characteristics to create new songs. Have groups come to the front and perform their songs.

Open books and ask students to look at the activities on the page. Explain to students that they are going to review what they have learned in this unit. Write the lesson objective on the board: *We're thinking about our learning adventure.*

Ask students if they can remember the things they learned in this unit, e.g., *How many characteristic words can you remember?* Put their ideas on the board.

- For each example (e.g., *characteristics*), ask students, *Where are you on your learning adventure?*

22 Listen and number

A:64

- Ask the students to look at the pictures and try to talk about the animals' characteristics.
- Have the students listen to the audio and number the pictures. They can check answers with a partner.
- Now ask students to work in pairs to help each other remember any of the words they couldn't remember.

1 It has a long tail and four paws.
2 It has soft fur and long whiskers. It's cute.
3 It has yellow wings and a beak.
4 It has a hard shell. It's slow.
5 It has sharp teeth. It's scary.
6 It's long. It doesn't have legs. It has red and black skin.
7 It's small. It doesn't have legs. It has fins.

23 Play a guessing game. Ask and answer.

- Ask students to work in pairs. They take turns to choose an animal from Activity 22. Their partner asks questions to find out which animal they have chosen.

24 Draw a pet. Ask and answer.

- Have students think of a pet and then draw it.
- Ask students to work in groups. Have them ask and answer questions about each others' pets.

Ask students how they feel about their learning in this unit. Ask students to tell you what they found easy and what they found the most difficult to learn in the unit.

- Students review the I Can statements at the bottom of the page and color each bar according to how confident they feel about the language point.
- Ask students, *Where are you on your learning adventure?* Students indicate where they think they are on the learning adventure poster. Tell students, *Good job!* to reinforce the progress they are making.

Pop Quiz: In groups of four, students tell the others the answers to the following questions: *Which is your favorite activity in the unit? Why? Which activity don't you like? Why? What is your favorite new word? Which word is the most difficult for you?*

Materials
Sheets of paper, colored pens or pencils, poster

Homework WB page 36

Lesson 10 SB page 45 or Poptropica English World

Learning Objective
Can use what I have learned in Unit 3

Warm-up

- Give some students a Picture Card (from 83–99) each. Call out three to five target vocabulary words. Ask a student to come to the front and choose an animal, without telling the class. Divide the rest of the class into two teams. The teams take turns asking the student questions to guess the animal, e.g., *Can you swim? Do you have wings?*

Open books and ask students to look at the activities on the page. Ask, *What are we learning today?* Write the lesson objective on the board: *We're learning about the physical characteristics of pets.*

Say, *dogs are better than cats*. Ask students to agree or disagree and give reasons, e.g., *Cats are small. Cats/dogs are cute. Dogs are scary. Cats have sharp claws.*, etc. Give pairs two minutes to think of their reasons. They might like to write their ideas in their notebooks. Write their suggestions on the board.

25 Draw or write. Then play.

- Direct students' attention to the two houses. Review any of the rooms and pre-teach *hands* and *backyard.* Explain that each student should draw two or three pets in some of the rooms, without showing them to their classmates. Then in pairs, they should ask and answer questions about the pets in their partners' houses, and draw the pets in the correct rooms.
- Read the conversation in the speech bubbles to model the language.
- Pair students and have them play the game. Once they are done, they should show each other their houses and see if they have drawn the correct pets in the correct rooms. The winner is the student with all the pets correctly drawn from the fastest pair.
- Invite individual students to show their 'houses' and describe the pets they have drawn, e.g., *I have three pets. There's a rabbit in my bathroom. It has long ears and a small tail. It has soft white fur. In my dining room, I have a dog.*, etc. This activity helps build students' confidence as they are using the language they have learned in a different context.

I want to know more

- Ask students to choose anything they enjoyed from the unit and to go and find out more. You might like to set this activity as homework with a quick feedback session at the beginning of the next class, e.g., find out more words for animal body parts and characteristics, think of more ways for caring for animals, find out some more information about animal life cycles.

Are you ready for Unit 4?

- Ask students if they are ready to move onto the next unit. Tell students that it is fine if they do not remember everything as they will continue to practice throughout the level.
- Encourage students to ask if they have any questions about what they learned in Unit 3.

You may wish to give Unit 3 test (see page 192) at this time.

Materials
Picture Cards 83–99, colored pens or pencils

Homework WB page 37

Unit 3 Story Cards

SB pages 46–47 or Poptropica English World

Learning Objectives
Can understand texts about other children's pets
Can ask and answer about pets

Recycled/Additional Language
I'm from (China, Japan, Colombia, Australia). He doesn't like pineapples. He likes apples and salad.
nuts, hamster wheel, fruit, iguana, duck

1 What do you know?

- Ask students if they have a pet or know someone with a pet. Brainstorm names of pets. Decide on the most common pets people have in your country.
- Bring a map of the world, or globe, and show it to the class. Locate your country on the map and say, *I'm from (Mexico).*

Open books and ask students to look at the activities on the page. Ask, *What are we learning today?* Write the lesson objective on the board: *We're learning about children and their pets from around the world.*

2 Listen and read.

A:65

- Tell students they are going to hear about the children's pets. Play the audio once for students to follow in their books. Then play each part separately, and ask questions to check comprehension, e.g., *What's the child's name? What's the pet's name? How old is the pet? What does his/her pet like?*

3 Match.

- Have students cover the four texts in Activity 1. Pair them and ask them to match each pet to his/her favorite food.
- Have students uncover the texts, and check the answers with the whole class.

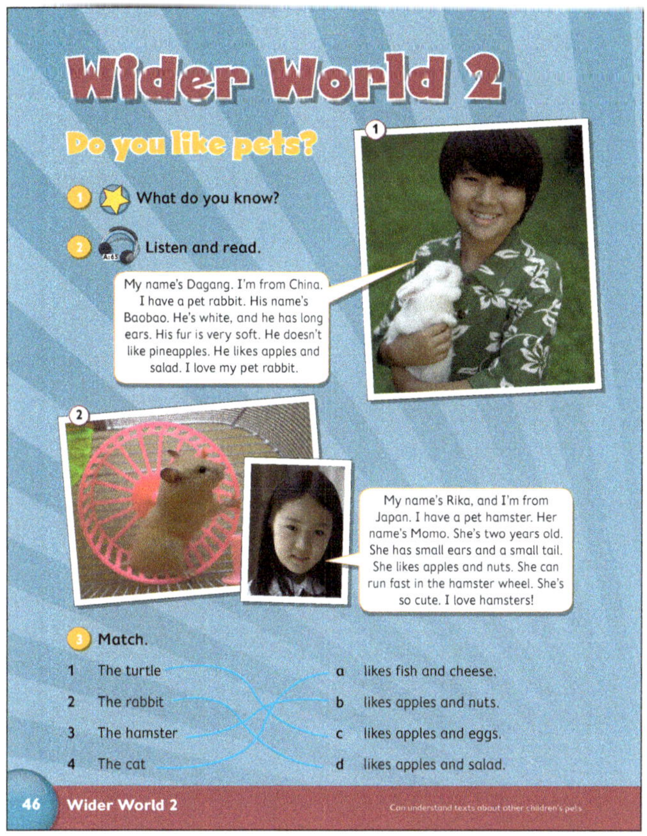
Wider World 2

Do you like pets?

1 What do you know?

2 Listen and read. A:65

1 My name's Dagang. I'm from China. I have a pet rabbit. His name's Baobao. He's white, and he has long ears. His fur is very soft. He doesn't like pineapples. He likes apples and salad. I love my pet rabbit.

2 My name's Rika, and I'm from Japan. I have a pet hamster. Her name's Momo. She's two years old. She has small ears and a small tail. She likes apples and nuts. She can run fast in the hamster wheel. She's so cute. I love hamsters!

3 Match.

1 The turtle — a likes fish and cheese.
2 The rabbit — b likes apples and nuts.
3 The hamster — c likes apples and eggs.
4 The cat — d likes apples and salad.

46 Wider World 2 Can understand texts about other children's pets

Materials
World map

I'm Pedro, and I'm from Colombia. I have a pet cat. Her name's Polly, and she's nine years old. She's white. She likes fish and cheese, but she doesn't like fruit. I love Polly.

I'm Jane, and I'm from Australia. I have a pet turtle. His name's Bruno. He has a small head and four strong legs. He's 15 years old. He has a very hard shell. He's big, and he likes apples and eggs.

4 Ask and answer.

parrot
iguana
duck
spider

1 Do you like these pets?
2 Why do you like them?
3 What's your favorite pet?

Tell the Class

Wider World 2 Can ask and answer about pets 47

Tell the Class

4 Ask and answer.

- Have students work in pairs. They take turns to ask and answer about the four animals using the questions on the page.
- Ask the children to think about which animals make good pets and why.

Point at the learning objective on the board. Ask students, *How many words do you know for pets now?* Give students a minute to tell their partner as many words for pets as they can.

- Ask students, *Where are you on your learning adventure?* Ask students which words they find easiest or most difficult to remember. Tell students, *Good job!* to reinforce the progress they are making.

Pop Quiz: As students are leaving the class, ask them to write three sentences about themselves, two that are true and one that is false. They say the three sentences to the class, who try to guess which statement is false, *e.g., I'm from Mexico. (true) I have a cat. (true) My cat likes apples. (false)*

4 Home

Unit Overview

Unit Objective

- I can talk about home

Language

Target Vocabulary	Furnishings: picture, stove, shower, sink, mirror, trash can, TV, computer, plant, closet, window Prepositions: next to, behind, above, below, in front of Household items: toothbrush, towels, pots, blankets, comb, shelf, pans, plates
Target Structures	There's a plant in the living room. There are two plants in the living room. The plant is below the mirror. / It's below the mirror. The plants are below the mirror. / They're below the mirror. Is the computer in the bedroom? Yes, it is. / No, it isn't. It's in the living room. Are the plates on the shelf? Yes, they are. / No, they aren't. They're in the sink.
Features	**Values:** Help at home. **Cross-curricular:** Art: Mosaics **Phonics:** *a_e, i_e, o_e* (cake, time, home)

Skills

Reading	• Can understand a simple story • Can understand details of a story	• Can understand a text about mosaics
Writing	• Can write simple answers about what's in my bedroom • Can complete simple sentences about where things are in the home (*Workbook*)	• Can make a mosaic picture • Can complete simple sentences about what I like and don't like doing to help at home (*Workbook*)
Listening	• Can identify home furnishings and where they are • Can identify household items	• Can understand a simple story • Can understand a text about mosaics
Speaking	• Can talk about where things are in a room • Can talk about where things are in the home	• Can role-play a story • Can talk about helping at home • Can pronounce the sounds *a_e, i_e,* and *o_e*

Lesson 1 SB page 48 or Poptropica English World

Learning Objective
Can identify home furnishings and where they are

Target Language
picture, stove, trash can, shower, window, mirror, sink, TV, sofa, computer, window, plant, closet, next to, behind, above, below, in front of

1 What do you know?

- Open books and ask students to look at the activities on the page. Ask, *What are we learning today?* Write the lesson objective on the board: *We're learning to talk about our home furnishings.*
- Close books. Ask students what English words they know related to houses, e.g., *living room, kitchen.* Write on board. Refer to the learning adventure poster and say, *Great! You are already moving along your learning adventure!*

2 A:66 Listen and find. What's missing?

- Use the Picture Cards of furnishings words (100–111) to teach the new vocabulary. Say the words and have students repeat.
- Ask questions about the main scene: *Who's this? Where are they?*
- Play the audio. Students listen to the dialog and find the items.

Fid: Welcome to my home. Here is the living room.
I like the computer in front of the window.
There are three green plants behind the sofa.
It's healthy.
Come into the bedroom. There is a closet next to the bed.
My books are above the bed.
Up to the kitchen. Hello Captain Conrad!
I like that picture.
Look out! The trash can is in front of you!
Oh no!
There is a sink in the bathroom. Wash your hands!
There is a mirror above the sink.
Look at your clean hands in the mirror.

3 A:67 Listen and match.

- Play the audio. Students listen and point to the items in the picture and repeat the words.

4 A:68 Listen and say.

- Play the audio and ask students to point to the items in the picture and say the words

1 There are three green plants behind the sofa.
2 There is a closet next to the bed.
3 There's a mirror above the sink. Look at our clean hands.
4 There's a trash can below the picture. Whoops Captain Conrad!
5 Is there a computer in front of the window? Yes, it's healthy.

Ask students how many words for furnishings they know now. Give students a minute to tell their partner the new words they know.

- Ask students to say where they are on their adventure now. Ask students which words they find easiest or most difficult to remember. Tell students, *Good job!* to reinforce the progress they are making.

Pop Quiz: Before they leave the classroom, show students a picture of furnishings, and ask them to say what it is and what room it's usually in.

Materials
Poster, Picture Cards 100–111

Homework WB page 38

Lesson 2 SB page 49 or Poptropica English World

Learning Objective
Can talk about where things are in a room

Target Language
There's a plant in the living room.
There are two plants in the living room.
The plant is below the mirror.
The plants are below the mirror.

Warm-up

- Shuffle Picture Cards (100–111) and choose one. Hold it up and say a sentence, e.g., *I have a mirror.* or *The mirror is above the sink.* Students take turns to choose a card and say a sentence.

Open books and ask students to look at the chant and the Look! box. Ask, *What are we learning today?* Write the lesson objective on the board: *We're learning to say where things are in a room.*

5 Listen and chant. (A:69, A:70)

- Read through the Look! box with the class and play the audio (A:71), then play the chant. Ask students to tell you what furnishings words they hear on the chant. Then ask them to point to the items in the main picture.
- Play the chant a few times and have students chant along. If students are confident, use the karaoke version.

6 Listen and circle the things you hear. Then say. (A:71)

- Play the audio. Have students listen and circle the items they hear.

There's a computer on the table.
There are two plants next to the sofa.
There's a mirror behind the lamp.
The boy is in front of the TV.

- Play the audio again, pausing after each sentence for students to point to the item(s) they have circled.
- Pair students and have them each take turns to describe the boy's room using *There's...* or *There are...* and the correct prepositions.
- Ask students to find the tifftiff plant in the main picture.
- Direct students' attention to the motorbike helmet card on page 49. Tell students to go online to the Poptropica English Island Adventure Game and find the item. Once students click on it, they are taken to a supplementary language task.

Pop Quiz: Before the end of the lesson, play a hide-and-seek game. Ask the students to close their eyes. Walk around the class and hide a small toy somewhere. Students open their eyes and ask about its location, e.g., *Is it under the desk? Is it above the door / behind the chair?* Answer their questions until students find the toy, then play the game again. The child who guesses correctly can hide the toy next time.

Materials
Picture Cards 100–111, one small toy

Homework WB page 39

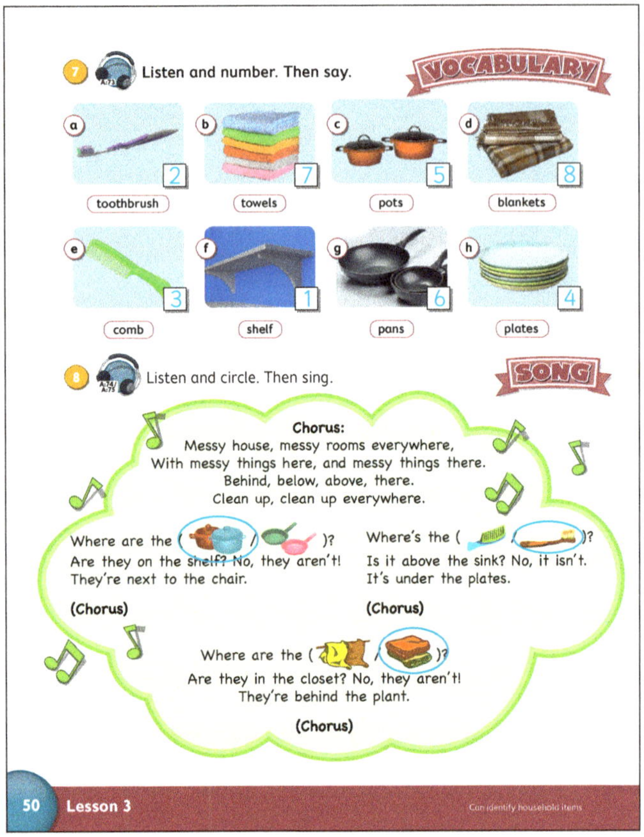

7 Listen and number. Then say. VOCABULARY

a toothbrush 2 | b towels 7 | c pots 5 | d blankets 8
e comb 3 | f shelf 1 | g pans 6 | h plates 4

8 Listen and circle. Then sing. SONG

Chorus:
Messy house, messy rooms everywhere,
With messy things here, and messy things there.
Behind, below, above, there.
Clean up, clean up everywhere.

Where are the (/)?
Are they on the shelf? No, they aren't!
They're next to the chair.

(Chorus)

Where's the (/)?
Is it above the sink? No, it isn't.
It's under the plates.

(Chorus)

Where are the (/)?
Are they in the closet? No, they aren't!
They're behind the plant.

(Chorus)

50 Lesson 3 Can identify household items

Lesson 3 SB page 50 or Poptropica English World

Learning Objective
Can identify household items

Target Language
toothbrush, towels, pots, blankets, comb, shelf, pans, plates

Warm-up

- Stick two or three large sheets of paper on the board. Invite two or three pairs of students to the front. Dictate a description of a room for the students to draw as quickly as possible. Say, e.g., *This is a living room. There's a sofa in the living room. There's a TV in front of the sofa. There are two plants behind the sofa.* etc. The winner is the pair who first completes the drawing correctly.

Open books and ask students to look at the activities on the page. Ask, *What are we learning today?* Write the lesson objective on the board: *We're learning words for household items.*

- Close books. Ask students what English words they know for household items, e.g., *computer, toothbrush.* Write these on board.
- Refer to the learning adventure poster and say, *Great! You are moving along your learning adventure!*

7 Listen and number. Then say.

- Introduce the new words with the Picture Cards of the household items (100–111). Hold them up one by one and ask students to repeat the words after you. Then ask students to look in their books and point at the words as you say them.
- Play the audio and have students number the items as they hear them. Then play the audio again for them to repeat the words.

1 shelf	**5** pots
2 toothbrush	**6** pans
3 comb	**7** towels
4 plates	**8** blankets

- Point to individual pictures and ask students to tell you the word.

8 Listen and circle. Then sing.

- Ask students about the picture choices, e.g., *What can you see?* Prompt students to answer, e.g., *pots or pans, comb or toothbrush, towels or blankets.*
- Play the song audio and have students listen.
- Play the audio again and ask students to circle the correct pictures. Have students check their answers with a partner. Read the lyrics and explain any words students may not know, e.g., *messy, clean up, shelf.*
- Invite students to sing the song. Display Picture Cards 112–119. Play the audio again and ask students to point to the cards as they sing along.
- If students are confident, use the karaoke version.

Ask students, *How many words for household items do you know now?* Give students a minute to tell their partner the new words they know.

- Ask students to say where they are on their adventure now. Ask students which words they find easiest or most difficult to remember. Tell students, *Good job!* to reinforce the progress they are making.

Pop Quiz: Play a memory game with a tray of household items, e.g. a comb, a toothbrush, a pot, a plate, a plant, a picture, a mirror, a pen. Students look at the tray for one minute. Cover the tray with a cloth and see if students can remember the 8 items.

Materials
Picture Cards 112–119, poster, 2–3 large sheets of paper, colored pens or pencils, tray, household items, cloth

Homework WB page 40

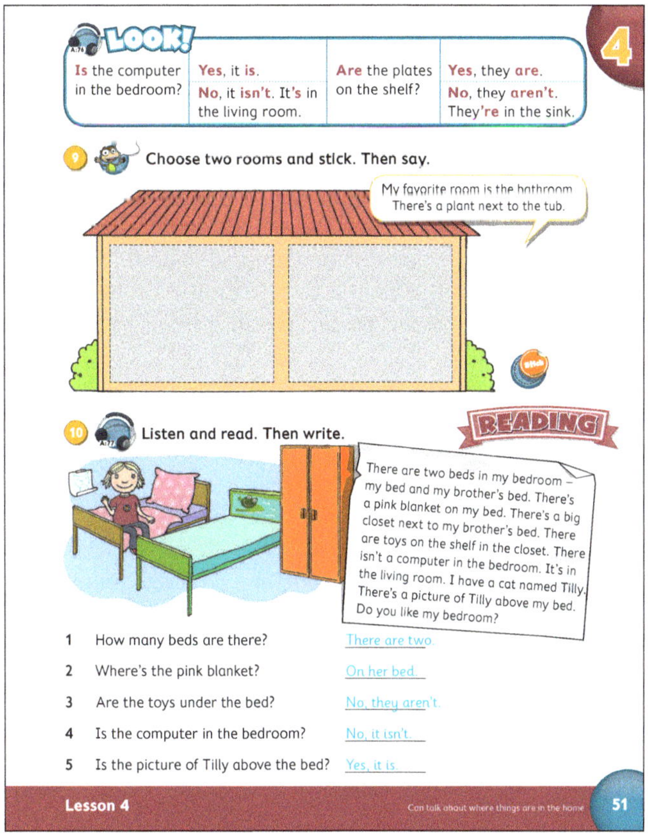

LOOK!

Is the computer in the bedroom?	Yes, it is. / No, it isn't. It's in the living room.	Are the plates on the shelf?	Yes, they are. / No, they aren't. They're in the sink.

9 Choose two rooms and stick. Then say.

10 Listen and read. Then write.

READING

There are two beds in my bedroom – my bed and my brother's bed. There's a pink blanket on my bed. There's a big closet next to my brother's bed. There are toys on the shelf in the closet. There isn't a computer in the bedroom. It's in the living room. I have a cat named Tilly. There's a picture of Tilly above my bed. Do you like my bedroom?

1 How many beds are there? There are two.
2 Where's the pink blanket? On her bed.
3 Are the toys under the bed? No, they aren't.
4 Is the computer in the bedroom? No, it isn't.
5 Is the picture of Tilly above the bed? Yes, it is.

Lesson 4 Can talk about where things are in the home 51

Lesson 4 SB page 51 or Poptropica English World

Learning Objective
Can talk about where things are in the home

Target Language
Is the computer in the bedroom?
Yes, it is. / No, it isn't. It's in the living room.
Are the plates on the shelf?
Yes, they are. / No, they aren't. They're in the sink.

Warm-up

- Put the Picture Cards of furnishings and household items (100–111; 112–119) in a bag filled with shredded paper. Have students sit in a circle and pass the bag around while music is playing. Stop the music. The student who is holding the bag picks out a card and identifies the picture. Give five points for each correct answer. The winner is the student with the most points.

Open books and ask students to look at the book and the Look! box. Ask, *What are we learning today?* Write the lesson objective on the board: *We're learning to talk about where things are.*

9 Choose two rooms and stick. Then say.

- Read through the Look! box with the class and play the audio (A:76).
- Have students look at the stickers at the back of the book and choose two of the rooms to stick on the empty spaces. Explain that they should choose the rooms they like most.
- Pair students and have them describe one of their favorite rooms. Model the language by pointing to the bathroom picture and reading the model sentences.
- Alternatively, have students play a guessing game. One student describes one of his/her rooms, while the other student tries to guess it, e.g., *In my favorite room, there's a telephone next to the mirror. (Your favorite room is the bedroom!) That's right!*

10 Listen and read. Then write.

A:77

- Ask students to look at the picture. Play the audio and have students listen. Play the audio again and have them follow. Ask them if they like the girl's bedroom.
- Have students read the questions and write their answers. They can check their answers with a friend.

Pop Quiz: Before the end of the lesson, ask students to play a guessing game. Think of a household item that they know, e.g. toothbrush. Students ask questions about the object to guess what it is, e.g., *Is it in the bedroom? (no) Is it in the bathroom? (yes) Is it in the shower? (no) Is it above the sink? (yes) Is it a toothbrush? (yes)* The student who guesses correctly then chooses another object for the class to guess.

Materials
Picture Cards 100–111; 112–119, a small bag, shredded paper, music CD, stickers

Homework WB page 41

Lesson 5 SB page 52 or Poptropica English World

Learning Objectives
Can understand a simple story
Can role-play a story

Additional Language
My lovely house! Look out! My poor kitchen!

Functional Language
Help! Quick..., Aaarrggh! Phew! Look out!

Warm-up

- Ask students what they can remember about the story from the previous episode. Use the Unit 3 Story Cards as prompts. Ask students where the characters were, what they saw in the zoo, and what the creatures looked like. Remind students that the characters are still looking for a tifftiff plant.

Open books and ask students to look at the story. Ask, *What are we learning today?* Write the lesson objectives on the board: *We're reading a story and we're role-playing a story.*

11 A:78 Talk about the pictures. Then listen and read.

- Direct students' attention to the story and ask questions about the characters and the scene: *Who can you see? Where are they? What are they doing? Where's the tifftiff plant?*
- Play the audio and have students listen and follow. Check understanding by pointing at the pictures and asking questions: *Where is the tifftiff plant in picture 2? Where are they in picture 6? Who has the tifftiff plant at the end?*
- Play the recording again, pausing after each line. Have students repeat.
- Play the audio again. Have students speak along and mime the actions.

Write the following quotes on the board: *Oh, no. My beautiful house.* and *Oh, no. My poor kitchen!* Tell students to work with a partner and think about why Fid made these comments. *What is his house usually like? What happens when Kim, Katy and the tricksters come? Does Fid like a messy house?* Give pairs two minutes to think of their answers. They might like to write their ideas in their notebooks. Write their suggestions on the board. Ask students to say why they chose their ideas.

12 Role-play the story.

- See the "How to use stories" section on page 22 for more ideas on how to build your students' confidence with role-plays.
- Divide students into groups of six (have one student play both tricksters). Give each group a set of cut-up Story Cards and have students place them in order.
- Divide students into groups and have them role-play the story. When you say, *change*, they should change character and role-play a new character. Rotate through the characters, giving students the chance to play each one.

You might like to give the students feedback on their role-play.

Pop Quiz: As students are leaving the class, ask if they can remember what Fid's house is like. Can they describe where things are?, e.g. *There's a sofa in the living room. There are two plants behind the sofa.*

Materials
Story Cards (Units 3 and 4)

Homework WB page 42

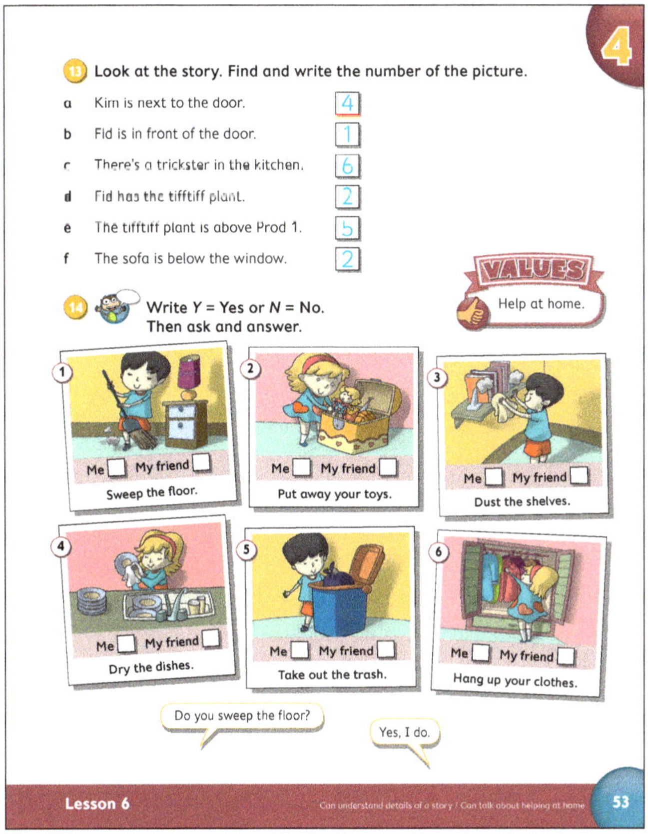

4

13 Look at the story. Find and write the number of the picture.

a Kim is next to the door. 4

b Fid is in front of the door. 1

c There's a trickster in the kitchen. 6

d Fid has the tifftiff plant. 2

e The tifftiff plant is above Prod 1. 5

f The sofa is below the window. 2

14 Write *Y* = Yes or *N* = No. Then ask and answer.

VALUES Help at home.

Lesson 6 Can understand details of a story / Can talk about helping at home 53

Lesson 6 SB page 53 or Poptropica English World

Learning Objectives
Can understand details of a story
Can talk about helping at home

Additional Language
sweep the floor, put away your toys, dust the shelves, dry the dishes, take out the garbage, hang up your clothes

Value
Help at home.

Open books and ask students to look at the activities on the page. Ask, *What are we learning today?* Write the lesson objectives on the board: *We're understanding details of a story, and we're talking about helping at home.*

Warm-up

- Play the story audio (track A:78) and review the story with the students. Then play the audio again. Pause at key moments and have students try to continue the story or say the next line. For example, stop after these points. *Do you have a tifftiff plant?* PAUSE *(Yes, it's on the table.)*
  Quick, PAUSE *(the trickster's in the yard)*
  It isn't your plant. PAUSE *(It's our plant.)*
  Look out! It's another trickster! PAUSE *(Oh, no. My poor kitchen!)*

13 Look at the story. Find and write the number of the picture.

- Have students work in pairs. They look carefully at the story frames and read the sentences, writing the number of the picture they describe.
- Have students check their answers with a partner.

14 Write Y = Yes or N = No. Then ask and answer.

- Read the value, *Help at home*. Ask students if they help at home, and to say what household chores they do to help Mom and Dad. Go through the phrases under each picture and read them with the whole class.
- Have students complete the boxes about themselves. Then pair students and have them ask each other questions to complete the box 'My friend'. Have a pair read the questions and answers in speech bubbles to model the language students should use in this activity.

Write the following questions on the board: *Why is it important to help at home? (It helps our family.) What other things can we do to help at home? (make our beds, wash the dishes, sweep the yard, ask Mom if she needs help, etc.)*

- Tell students to work with a partner. Give pairs two minutes to discuss and note down their answers. Ask students to share their answers with the class.

Pop Quiz: Before the end of the lesson, play an acting game. Students act out one of the six activities from Activity 14, e.g. dusting shelves, sweeping the floor, etc. The other students guess the activity.

Homework WB page 43

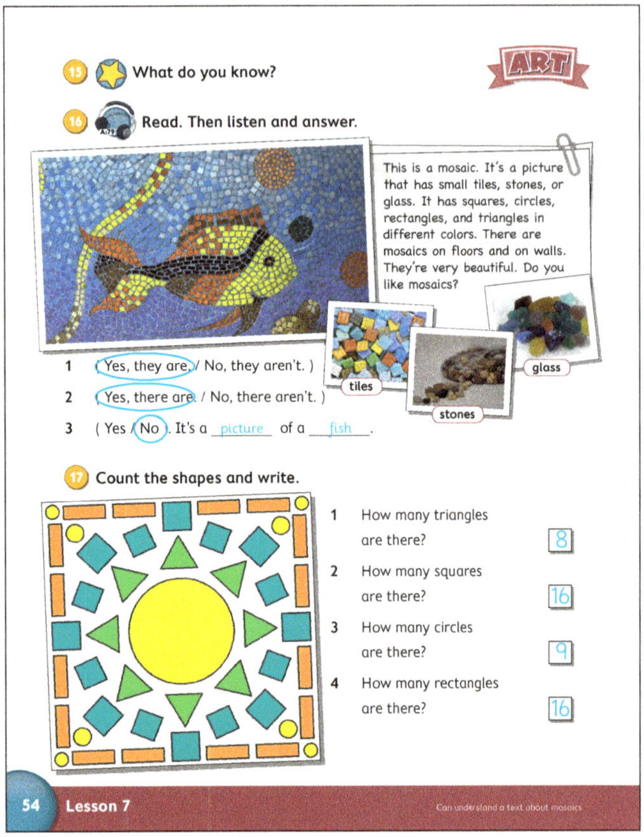
15 What do you know?

ART

16 Read. Then listen and answer.

This is a mosaic. It's a picture that has small tiles, stones, or glass. It has squares, circles, rectangles, and triangles in different colors. There are mosaics on floors and on walls. They're very beautiful. Do you like mosaics?

tiles

stones

glass

1 (Yes, they are. / No, they aren't.)
2 (Yes, there are. / No, there aren't.)
3 (Yes / No). It's a picture of a fish.

17 Count the shapes and write.

1 How many triangles are there? 8
2 How many squares are there? 16
3 How many circles are there? 9
4 How many rectangles are there? 16

54 Lesson 7 Can understand a text about mosaics

Lesson 7 SB page 54 or Poptropica English World

Learning Objective
Can understand a text about mosaics

Additional Language
mosaic, picture, tiles, stones, glass, squares, circles, rectangles, triangles, shapes, different, floors, walls, very beautiful

Warm-up

- Tell the class they are going to mix colors to create new ones, using colored pencils. Give them sheets of paper and say, *Yellow and blue make....* Students mix the colors and say, *Green!* Ask individual students to write the *formula* on the board, e.g., *yellow + blue = green.*

15 What do you know?

- Open books and ask students to look at the activities on the page. Ask, *What are we learning today?* Write the lesson objective on the board: *We're learning about mosaics.*
- Close books. Ask students what they know about mosaics. Write their ideas on the board.
- Refer to the learning adventure poster and say, *Great! You are moving along your learning adventure!*

16 A:79 Read. Then listen and answer.

- Focus on the picture of the mosaic and ask, *What's this? (mosaic)* Say the word and ask students to repeat after you. Then look at each of the materials and ask students to repeat the words *(tiles, stones, glass).*
- Draw shapes (*a triangle, square, circle* and *rectangle*) on the board and say the names for students to repeat. Have students copy the words in their notebooks, draw the shapes and color them in. Students hold up their notebooks and say, *It's a (blue) (square).*
- Pair students and have them read the text.
- Play the audio. Ask students to listen carefully.

> **1** Are mosaics colorful?
> **2** Are there mosaics on floors?
> **3** Look at the picture. Is it a picture of a flower?

- Play the audio again pausing after each question to allow students to circle the answers.
- Play the audio again. Repeat each question and have students find the answers in the text or the picture.

17 Count the shapes and write.

- Focus on the picture. Ask, *What color are the triangles? What's blue?* Have students answer.
- Repeat with the other shapes.
- Ask individual students to read the questions to the class. Students count the shapes and write the answers individually. Check the answers as a class.
- For further practice, give a copy of Activity Sheet 3 (see page 157) to each student. Have them draw a picture of each item as indicated in each box. They should use the shape in the middle as a prompt and draw different shapes around it to create a mosaic of the item. Have students color in all the shapes. Pair students and have them ask and answer questions about the mosaics, e.g., *How many circles are there in your sun?* Display students' drawings in the classroom.

Ask the students: *Have you ever seen a mosaic? Where? What picture did it show? Do you think this type of art is new or has it been around for a long time?*

- Ask students, *Where are you on your learning adventure?* Tell students, *Good job!* to reinforce the progress they are making.

Pop Quiz: Before the end of the lesson, draw a square on the board and write the word *mosaic* in the square. Invite students to come to the front and add to your mosaic by drawing more squares with words related to mosaics in them, e.g., *tiles, stones, colors.*

Materials
Colored pens or pencils, sheets of paper, poster, Activity Sheet 3

Homework WB page 44

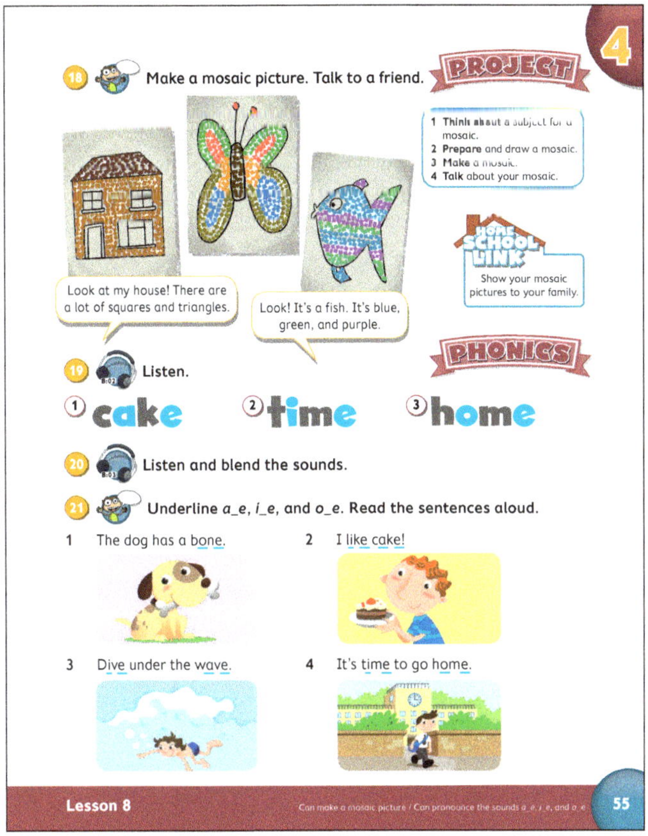
18 Make a mosaic picture. Talk to a friend. PROJECT 4

1 Think about a subject for a mosaic.
2 Prepare and draw a mosaic.
3 Make a mosaic.
4 Talk about your mosaic.

Look at my house! There are a lot of squares and triangles.

Look! It's a fish. It's blue, green, and purple.

HOME SCHOOL LINK Show your mosaic pictures to your family.

PHONICS

19 Listen.

1 cake 2 time 3 home

20 Listen and blend the sounds.

21 Underline a_e, i_e, and o_e. Read the sentences aloud.

1 The dog has a bone.
2 I like cake!
3 Dive under the wave.
4 It's time to go home.

Lesson 8 Can make a mosaic picture / Can pronounce the sounds a_e, i_e, and o_e 55

Lesson 8 SB page 55 or Poptropica English World

Learning Objectives
Can make a mosaic picture
Can pronounce the sounds *a_e, i_e*, and *o_e*

Warm-up

- Prepare large letter cards to review the sounds and letters. Put the letter cards on the board. Say a letter-sound and choose a student to come to the front and touch the correct letter.

Open books and ask students to look at the activities on the page. Ask, *What are we learning today?* Write the lesson objective on the board: *We're learning to make a mosaic picture and we're learning to pronounce the sounds* a_e, i_e, *and* o_e.

18 Make a mosaic picture. Talk to a friend.

- Show students the example mosaic pictures in their books. Explain that they are going to make their own picture. Ask students to think about a subject for their mosaic.
- Provide the materials they need. Give students time to draw an outline on a large sheet of paper and tear or cut squares from colored paper or magazines. They then stick the squares onto the outline to make mosaics.
- Display the mosaics around the classroom. Have students describe their mosaic to a partner.

You may also wish to give students feedback on their projects

- **Home-School link:** Read the instruction with the class: *Show your mosaic pictures to your family.* Ask students to do this at home.

19 Listen.

- Explain that although these letters are not together in a word, they are a team and together they make a new sound.
- Have students open their books and look at the three words, *cake, time* and *home*. Explain to students that they are going to read and pronounce the sounds *a_e, i_e*, and *o_e*. Play the audio..

1 a e cake	**2** i e time	**3** o e home

20 Listen and blend the sounds.

- Write a word on the board. Underline each phoneme in the word, e.g., *c a ke* as you sound it out, *c-a-ke.* As a group, chorus the sounding out and word again, *c-a-ke cake.* Now repeat with the other words.
- Turn to the book and do the activity on the page.

1 c ake cake	**2** t ime time	**3** h ome home

21 Underline *a_e, i_e*, and *o_e*. Read the sentences aloud.

- Write one of the sentences on the board. Ask students to scan the sentence to find the target graphemes. Now run your finger under the sentence as you sound out and read the words. Have students repeat. Have students open their books to find the same sentence on the page, then underline the target graphemes and read it aloud. Repeat with the other sentences.

Pop Quiz: Before the end of the lesson, write *not* and *note* on the board. Say, *not* quickly then say, *note* very slowly. Then say a mixture of words with short (*hit, pot, mat, dog, cat)* and long *(cake, shape, dive, bone, home)* sounds and ask students to say which they are.

Materials
Letter cards (Units 1 and 2), large sheets of paper, squares from colored paper or magazines

Homework WB page 45

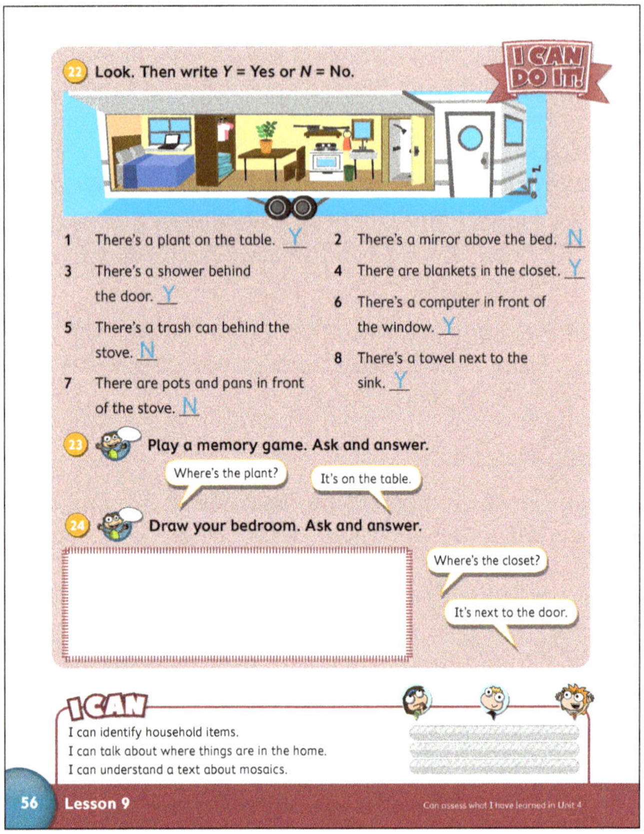
22 Look. Then write Y = Yes or N = No.

I CAN DO IT!

1 There's a plant on the table. Y
2 There's a mirror above the bed. N
3 There's a shower behind the door. Y
4 There are blankets in the closet. Y
5 There's a trash can behind the stove. N
6 There's a computer in front of the window. Y
7 There are pots and pans in front of the stove. N
8 There's a towel next to the sink. Y

23 Play a memory game. Ask and answer.

Where's the plant?
It's on the table.

24 Draw your bedroom. Ask and answer.

Where's the closet?
It's next to the door.

I CAN

I can identify household items.
I can talk about where things are in the home.
I can understand a text about mosaics.

56 Lesson 9 Can assess what I have learned in Unit 4

Lesson 9 SB page 56 or Poptropica English World

Learning Objective
Can assess what I have learned in Unit 4

Warm-up

- Divide the class into small groups. Each group chooses four words from this unit and writes the letters in scrambled order. Groups exchange words and unscramble them. Then they read them to the class. You may turn this activity into a class competition by setting a time limit.

Open books and ask students to look at the activities on the page. Explain to students that they are going to review what they have learned in this unit. Write the lesson objective on the board: *We're thinking about our learning adventure.*

- Ask students if they can remember the things they learned in this unit, e.g., *How many furnishings words can you remember?* Put their ideas on the board.
- For each example (e.g., *furnishings*), ask students, *Where are you on your learning adventure?*

22 Look. Then write Y = Yes or N = No.

- Ask the students to look at the picture of the caravan and say what they can see inside.
- Have the students work in pairs and read the sentences under the picture. They decide together whether the sentences are true or false and write *Y* or *N* accordingly.
- Now ask students to work in pairs to help each other remember any of the words they couldn't remember.

23 Play a memory game. Ask and answer.

- Put students in pairs. Ask them to take turns to close their books. Their partner looks at the picture of the caravan, and asks questions about the location of things in the picture. Once they have answered five or six questions, they switch roles.

24 Draw your bedroom. Ask and answer.

- Ask students to draw a picture of their bedroom. In pairs, they ask and answer about their pictures.

Ask students how they feel about their learning in this unit. Ask students to tell you what they found easy and what they found the most difficult to learn in the unit.

- Students review the I Can statements at the bottom of the page and color each bar according to how confident they feel about the language point.
- Ask students, *Where are you on your learning adventure?* Students indicate where they think they are on the learning adventure poster. Tell students, *Good job!* to reinforce the progress they are making.

Pop Quiz: Before the end of the lesson, ask students to close their eyes while you move something in the classroom. They open their eyes and look for the change, e.g., *The trash can is under the desk. The book is next to the computer.*

Materials
Poster

Homework WB page 46

Lesson 10 SB page 57 or Poptropica English World

Learning Objective
Can use what I have learned in Unit 4

Warm-up

- Play the audio for the chant (A:69). Have students chant along. Then play the chant again and when it gets to the furnishings, turn the audio volume down low and hold up a Picture Card (from 100–111; 112–119) with a different item on, e.g., *closet.* Students complete the chant with the new item you are holding up. Use a different Picture Card (100–111; 112–119) for every number mentioned in the chant.

Open books and ask students to look at the activities on the page. Ask, *What are we learning today?* Write the lesson objective on the board: *We're learning about things in the home.*

Say: *The bedroom is the best room in the house.* Ask learners to agree or disagree and give reasons. e.g., *You sleep there. Your toys are there. Your bed and clothes are in the bedroom. Food is in the kitchen. You wash in the bathroom.*, etc. Give pairs two minutes to think of their reasons. They might like to write their ideas in their notebooks. Write their suggestions on the board.

25 Spot the difference. Talk with a friend.

- Have the students work in pairs. Each student covers one of the pictures. Then they ask and answer questions in order to find the eight differences between the two pictures.
- When they have found the differences, they look at both pictures side-by-side to check that they have found all the differences. This activity helps build students' confidence as they are using the language they have learned in a different context.

I want to know more

- Ask students to choose anything they enjoyed from the unit and to go and find out more. You might like to set this activity as homework with a quick feedback session at the beginning of the next class, e.g., find out more words for furnishing and household items, think of more ways to help out in the house, find out some language about the shapes in mosaics.

Are you ready for Unit 5?

- Ask students if they are ready to move onto the next unit. Tell students that it is fine if they do not remember everything as they will continue to practice throughout the level.
- Encourage students to ask if they have any questions about what they learned in Units 3 and 4.

You may wish to give Unit 4 test (see page 194) at this time.

Materials
Picture Cards 100–111; 112–119

Homework WB page 47

Unit 4 Story Cards

Review Units 3 and 4

SB pages 58–59 or Poptropica English World

Learning Objectives
Can talk about pets and where pets are
Can talk about home and where things are

Warm-up

- Have students sit in a circle. Assign each student an animal body part or characteristic. Stand in the middle of the circle and call out a sentence with that word, e.g., *They have wings.* All students who have been assigned the word *wings* should get up and change places with one another. Once the class is familiar with the game, you could allow one of the students to take your place. The student without a seat calls out the sentence and tries to take a seat as the others change places.

Open books and ask students to look at the activities on the page. Ask, *What are we learning today?* Write the lesson objective on the board: *We're talking about pets and home, and where things are.*

1 Listen and check (✓).

- Have students look at the pictures. Point to each picture and have students name the pets, e.g., *rabbit, cat, hamster.*
- Play the audio and have students listen for the pet being described.

> I have a pet. It's small and white. It has soft fur. It has four short legs and small ears. It has big teeth. It has a small head. It doesn't have blue eyes. It's so cute! Can you find it?

- Play the audio again and have students check the correct box. Ask students to tell you which sentence helped them work out the correct pet. (*It doesn't have blue eyes.*)
- Pair up students. Have each student choose a pet and describe it to his/her partner, who should try to guess the animal.

2 Ask and answer.

- Do a quick review of the prepositions with Picture Cards 107–111. Hold up a Picture Card and ask students to make a sentence with it, e.g., *next to – The fish is next to the window.*
- Pair students and have them look at the pictures and ask questions about the location of the pets. Continue until each student in the pair has had a chance to ask and answer about all pictures.

Materials
Picture Cards 107–111

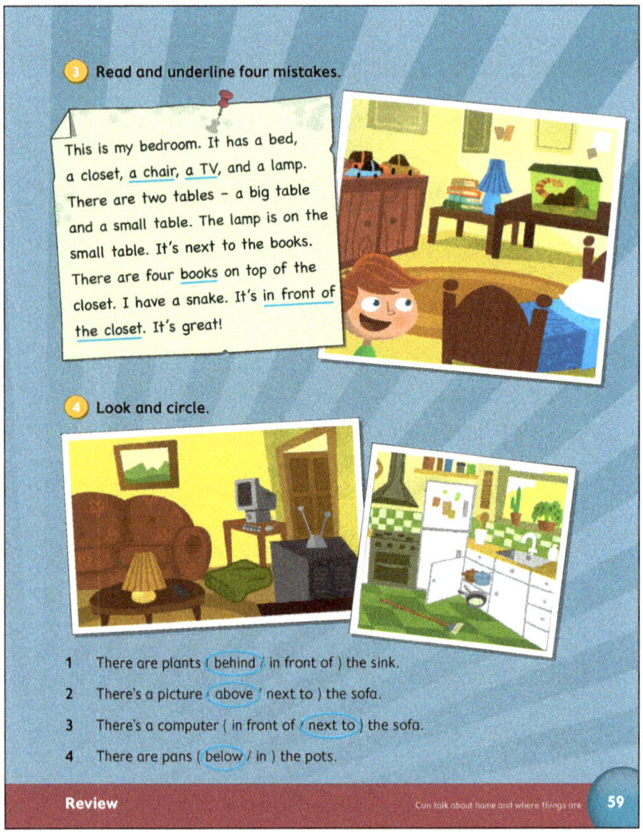
3 Read and underline four mistakes.

This is my bedroom. It has a bed, a closet, a chair, a TV, and a lamp. There are two tables – a big table and a small table. The lamp is on the small table. It's next to the books. There are four books on top of the closet. I have a snake. It's in front of the closet. It's great!

4 Look and circle.

1 There are plants (behind / in front of) the sink.
2 There's a picture (above / next to) the sofa.
3 There's a computer (in front of / next to) the sofa.
4 There are pans (below / in) the pots.

Review Can talk about home and where things are 59

3 Read and underline four mistakes.

- Point to the picture and the text, and explain the activity. Pair up students and have them work together.
- Ask individual students to read the text sentence by sentence. After each one, ask the class, e.g., *Is there a mistake?* Have students call out the mistakes and the correct word, e.g., *It has a bed, a cupboard and a lamp.* Have students cross out the wrong words and write the correct ones above them.
- Ask students to read the corrected descriptions to each other.

4 Look and circle.

- Have students work in pairs. They look at the two pictures and describe the rooms to each other, e.g., *This is a living room. There's a sofa, a TV, a table, and a lamp.*
- Have students read the sentences and circle the correct words to describe the rooms.
- Check their answers by asking students to read the sentences and say which room they refer to.

Watch the video story *Where's Hoopla?* on Poptropica English World. Ask students what happened in the story. Watch again, stopping at key points, and ask them about the language, the images, or the story. Ask the students to role-play the story. Assign the roles of two of the characters to confident speakers and let other students play the other parts. Encourage them to say as much of the dialog as they can and prompt them where necessary.

Point at the learning objective on the board. Ask students, *How many words do you know for the home now?* Give students a minute to tell their partner as many words for furnishings and the home as they can.

- Ask students, *Where are you on your learning adventure?* Ask students which words they find easiest or most difficult to remember. Tell students, *Good job!* to reinforce the progress they are making.

Pop Quiz: Before the end of the lesson, write these headings on the board: *Pet, Preposition, Furnishings, Room*, and have students brainstorm several words to write under each category. Write the words on the board under the headings. Then ask students to choose a word from each category and make a sentence, e.g., *There's a rabbit under the sofa in the living room.*

You may wish to give Review Test 2 (see page 208) at this time.

5 Clothes

Unit Overview

Unit Objective

- I can talk about clothes

Language

Target Vocabulary	Clothing: a baseball cap, a sweatsuit, a polo shirt, shirt, shorts, jeans, a belt, a uniform, a jacket, a sweatshirt, flip-flops, sneakers, sandals, beanie, hiking boots, scarf, tights, ski jacket, wool sweater Material/style: plain, colorful, fancy
Target Structures	What are you wearing? I'm wearing a baseball cap/sandals. What's he/she wearing? He/She's wearing a baseball cap/sandals. Are you wearing a baseball cap/sandals? Yes, I am. / No, I am not. Is he/she wearing a baseball cap/sandals? Yes, he/she is. / No, he/she isn't. This is my favorite scarf. These are my favorite tights. I love my scarf/tights.
Features	**Values:** Be polite. **Cross-curricular:** Social science: Household chores. **Phonics:** *sc, sk, sm, sn, sp, squ, st, sw* (scarf, skate, smell, snip, spoon, squid, star, swim)

Skills

Reading	• Can understand a simple story • Can understand details of a story	• Can identify household chores
Writing	• Can use polite phrases in English • Can make a chores chart • Can complete simple sentences about what people are wearing (*Workbook*)	• Can write simple sentences about what people are wearing (*Workbook*) • Can write about my favorite clothes (*Workbook*)
Listening	• Can identify clothing items • Can understand a simple story	• Can identify more clothing items and words that describe them
Speaking	• Can ask and answer about what people are wearing • Can talk about favorite clothes	• Can role-play a story • Can pronounce the sounds *sc, sk, sm, sn, sp, squ, st,* and *sw*

Lesson 1 SB page 60 or Poptropica English World

Learning Objective
Can identify clothing items

Target Language
a baseball cap, a sweatsuit, a polo shirt, a shirt, shorts, jeans, a belt, a uniform, a jacket, a sweatshirt, flip-flops, sneakers, sandals

1 What do you know?

- Open books and ask students to look at the activities on the page. Ask, *What are we learning today?* Write the lesson objective on the board: *We're learning to talk about our clothes.*
- Close books. Ask students what English words they know for clothes, e.g., *T-shirt, jeans,* etc. Write on board.
- Refer to the learning adventure poster and say, *Great! You are already moving along your learning adventure!*

2 Listen and find. What's missing?

B:05

- Use the Picture Cards of clothes (120–129) to teach the new vocabulary. Say the words and have students repeat.
- Play the audio. Students listen to the dialog and circle the pictures when they hear the related words. Ask, *What's missing? (sweatshirt, polo shirt, and shorts)*

LL: Hello, Captain Conrad. What are you wearing?
CC: I'm wearing my uniform. It's white and purple, and has a white belt.
I wear this for work every day. At home, I wear jeans and sneakers.
LL: Hmmm... Very clean uniform!
Hello, Fashionista. Can I help you?
F: Yes, please. I love clothes. Do you have my blue jacket?
LL: Here it is.
F: Thank you. Oh, and that's my yellow and white sweatsuit.
LL: Oh, yes, here you are.
Are you wearing flip-flops?
F: Yes, I am. You have my pink sandals.
LL: Oh, yes.
F: And where's my green baseball cap?
CC: Oh, dear! Prod 1 is wearing your baseball cap!

3 Listen and number.

B:06

- Ask questions about the main scene again.
- Ask students to look at the picture and listen. Play the audio again. Students find the items and number them.

1 Captain Conrad is wearing a purple and white uniform.
2 The flip-flops are blue.
3 The jacket is blue.
4 Prod 1 has a green baseball cap.
5 The jeans are blue.
6 The sweatsuit is yellow and white.
7 Fashionista has a white belt.
8 I like these purple and pink sneakers.
9 There's a red polo shirt.
10 I like these pink sandals.
11 Prod 2 is wearing a big sweatshirt.
12 There's a yellow and green shirt.

4 Listen and say.

B:07

- Play the audio. Students listen and point to the items in the picture, and repeat the words.

Ask students how many words for clothes they know now. Give students a minute to tell their partner the new words they know.

- Ask students to say where they are on their adventure now. Tell students, *Good job!* to reinforce the progress they are making.

Pop Quiz: As students are leaving the class, show them pictures of clothes, and ask them to describe the items, e.g., *It's a red sweatshirt.*

Materials
Poster, Picture Cards 120–129, pictures of clothes

Homework WB page 48

Lesson 2 SB page 61 or Poptropica English World

Learning Objective
Can ask and answer about what people are wearing

Warm-up

- Divide students into two teams and have them stand in two lines. Whisper a clothing word to the first student in each line. Have him/her whisper the word to the next student, and so on. Have the last student in each line go to the board and draw the item. Have the first student go to the back of the line. Continue with other words.

Open books and ask students to look at the chant and the Look! box. Ask, *What are we learning today?* Write the lesson objective on the board: *We're learning to ask and answer questions about clothes.*

5 Listen and chant. B:08 B:09

- Play the chant about clothes. Ask students to tell you what new words they hear on the chant. Then ask them to point to the items in the main picture.
- Play the chant a few times and have students chant along. If students are confident, use the karaoke version.

6 Look at Laurence Laundry, Fashionista and PROD 2. Then ask and answer.

- Read through the Look! box with the class and play the audio (track B:10). Then ask the students to work in pairs. Have them find the characters in the scene and look at their clothes.
- Have students read the speech bubble text, and match them to the characters. Check answers by calling out the characters' names and having students say the correct sentences.
- Read the model conversation with a student. In pairs, have students practice asking and answering questions about each character.
- Ask students if they can see the tifftiff plant in the scene and to say where it is.
- Direct students' attention to the ladder card on page 60. Tell students to go online to the Poptropica English Island Adventure Game and find the item. Once students click on it, they are taken to a supplementary language task.

Pop Quiz: Before the end of the lesson, play a memory game. Ask pairs of volunteers to face each other for 5 seconds, then turn around and stand back to back and describe what their partner is wearing. If they usually wear uniform and all look the same, bring in some props to make the game more challenging, e.g. belts, baseball caps, flip-flops, etc.

Materials
Some clothing items (belt, flip-flops, etc)

Homework WB page 49

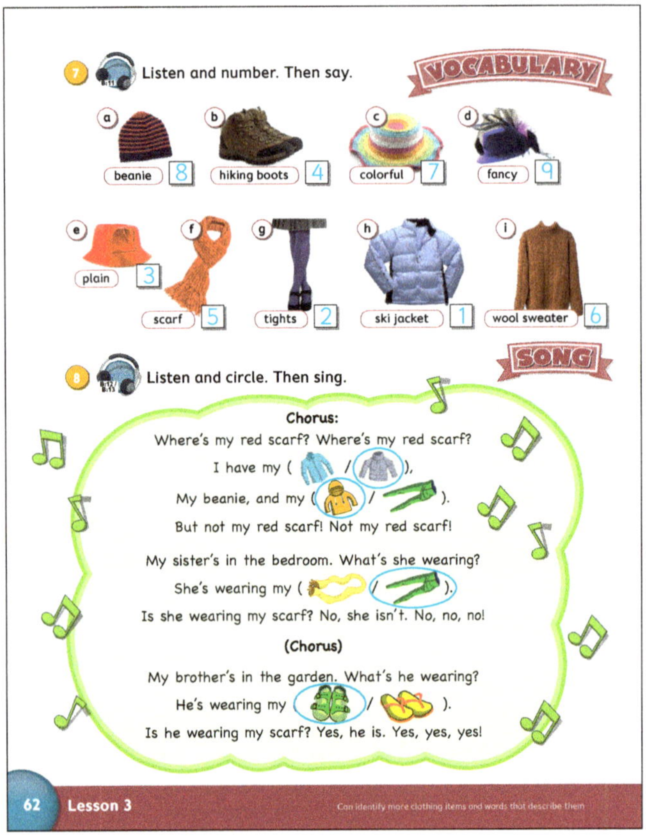

7 Listen and number. Then say. VOCABULARY

a beanie 8 | b hiking boots 4 | c colorful 7 | d fancy 9

e plain 3 | f scarf 5 | g tights 2 | h ski jacket 1 | i wool sweater 6

8 Listen and circle. Then sing. SONG

Chorus:
Where's my red scarf? Where's my red scarf?
I have my (/),
My beanie, and my (/).
But not my red scarf! Not my red scarf!

My sister's in the bedroom. What's she wearing?
She's wearing my (/).
Is she wearing my scarf? No, she isn't. No, no, no!

(Chorus)

My brother's in the garden. What's he wearing?
He's wearing my (/).
Is he wearing my scarf? Yes, he is. Yes, yes, yes!

62 Lesson 3

Lesson 3 SB page 62 or Poptropica English World

Learning Objective
Can identify more clothing items and words that describe them

Target Language
wool sweater, hiking boots, colorful, fancy, scarf, tights, ski jacket, beanie, plain

Warm-up

- Play the chant audio (track B:08). Divide the class into two groups: one group asks the questions, the other gives the answers.

Open books and ask students to look at the activities on the page. Ask, *What are we learning today?* Write the lesson objectives on the board: *We're learning more clothes words and ways to describe clothes.*

- Close books. Ask students what English words they know for describing clothes, e.g., *wool sweater, colorful scarf.* Write on board.
- Refer to the learning adventure poster and say, *Great! You are moving along your learning adventure!*

7 Listen and number. Then say.

B:11

- Introduce the new words with Picture Cards 130–138. Hold them up one by one and ask students to repeat the words after you. Then ask students to look in their books and point at the words as you say them.
- Play the audio and have students number the words as they hear them. The play it again and have them repeat.
- Point to individual pictures and ask students to tell you the word.

1 ski jacket
2 tights
3 plain
4 hiking boots
5 scarf
6 wool sweater
7 colorful
8 beanie
9 fancy

8 Listen and circle. Then sing.

B:12 B:13

- Ask students what clothing items they can see in the choices in brackets. Point to each one in turn and ask, *What's this? / What are these?*
- Play the song audio and have students listen.
- Play the audio again and ask students to circle the item they hear. Have students check their answers in pairs. Invite different pairs to come to the front and write the names of the clothing items they circled.
- Invite students to sing the song. Play the audio again and ask students to mime putting on the clothing items as they sing the song.
- If students are confident, use the karaoke version.

Ask students, *How many words for clothes do you know now?* Give students a minute to tell their partner the new words they know.

- Ask students to say where they are on their adventure now. Ask students which words they find easiest or most difficult to remember. Tell students, *Good job!* to reinforce the progress they are making.

Pop Quiz: As students are leaving the class, show them pictures from a fashion magazine with models wearing a variety of clothing. Ask each student to make a true sentence about the models, e.g., *He's wearing a plain scarf. She's wearing fancy tights.*

Materials
Poster, Picture Cards 130–138, pictures of models wearing a variety of clothing

Homework WB page 50

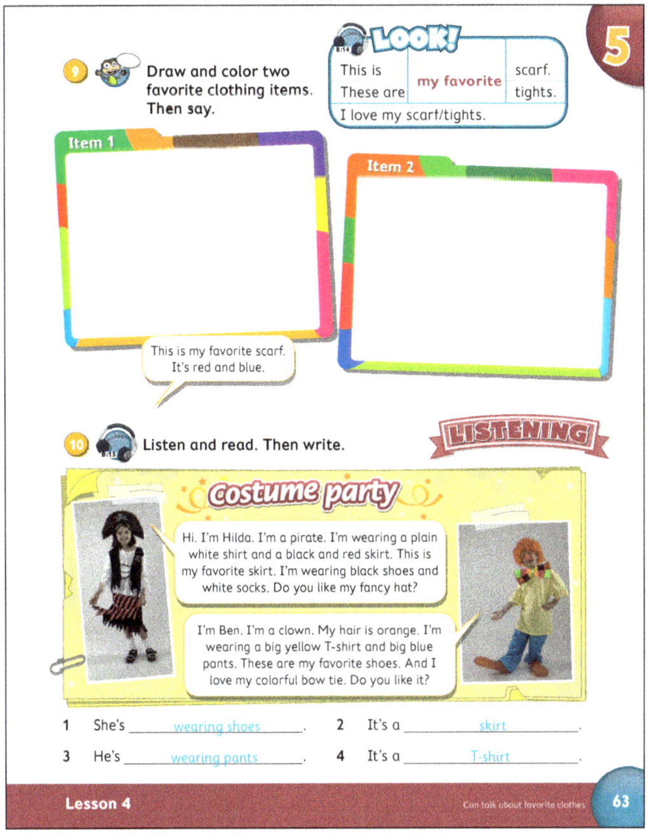
5

9 Draw and color two favorite clothing items. Then say.

LOOK!

This is	my favorite	scarf.
These are		tights.

I love my scarf/tights.

Item 1

This is my favorite scarf. It's red and blue.

Item 2

10 Listen and read. Then write.

LISTENING

Costume party

Hi. I'm Hilda. I'm a pirate. I'm wearing a plain white shirt and a black and red skirt. This is my favorite skirt. I'm wearing black shoes and white socks. Do you like my fancy hat?

I'm Ben. I'm a clown. My hair is orange. I'm wearing a big yellow T-shirt and big blue pants. These are my favorite shoes. And I love my colorful bow tie. Do you like it?

1 She's wearing shoes.
2 It's a skirt.
3 He's wearing pants.
4 It's a T-shirt.

Lesson 4 Can talk about favorite clothes 63

Lesson 4 SB page 63 or Poptropica English World

Learning Objective
Can talk about favorite clothes

Target Language
This is my favorite scarf. These are my favorite tights. I love my scarf/tights.

Warm-up

- Prepare sets of word cards for the clothing items mentioned in the song on page 62. Give a set to each student. Play the song (track B:12). Have students listen and hold up the correct cards when they hear the words mentioned in the song.

Open books and ask students to look at the book and the Look! box. Ask, *What are we learning today?* Write the lesson objective on the board: *We're learning to talk about our favorite clothes.*

9 Draw and color two favorite clothing items. Then say.

- Explain to students that they will now draw two of their favorite clothing items in the spaces provided and color them.
- When they are finished, focus on the sentences in the Look! box and play the audio (track B:14). Ask students to read the text aloud.
- Pair students and have them describe their favorite clothes to each other.

10 B:15 Listen and read. Then write.

- Focus students' attention on the two children and have them identify the costumes. Explain what a fancy dress show is (a show where everyone dresses up in a costume). Say, e.g., *Look! She's a pirate. He's a clown!*
- Ask them to find the sentences with the word *favorite* in and write them on the board. *(This is my favorite skirt. These are my favorite shoes.)* Explain that the words *This is* refer to one thing *(a skirt)*, and the words *These are* refer to two or more things *(two shoes).*
- Explain to students that they will listen to some sentences and questions about the two children. Play the audio and have students listen and follow.

1 Hilda isn't wearing sandals. What's she wearing?
2 Hilda is wearing something black and red. What is it?
3 Ben isn't wearing shorts. What's he wearing?
4 Ben is wearing something yellow. What is it?

- Play the audio, pausing after each question. Have students listen and write the answers.
- Check the answers by inviting individual students to come to the front and write the completed sentences on the board.
- For further practice, divide students into groups of four (two pairs) and give each group a copy of Activity Sheet 4 (see page 158). The first pair has a minute to try to memorize the position of the clothing items on the sheet. This pair then turns their back while the second pair uses the four number cards to cover up four of the items. The first pair then turns around and tries to remember which four items have been covered up. They call out the items in order, using the numbers, e.g., *Number 1, shorts.* When they finish, have pairs change roles and play again.

Pop Quiz: Before the end of the lesson, ask students to look through fashion magazines and choose a favorite item to show the class and say, e.g., *This is my favorite skirt. I love these sandals.*

Materials
Word cards, Activity Sheet 4, fashion magazines

Homework WB page 51

Lesson 5 SB page 64 or Poptropica English World

Learning Objectives
Can understand a simple story
Can role-play a story

Functional Language
There! Hee, hee! Look...it's up there!

Warm-up

- Ask questions about the story from Unit 4, e.g., *Where were they? Where was the tifftiff plant?*

Open books and ask students to look at the story. Ask, *What are we learning today?* Write the lesson objective on the board: *We're reading a story and we're role-playing a story.*

11 Talk about the pictures. Then listen and read.

B:16

- Direct students' attention to the story and ask questions about the characters and the scene: *Who can you see? Where are they? What are they doing? What's he wearing? Where's the tifftiff plant?*
- Play the audio and have students listen and follow. Check understanding by pointing at the pictures and asking questions: *Who has the tifftiff plant in picture 2? What clothes are in picture 2? What's PROD 2 wearing in picture 5? Do they have the tifftiff plant at the end?*
- Play the recording again, stopping after each line. Have students repeat.
- Play the audio again. Have students speak along and mime the actions.

Think of a question that has the answer, *No, he isn't.* Write the answer, *No, he isn't.* on the board, but don't tell the students the question. Students need to find the correct question for your answer. Possible questions are: *Is Kim wearing shorts? Is PROD 2 happy? Is PROD 1 wearing a baseball cap? Is the trickster wearing flip-flops?* Accept all suggestions before revealing the question you had been thinking about.

12 Role-play the story.

- See the "How to use stories" section on page 22 for more ideas on how to build your students' confidence with role-plays.
- Divide students into groups of five. Give each group a set of cut-up Story Cards and have students place them in order.
- Divide students into groups and have them role-play the story. When you say, *change*, they should change character and role-play a new character. Rotate through the characters giving students the chance to play each one.

You might like to give the students feedback on their role-play

Pop Quiz: Before the end of the lesson, ask students if they can remember what clothes were in the laundry. Can they describe them? (e.g., *There's a fancy blue and yellow dress. There's a red jacket. There are green pants.*)

Materials
Story Cards

Homework WB page 52

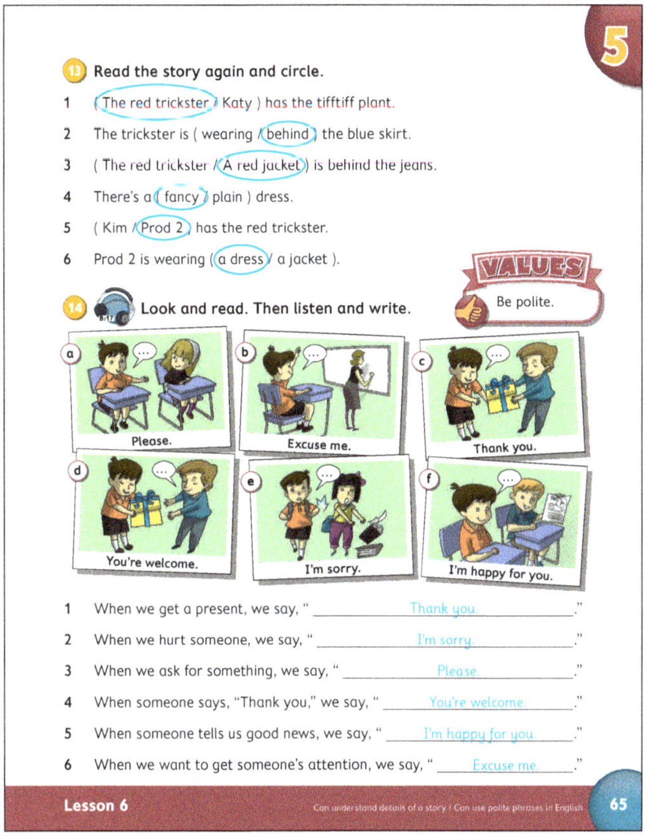

5

13 Read the story again and circle.

1 (The red trickster / Katy) has the tifftiff plant.
2 The trickster is (wearing / behind) the blue skirt.
3 (The red trickster / A red jacket) is behind the jeans.
4 There's a (fancy / plain) dress.
5 (Kim / Prod 2) has the red trickster.
6 Prod 2 is wearing (a dress / a jacket).

VALUES
Be polite.

14 B:17 Look and read. Then listen and write.

1 When we get a present, we say, "Thank you."
2 When we hurt someone, we say, "I'm sorry."
3 When we ask for something, we say, "Please."
4 When someone says, "Thank you," we say, "You're welcome."
5 When someone tells us good news, we say, "I'm happy for you."
6 When we want to get someone's attention, we say, "Excuse me."

Lesson 6 Can understand details of a story / Can use polite phrases in English 65

Lesson 6 SB page 65 or Poptropica English World

Learning Objectives
Can understand details of a story
Can use polite phrases in English

Additional Language
Be polite.
please, excuse me, thank you, you're welcome, I'm sorry
I'm happy for you.

Value
Be polite.

Open books and ask students to look at the activities on the page. Ask, *What are we learning today?* Write the lesson objective on the board: *We're understanding details of a story, and we're learning how to be polite.*

Warm-up

- Play the story audio (B:16) again and review the story with students. Ask questions about each story frame: *Who's this? What color is the shirt,* etc.

13 Read the story again and circle.

- Have students work in pairs. They look carefully at the story frames and read the story again. Then have them read the sentences and circle the correct words.
- Have students read the statements to check that they are correct.

14 B:17 Look and read. Then listen and write.

- Read the value, *Be polite.* Direct students' attention to the pictures of the children. Point to each one and explain, e.g., *The boy is asking for something.* Then ask, e.g., *What's he saying? (please)* Explain the value and have students think about ways of being polite.
- Play the audio and have students listen. Then play it again, pausing after each line, and have students say the polite expression.

1 When we get a present, we say, "Thank you."
2 When we hurt someone, we say, "I'm sorry."
3 When we ask for something, we say, "Please."
4 When someone says, "Thank you," we say, "You're welcome."
5 When someone tells us good news, we say, "I'm happy for you."
6 When we want to get someone's attention, we say, "Excuse me."

- Pair students and have them work together to complete the sentences with the correct expressions.
- Check answers by inviting individual students to read the completed sentences.
- Write the following questions on the board: *Why is it important to be polite? (People are happy.) What other things can we do to be polite? (Ask people if they need help. Wait in line. Smile when you say "thank you.")*
- Tell students to work with a partner. Give pairs two minutes to discuss and note down their answers. Ask students to share their answers with the class.

Pop Quiz: Before the end of the lesson, play an acting game. Students role-play one of the six activities from the values on Activity 14, in front of the class.

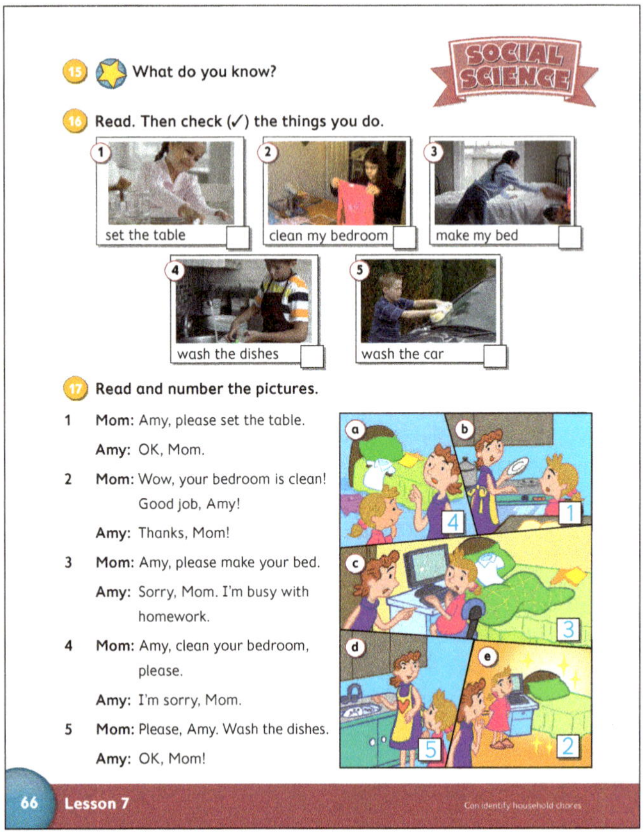

SOCIAL SCIENCE

15 What do you know?

16 Read. Then check (✓) the things you do.

1 set the table
2 clean my bedroom
3 make my bed
4 wash the dishes
5 wash the car

17 Read and number the pictures.

1 **Mom:** Amy, please set the table.
Amy: OK, Mom.

2 **Mom:** Wow, your bedroom is clean! Good job, Amy!
Amy: Thanks, Mom!

3 **Mom:** Amy, please make your bed.
Amy: Sorry, Mom. I'm busy with homework.

4 **Mom:** Amy, clean your bedroom, please.
Amy: I'm sorry, Mom.

5 **Mom:** Please, Amy. Wash the dishes.
Amy: OK, Mom!

66 Lesson 7 Can identify household chores

Lesson 7 SB page 66 or Poptropica English World

Learning Objective
Can identify household chores

Additional Language
set the table, clean the bedroom, make my bed, wash the dishes, wash the car

Warm-up

- Use the Picture Cards 100–111 and 112–119 to review furnishings/household items vocabulary. Choose several Cards and stick them on the board. Then write the matching words next to them, leaving out a letter in each word. Ask students to complete the words.

15 What do you know?

- Open books and ask students to look at the activities on the page. Ask, *What are we learning today?* Write the lesson objective on the board: *We're learning about household chores.*
- Close books. Ask students what they know about different household chores. Write their ideas on the board.
- Refer to the learning adventure poster and say, *Great! You are moving along your learning journey!*

16 Read. Then check (✓) the things you do.

- Ask students if they help at home and elicit some expressions for household chores, e.g., *wash the dishes, make my bed, tidy up my room, feed the dog.*, etc.
- Point to each picture and read the sentence underneath. Then ask students, e.g., *Do you help set the table at home?* The students who answer *yes* should check the corresponding picture.
- Invite individual students to read the sentences they have checked.

17 Read and number the pictures.

- Focus students' attention on the picture and the mini-conversations. Ask students to explain the situation. *(The mom wants her daughter to help at home.; The girl is sometimes busy.)*
- Pair students and have them work out what the mom is asking Amy to do in each picture.
- Then have students read the conversations in pairs and match them to the pictures.
- Check answers by inviting pairs to read the conversations in turn, and identifying the corresponding picture.

Ask the students: *Why is it important to help at home?* Accept any answers and promote discussion. Point to the lesson objective on the board. Ask learners what they know now about helping at home. Give learners two minutes to tell their partner what they know.

- Ask students: *Where are you on your learning adventure?* Tell students, *Good job!* to reinforce the progress they are making.

Pop Quiz: Before the end of the lesson, ask students to think about three things they can do to help when they get home, e.g., *I can feed the dog. I can clean my bedroom. I can wash the dishes.*

Materials
Picture Cards 100–111; 112–119, poster

Homework WB page 54

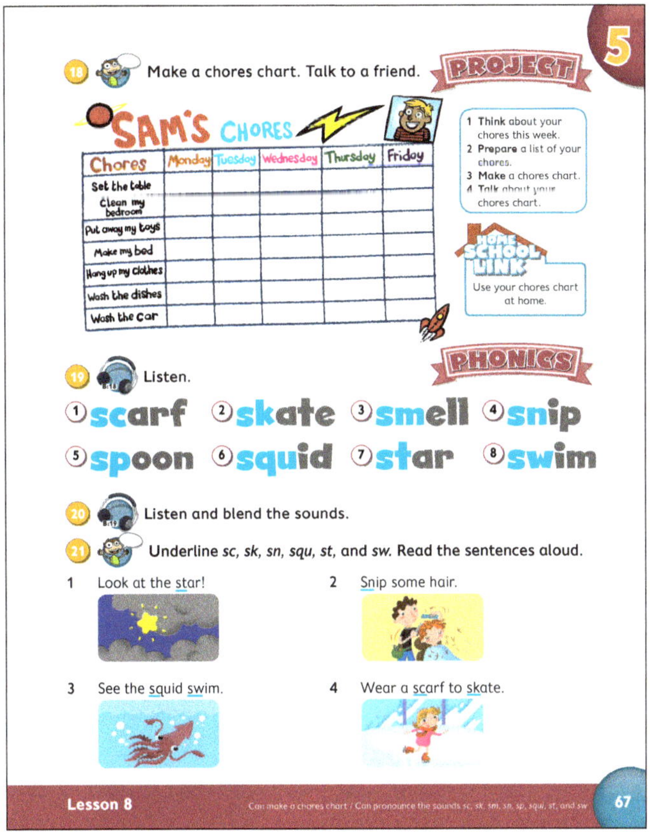

Lesson 8 SB page 67 or Poptropica English World

Learning Objectives
Can make a chores chart
Can pronounce the sounds *sc, sk, sm, sn, sp, squ, st,* and *sw.*

Warm-up

- Prepare large letter cards to review the sounds and letters. Show the cards in random order and have the students chorus the letter-sounds.

Open books and ask students to look at the activities on the page. Ask, *What are we learning today?* Write the lesson objectives on the board: *We're learning to make a chores chart, and we're learning to pronounce* sc, sk, sm, sn, sp, squ, st *and* sw.

18 Make a chores chart. Talk to a friend.

- Show students the example chores chart in their books. Explain that they are going to make their own charts. Ask students to think about the chores they do over an average week and have them write a list.

Look at the chores chart in the book. Ask students: *Is it good? Why?* Write their ideas on the board.

- Provide the materials they need and give students time to make their charts. Ask them to check the chart according to the chores they do over the next week.
- Have the students talk to a partner about their charts.
- Display the charts in the classroom.

You may also wish to give students feedback on their projects.

- **Home-School link:** Read the instruction with the class: *Use your chores chart at home.* Ask students to do this at home.

19 Listen.

B:18

- Have students open their books and look at the eight words, *scarf, skate, smell, snip, spoon, squid, star,* and *swim.* Explain to students that they are going to read and pronounce the sounds *sc, sk, sm, sn, sp, squ, st,* and *sw.* Play the audio.

1 sk	scarf	**2** sk	skate	**3** sm	smell
4 sn	snip	**5** sp	spoon	**6** squ	squid
7 st	star	**8** sw	swim		

20 Listen and blend the sounds.

- Write a word on the board. Underline each phoneme in the word, e.g., *s p oo n* as you sound it out, *s-p-oo-n.* Now have the students repeat. Repeat with the other words.
- Do the activity on the page.

1 sk ar f	scarf	**2** sk ate	skate
3 sm e ll	smell	**4** sn i p	snip
5 sp oo n	spoon	**6** squ i d	squid
7 st ar	star	**8** sw i m	swim

21 Underline *sc, sk, sn, squ, st,* and *sw.* Read the sentences aloud.

- Have students work individually. First they should hide the illustrations with a ruler or notebook. Once they have underlined the graphemes and read the sentences aloud, they can reveal the illustrations. Put students in pairs to read the sentences.

Pop Quiz: Before the end of the lesson, write *S* in a sunshine in the middle of the board and these consonants emanating from the sun's rays around it: *c, k, m, n, p, qu, t, w.* Ask volunteers to come to the front, write a word at the end of each ray that begins with *s* + one of the consonants, and say the word.

Materials
Letter cards (Units 1 and 2)

Homework WB page 55

Lesson 9 SB page 68 or Poptropica English World

Learning Objective
Can assess what I have learned in Unit 5

Warm-up

- Write jumbled clothing words on the board. Invite students to come to the front, write the word correctly, and stick Picture Cards 120–138 next to it.

Open books and ask students to look at the activities on the page. Explain to students that they are going to review what they have learned in this unit. Write the lesson objective on the board: *We're talking about our learning adventure.*

- Ask students if they can remember the things they learned in this unit, e.g., *How many clothes words can you remember?* Put their ideas on the board.
- For each example (e.g., *clothes*), ask students, *Where are you on your learning adventure?*

22 B:20 Listen and match.

- Ask students to look at the pictures and talk about what the children are wearing.
- Have the students listen to the audio and number the pictures according to the descriptions they hear. Have them check answers with a partner.
- Ask students to work in pairs to help each other remember any of the words they couldn't remember.

1 Hi, I'm Rob. I'm wearing a wool sweater, pants and hiking boots.
2 My name's Beth. I'm wearing a plain sweatshirt and shorts. Do you like my fancy flip-flops?
3 I'm Harry. I'm wearing a sweatsuit and a baseball cap.
4 Hello. I'm Suzy. I'm wearing a polo shirt and a skirt. I'm wearing colorful tights, too.
5 I'm Matt. I'm wearing a beanie and a colorful scarf. I'm wearing a ski jacket.
6 My name's Lulu. I'm wearing my school uniform. I have a fancy hat, a dress, socks, and sandals. Do you have a uniform?

23 Look at Activity 22. Play a guessing game. Ask and answer.

- Ask students to work in pairs. They take turns to choose one of the children from Activity 22. Their partner asks questions in order to find out which child they have chosen.

24 What are you wearing? Draw and write.

- Ask students to draw themselves in the clothes they are wearing and write about their pictures.

Ask students how they feel about their learning in this unit. Ask students to tell you what they found easy and what they found the most difficult to learn in the unit.

- Students review the I Can statements at the bottom of the page and color each bar according to how confident they feel about the language point.
- Ask students, *Where are you on your learning adventure?* Students indicate where they think they are on the learning adventure poster. Tell students, *Good job!* to reinforce the progress they are making.

Pop Quiz: In groups of four, students tell the others the answers to the following questions: *Which is your favorite activity in the unit? Why? Which activity don't you like? Why? What is your favorite new word? Which word is the most difficult for you?*

Materials
Picture Cards 120–138, poster

Homework WB page 56

Lesson 10 SB page 69 or Poptropica English World

Learning Objective
Can use what I have learned in Unit 5

Warm-up

- Draw a simple picture of a clothing item, one line at a time on the board. Each time you draw a line, have students try to guess what you are drawing by asking, e.g., *Is it a baseball cap? Are these sneakers?* The first student who guesses correctly draws the next picture.

Open books and ask students to look at the activities on the page. Ask, *What are we learning today?* Write the lesson objective on the board: *We're learning to talk about clothes.*

Make a statement: *School uniforms are great.* Give pairs two minutes to think about this statement and whether or not they agree with it. They might like to write their ideas in their notebooks. Write their suggestions on the board.

25 Stick. Then ask, answer, and draw.

- Direct students' attention to the clothing stickers at the back of the book and ask them to choose their favorite items for themselves, and stick them on the 'Me' figure. Make sure they don't show them to other classmates.
- Explain the game to the class. Students try to guess the clothing items their friend/partner has chosen by asking questions. When they guess an item, they draw it in the "My friend" box.
- Pair students. Have them play the game until they have drawn the items on their 'friends'.
- Have students walk around the class and find new partners to tell about their favorite clothes and their friend's picture, e.g., *Look at my picture. This is my favorite polo shirt. These are my favorite jeans. I love my scarf and my hiking boots. Look at my friend's favorite clothes.* This activity helps build students' confidence as they are using the language they have learned in a different context.

I want to know more

- Ask students to choose anything they enjoyed from the unit and to go and find out more. You might like to set this activity as homework with a quick feedback session at the beginning of the next class, e.g. find out more words for clothes, think of more ways to be polite, think of more household chores.

Are you ready for Unit 6?

- Ask students if they are ready to move onto the next unit. Tell students that it is fine if they do not remember everything as they will continue to practice throughout the level.
- Encourage students to ask if they have any questions about what they learned in Unit 5.

You may wish to give Unit 5 test (see page 196) at this time.

Materials
Colored pens or pencils, stickers

Homework WB page 57

Unit 5 Story Cards

Wider World 3

SB pages 70–71 or Poptropica English World

Learning Objectives
Can understand texts about school uniforms
Can talk about what I'm wearing

Additional Language
I'm from (Mexico/the United Kingdom/Canada/China).
comfortable

1 What do you know?

Discuss wearing uniforms with the class. Ask: *Do you wear uniforms? In which countries do they think students wear uniforms?*

Open books and ask students to look at the activities on the page. Ask, *What are we learning today?* Write the lesson objective on the board: *We're learning about school uniforms around the world.*

2 Listen and read.

B:21

- Point at the pictures. Ask questions, e.g., *Where do you think he/she is from? Is he/she wearing a uniform?* Encourage students to answer without reading the text.
- Play the audio and have students listen and follow. Then play each part separately and ask questions to check comprehension, e.g., *What's the child's name? Do they have uniforms at school? What's he/she wearing?*, etc.

3 Write C (Clara), S (Scott), E (Emma), or J (Jiaming).

- Have students work in pairs. They read the sentences and decide which child they relate to, then write that child's initial at the end of each sentence.
- Check their answers by reading out the sentences and having students call out the children's names.

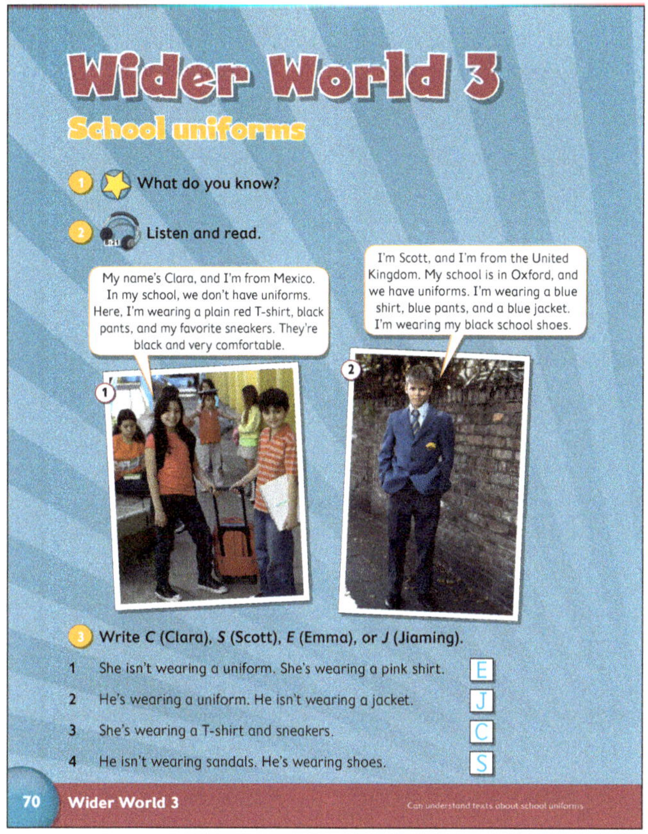

Wider World 3
School uniforms

1 What do you know?

2 Listen and read.

3 Write *C* (Clara), *S* (Scott), *E* (Emma), or *J* (Jiaming).

1 She isn't wearing a uniform. She's wearing a pink shirt. E
2 He's wearing a uniform. He isn't wearing a jacket. J
3 She's wearing a T-shirt and sneakers. C
4 He isn't wearing sandals. He's wearing shoes. S

Materials
World map

Tell the Class

4 Ask and answer.

- Have students work in small groups. They take turns to ask and answer the three questions.
- Then have a class discussion about school uniforms using the questions as prompts.
- Ask the children to think about how their clothes or school uniforms are similar to those of the children from around the world, and how they are different.

Point at the learning objective on the board. Ask students, *How many words do you know for clothes now?* Give students a minute to tell their partner as many clothes words as they can.

- Ask students, *Where are you on your learning adventure?* Ask students which words they find easiest or most difficult to remember. Tell students, *Good job!* to reinforce the progress they are making.

Pop Quiz: As students are leaving the class, ask them to make two statements about their own clothes, one positive and one negative, e.g., *I'm wearing a white shirt. I'm not wearing a uniform.*

6 Sports

Unit Overview

Unit Objective

- I can talk about sports

Language

Target Vocabulary	Abilities: do taekwondo, catch a ball, play tennis, run, play baseball, ride a bike, play basketball, play soccer Sports facilities: gym, baseball field, basketball court, running track, stadium, ski slope, beach, swimming pool, tennis court, soccer field
Target Structures	I/He/She can run and jump. I/He/She can run, but I/he/she can't jump. Can you/he/she play tennis? Yes, I/he/she can. / No, I/he/she can't. I/He/She was at the gym. I/He/She wasn't at the gym. I/He/She was at the baseball field.
Features	**Values:** Be active. Exercise every day. **Cross-curricular:** Health: Exercise **Phonics:** *bl, fl, gl, pl, sl* (black, flag, float, glass, plate, sleep)

Skills

Reading	• Can understand a simple story • Can understand details of a story • Can understand fitness instructions and which activities are healthy
Writing	• Can make a healthy living poster • Can complete simple sentences about what people can and can't do (*Workbook*) • Can complete simple sentences about where people were using was and wasn't (*Workbook*) • Can write simple sentences about my exercise plan (*Workbook*)
Listening	• Can identify sports and abilities • Can identify sports facilities • Can understand a simple story • Can understand fitness instructions and which activities are healthy
Speaking	• Can ask and answer about what people can and can't do • Can talk about where people were using *was* and *wasn't* • Can role-play a story • Can talk about being active and exercising every day • Can pronounce the sounds *bl, fl, gl, pl,* and *sl*

Lesson 1 SB page 72 or Poptropica English World

Learning Objective
Can identify sports and abilities

Target Language
do taekwondo, catch a ball, play tennis, run, play baseball, ride a bike, play basketball, play soccer

1 What do you know?

- Open books and ask students to look at the activities on the page. Ask, *What are we learning today?* Write the lesson objective on the board: *We're learning to talk about sports and abilities.*
- Close books. Ask students what English words they know for sports/activites, e.g., *jump, climb.* Write on board. Refer to the learning adventure poster and say, *Great! You are already moving along your learning journey!*

2 B:22 Listen and find. What's missing?

- Using the Picture Cards of sports words or drawings on the board, teach the new vocabulary. Say the words and have students repeat.
- Play the audio. Students listen to the dialog and circle the pictures when they hear the related words. Ask, *What's missing? (baseball)*

Arnold: Hello! Welcome to the sports centre. Do you like sports?
Katy: Yes, I do. I can ride a bike.
Arnold: Can you run?
Kim: Yes. I can run fast and I can play soccer.
Arnold: Can you play basketball?
Katy: Yes, I can. PROD 2, here catch!
PROD 2: I can catch a ball. I have long arms!
Arnold: Ha ha! Can you play tennis?
PROD 2: No, I can't.
PROD 1: I can do taekwondo! Look!
PROD 2: Ouch!

3 B:23 Listen and number.

- Ask questions about the main scene: *Who's this? Where are they?* Call out the sport words and have students find and point.
- Ask students to look at the pictures in their books and listen. Play the audio again and ask them to find the items and number them.

1 Do you want to play tennis?
2 She can ride a bike. Look! Her bike is red.
3 Can you do taekwondo?
4 Can you catch a ball?
5 He can run fast!
6 Do you like to play soccer?
7 Do you like to play baseball?
8 He can play basketball. He can jump really high.

4 B:24 Listen and say.

- Play the audio. Students listen and point to the items in the picture and repeat the words.

Ask learners how many words for sports they know now. Give students a minute to tell their partner the new words they know. Ask students to say where they are on their adventure now. Ask students which word they find easiest or most difficult to remember. Tell students, *Good job!* to reinforce the progress they are making.

Pop Quiz: As students are leaving the class, ask volunteers to mime playing a sport for the class to guess.

Materials
Poster, Picture Cards 139–146

Homework WB page 58

Lesson 2 SB page 73 or Poptropica English World

Learning Objective
Can ask and answer about what people can and can't do

Target Language
I/He/She can/can't run and jump.
I/He/She can run, but I/he/she can't jump.
Can you/he/she play tennis?
Yes, I/he/she can. / No, I/he/she can't.

Warm-up

- Show Picture Cards 139–146 in turn, and say something for each one, e.g., *I can run.* Deliberately make some mistakes, e.g., say the wrong sports or activity. Have students call out *true* or *false.*

Open books and ask students to look at the chant and the Look! box. Ask, *What are we learning today?* Write the lesson objective on the board: *We're learning to say which sports we can and can't do.*

5 Listen and chant. (B:25, B:26)

- Play the chant. Ask students to tell you what sports and activities they hear on the chant. Then ask them to point to the items in the main picture.
- Play the chant a few times and have students chant along. If students are confident, use the karaoke version.

6 Listen and ✓ = can or ✗ = can't. Then ask and answer.

- Read through the Look! box with the class and play the audio (track B:27).
- Have students listen to the activity audio and mark checks and crosses in the chart. Then, in pairs, they ask each other questions about Kim and Katy.

Arnold: So Katy, you can ride a bike and you can play basketball.
Katy: Yes, that's right. I can run fast too, but I can't play soccer.
Arnold: Can Kim play soccer?
Katy: Yes, he can. He can play soccer and he can run fast. He can ride a bike, but he can't play basketball.
Arnold: Can he play tennis?
Katy: Yes, he can. I can play tennis too.

- For further practice pair the students and give a copy of Activity Sheet 5 (see page 159) to each student. Students cut out the pictures at the bottom of the Activity Sheet. Put a divider between Student 1 and Student 2 so that they cannot see each other's sheets. Have students stick four sports/activities they can do into the first box without telling their partners. Then have students guess what their partner can do, e.g., *Can you run?* (*No, I can't. / Yes, I can.*) When a student makes a correct guess, he/she sticks the sport into the second box.
- Direct students' attention to the exercise bike card on page 73. Tell students to go online to the Poptropica English Island Adventure Game and find the item. Once students click on it, they are taken to a supplementary language task.

Pop Quiz: As students are leaving the class, hand them two Picture Cards (from 139–146) showing sports. They make true statements about the sports shown, joining the statements with *and* or *but*, e.g., *I can play soccer, but I can't play tennis. I can run and I can play baseball.*

Materials
Picture Cards 139–146, Activity Sheet 5

Homework WB page 59

Lesson 3 SB page 74 or Poptropica English World

Learning Objective
Can identify sports facilities

Target Language
gym, baseball field, basketball court, running track, stadium, ski slope, beach, swimming pool, tennis court, soccer field

Warm-up

- Put students into three teams. Place a selection of the Picture Cards (61–87) across the board. Have students line up in three rows and face the front. Go to the back of the room. Ask the last student in each row to turn to you. Silently say the name of one of the Picture Cards (or show the word matching the Card). Have each student whisper the name to the student in front of him/her. The last student in the row goes to the board and taps the Picture Card as he/she says the name. The first student to do so correctly gets five points for his/her team. The three students nearest the board go to the back of the rows. Repeat the activity.

Open books and ask students to look at the activities on the page. Ask, *What are we learning today?* Write the lesson objective on the board: *We're learning the names of places where you can do sports.*

- Close books. Ask students what English words they know for sports facilities, e.g. *gym, swimming pool.* Write on board.
- Refer to the learning adventure poster and say, *Great! You are moving along your learning adventure!*

7 Listen and number. Then say.

B:29

- Introduce the new vocabulary with Picture Cards 139–156. Hold them up one by one and ask students to repeat the words after you. Then ask students to look in their books and point at the words as you say them.
- Play the audio and have students number the words as they hear them. Then play the audio again and have students repeat.
- Point to individual pictures and ask students to tell you the word.

8 Listen and circle. Then sing.

B:30
B:31

- Focus students' attention on the pictures and ask about each child, e.g., *Can she play basketball? (Yes, she can.) Where is she? (at the gym).*
- Play the audio. Have students listen and circle the correct words.
- Play the song again and have students complete the missing words.
- Play the song again and ask students to sing along. If students are confident, use the karaoke version.

Ask students, *How many words for sports facilities do you know now?* Give students a minute to tell their partner the new words they know.

- Ask students to say where they are on their adventure now. Ask students which words they find easiest or most difficult to remember. Tell students, *Good job!* to reinforce the progress they are making.

Pop Quiz: Play a miming game. Mime doing a sport at one of the places in Activity 7. Then ask, *Where am I?* Students guess: *You're at the (swimming pool).* Students take turns to mime.

Materials
Picture Cards 61–87; 139–156, poster

Homework WB page 60

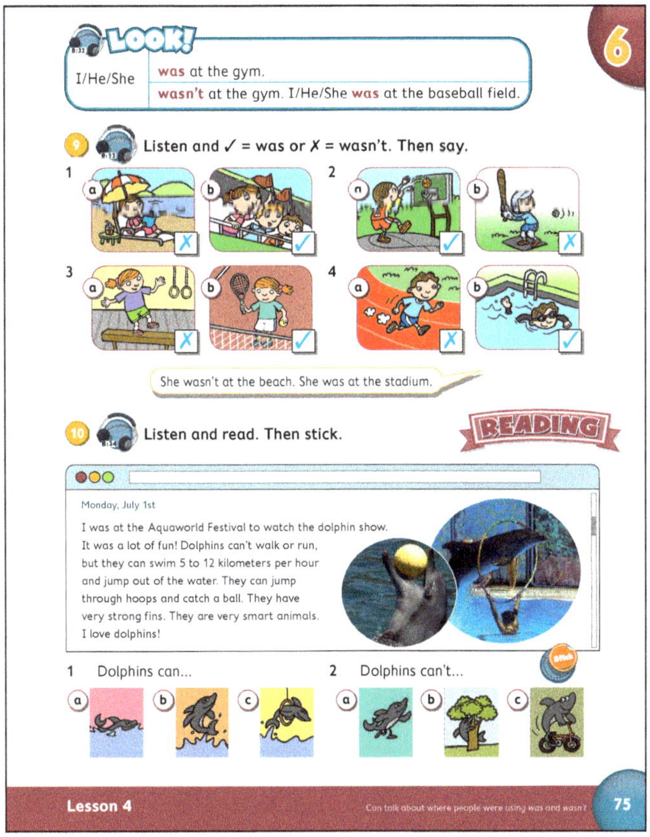

LOOK!

I/He/She	was at the gym.
	wasn't at the gym. I/He/She was at the baseball field.

9 Listen and ✓ = was or ✗ = wasn't. Then say.

She wasn't at the beach. She was at the stadium.

10 Listen and read. Then stick. READING

Monday, July 1st

I was at the Aquaworld Festival to watch the dolphin show. It was a lot of fun! Dolphins can't walk or run, but they can swim 5 to 12 kilometers per hour and jump out of the water. They can jump through hoops and catch a ball. They have very strong fins. They are very smart animals. I love dolphins!

1 Dolphins can... 2 Dolphins can't...

Lesson 4 Can talk about where people were using was and wasn't 75

Lesson 4 SB page 75 or Poptropica English World

Learning Objective
Can talk about where people were using *was* and *wasn't*

Target Language
I/He/She was at the gym.
I/He/She wasn't at the gym.
I/He/She was at the baseball field.

Warm-up

- Have students review sports vocabulary. Put Picture Cards 139–156 in a bag and call a student to the front to draw a card from the bag and hold it up. Choose a student to say the word. If he/she gets the sport name correct, he/she gets to draw the next card.

Open books and ask students to look at the book and the Look! box. Ask, *What are we learning today?* Write the lesson objective on the board: *We're learning to say where people were in the past.*

9 Listen and ✓ = was or ✗ = wasn't. Then say.

- Play the audio, pausing after each question to allow students to check the correct picture.

1 She wasn't at the beach. She was at the stadium.
2 He wasn't at the baseball field. He was at the basketball court.
3 She wasn't at the gym. She was at the tennis court.
4 He wasn't at the running track. He was at the swimming pool.

- Read through the Look! box with students and play the audio (track B:32). Play the audio for Activity 9 again. Pause after each question and have students call out the correct answers, e.g., *1b*.
- Put students in pairs and have them say to each other where each child was. Use the model sentences to demonstrate the language.

10 Listen and read. Then stick.

- Pair students and have them read the text and underline any words they don't understand. Play the audio. Have students listen and follow in their books.
- Have students find the stickers at the back of their books. Ask a question about each one, e.g., *Can dolphins climb trees?* Have students call out the answers, e.g., *No, they can't.* Have students stick the sticker under the correct heading. Do the same for the other stickers.

Pop Quiz: Before the end of the lesson, show students a picture of a sporty-looking person and explain that yesterday, he or she went to lots of different places to practice sports. Show students Picture Cards (from 139–156) of different sports facilities and ask them to make sentences in the past tense, e.g., *He/She was at the gym.*

Materials
Picture Cards 139–156, bag, stickers, pictures of a sporty-looking person and different sports facilities

Homework WB page 61

Lesson 5 SB page 76 or Poptropica English World

Learning Objectives
Can understand a simple story
Can role-play a story

Functional Language
Hmph! good at..., Let's find...

Warm-up

- Ask students what they can remember about the story from the previous episode. Use the Unit 5 Story Cards as prompts. Ask what they saw in the laundrette and what happened to the tifftiff plant.

Open books and ask students to look at the story. Ask, *What are we learning today?* Write the lesson objectives on the board: *We're reading a story and we're role-playing a story.*

11 Talk about the pictures. Then listen and read.

B:35

- Direct students' attention to the story and ask questions about the characters and the scene: *Who can you see? Where are they? What are they doing? Can you see the tifftiff plant?*
- Play the audio and have students listen and follow. Check understanding by pointing at the pictures and asking questions: *Can PROD 2 swim? Can PROD 1 run fast? Can they see the tifftiff plant in picture 6?*
- Play the recording again, pausing after each line. Have students repeat.
- Play the audio again. Have students speak along and mime the actions.

Write the following answers on the board: *Yes, he can.* and *No, he can't.* Think of one question for each answer, but don't tell the students. *(Can the trickster run fast? Can PROD 1 fly?)* Students need to find the correct question for each of your answers. Give pairs two minutes to think of some possible questions. They might like to write their ideas in their notebooks. Write their suggestions on the board. Ask students to say why they chose their ideas.

12 Role-play the story.

- See the "How to use stories" section on page 22 for more ideas on how to build your students' confidence with role-plays.
- Divide students into groups of six. Give each group a set of cut-up Story Cards and have students place them in order.
- Divide students into groups and have them role-play the story. When you say, *change*, they should change character and role-play a new character. Rotate through the characters giving students the chance to play each one.

You might like to give the students feedback on their role-play.

Pop Quiz: As students are leaving the class, ask students if they can remember which sports PROD1 and PROD 2 do in the gym.

Materials
Story Cards (Units 5 and 6)

Homework WB page 62

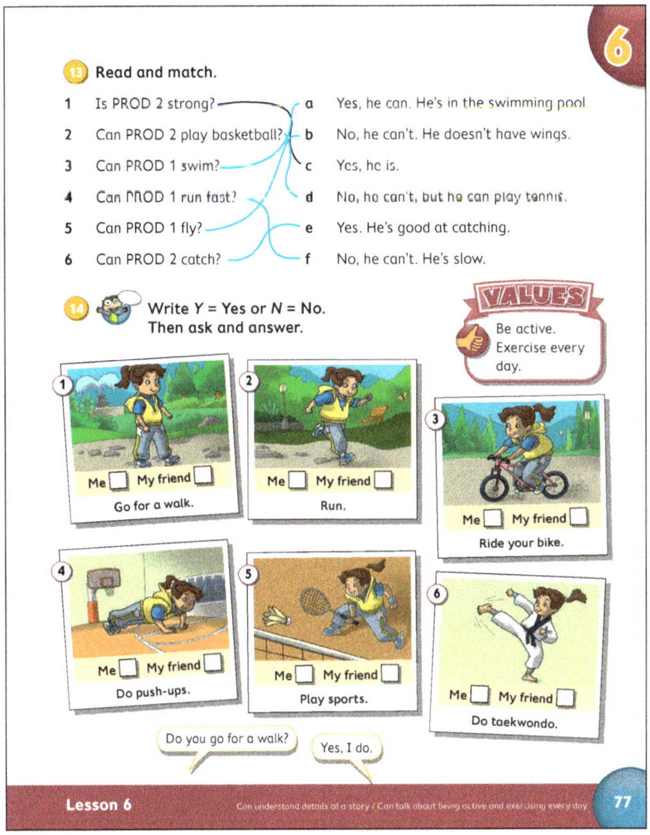

6

13 Read and match.

1 Is PROD 2 strong? — a Yes, he can. He's in the swimming pool.
2 Can PROD 2 play basketball? — b No, he can't. He doesn't have wings.
3 Can PROD 1 swim? — c Yes, he is.
4 Can PROD 1 run fast? — d No, he can't, but he can play tennis.
5 Can PROD 1 fly? — e Yes. He's good at catching.
6 Can PROD 2 catch? — f No, he can't. He's slow.

14 Write *Y* = Yes or *N* = No. Then ask and answer.

VALUES
Be active. Exercise every day.

1 Me ☐ My friend ☐ Go for a walk.
2 Me ☐ My friend ☐ Run.
3 Me ☐ My friend ☐ Ride your bike.
4 Me ☐ My friend ☐ Do push-ups.
5 Me ☐ My friend ☐ Play sports.
6 Me ☐ My friend ☐ Do taekwondo.

Do you go for a walk?
Yes, I do.

Lesson 6 Can understand details of a story / Can talk about being active and exercising every day 77

Lesson 6 SB page 77 or Poptropica English World

Learning Objectives
Can understand details of a story
Can talk about being active and exercising every day

Value
Be active. Exercise every day.

Open books and ask students to look at the activities on the page. Ask, *What are we learning today?* Write the lesson objectives on the board: *We're understanding details of a story, and we're learning how to be active.*

Warm-up

- Write some key words from the unit on the board, (e.g., *baseball, tennis, stadium, gym*), leaving out a letter in each word. Ask students to come to the front and complete the words.

13 Read and match.

- Have students work in pairs. They look carefully at the story frames and match the questions and answers.
- Have students read the questions and answers in pairs to check that they are correct.

14 Write Y = Yes or N = No. Then ask and answer.

- Read the value, *Be active. Exercise every day.* Direct students' attention to the activities. Talk about the importance of an active lifestyle and exercise. Ask why they think exercise is good for them, e.g., *I won't get sick so easily. I will grow taller and stronger.* Ask them if they do any activities or sports with their family, and how often.
- Point to each picture and have students read the phrases. Ask questions, e.g., *Do you go walking?* Have students write *Y* or *N* for themselves. Then pair students and have them ask each other questions, and complete the boxes for their partners.
- Talk about how many hours a week students spend doing exercise, how much time they spend watching TV or playing a computer game. Talk about team sports, and how they can help friendships and encourage cooperation.

Ask students to look at the six pictures again and to consider where they can do these activities (e.g., *the park, the gym*) and what they need in order to do them (e.g., *sneakers, a bike, a racket*). There is no correct answer, but this will extend students' thinking on the value.

Pop Quiz: Before the end of the lesson, ask students to come up with a list of things they can do to be active. Write their ideas on the board, e.g., *go for a walk, ride my bike to school, play sports, go to the gym, take the dog for a walk.*

Homework WB page 63

Lesson 7 SB page 78 or Poptropica English World

Learning Objective
Can understand fitness instructions and which activities are healthy

Additional Language
stretch your arms, bend your knees, twist your body to the left/right, turn around

Warm-up

- Cut a hole in a sheet of paper and hold it over one of the Picture Cards (from 139–156), so students can only see a part of the card. Have students try to guess the item. *(Can he/she run? Is this a gym / Was he/she at the gym?)* Continue with the other cards.

15 What do you know?

- Open books and ask students to look at the activities on the page. Ask, *What are we learning today?* Write the lesson objective on the board: *We're learning about staying fit and healthy.*
- Close books. Ask students what they know about staying fit and healthy. Write their ideas on the board. Refer to the learning adventure poster and say, *Great! You are moving along your learning journey!*

16 Listen and do.

B:36

- Point to the pictures and read the phrases to pre-teach unfamiliar language such as, *stretch*, *bend*, and *twist*. Have students repeat after you and mime the actions.
- Play the audio and have students listen and point to the picture when they hear the instruction.

> Stand up.
> Stretch your arms up, up, up.
> Bend your knees.
> Count to 10.
> 1, 2, 3, 4, 5, 6, 7, 8, 9, 10
> Stand up.
> Twist your body to the left.
> Do it five times.
> 1, 2, 3, 4, 5
> Twist your body to the right.
> Do it five times.
> 1, 2, 3, 4, 5
> Turn around.
> Now start again.

- Play the audio again and have students do the actions.

17 Which activities are healthy? Write ✓ or ✗.

- In pairs, have students look at the pictures and read the activities. They mark a check next to the activities that are healthy, and a cross next to the activities that are not.
- Check that the whole class agrees by reading the activities out loud and have students react by putting their thumbs up for healthy activities, and down for activities that are not so healthy.

Ask students: *What do you know about staying healthy? What simple things could you do to make your life healthier? Could you build in more exercise every day or stop drinking soda?* Give learners two minutes to tell their partner what they know. Ask students, *Where are you on your learning adventure?* Tell students, *Good job!* to reinforce the progress they are making.

Pop Quiz: Before the end of the lesson, play a game of *Simon says*, using the actions in Activity 16, plus other actions they know, e.g., *clap, jump, stamp, wave, sit down.*

Materials
A sheet of paper, Picture Cards 139–156, poster

Homework WB page 64

6

PROJECT

18 Make a healthy living poster. Talk to a friend.

1 Think about healthy living.
2 Choose examples of healthy living.
3 Make a healthy living poster.
4 Talk about your poster.

HOME SCHOOL LINK
Show your poster to your family.

PHONICS

19 Listen.

1 black 2 flag 3 glass
4 plate 5 sleep

20 Listen and blend the sounds.

21 Underline *bl*, *fl*, *gl*, *pl*, and *sl*. Read the sentences aloud.

1 I want a glass of pink milk. 2 Go to sleep.

3 There's plum jam on the spoon. 4 Look at the black flag.

Lesson 8 Can make a healthy living poster / Can pronounce the sounds *bl*, *fl*, *gl*, *pl*, and *sl* 79

Lesson 8 SB page 79 or Poptropica English World

Learning Objectives
Can make a healthy living poster
Can pronounce the sounds *bl, fl, gl, pl, and sl*

Warm-up

- Put the letter cards on the board. Say a letter-sound and choose a student to come to the front and touch the correct letter. Repeat until everyone has had a go.

Open books and ask students to look at the activities on the page. Ask, *What are we learning today?* Write the lesson objectives on the board: *We're learning to make posters about healthy living, and we're learning to pronounce* bl, fl, gl, pl, *and* sl.

18 Make a healthy living poster. Talk to a friend.

- Show students the example posters in their books. Ask students to think about healthy living and to talk to a friend about what they know.

Look at the posters in the Student Book and ask: *Are they good? Why?* Write their ideas on the board.

- Provide the materials and give students time to make their posters. Ask them to think about what information they are going to include and how they are going to present it (pictures, words or both).
- Display the posters around the classroom. Have students describe their posters to a partner.
- Display the healthy living posters in the classroom.

You may also wish to give students feedback on their projects.

- **Home-School link:** Read the instruction with the class: *Show your poster to your family.* Ask students to do this at home.

19 B:37 Listen.

- Have students open their books and look at the five words, *black, flag, glass, plate,* and *sleep.* Explain to students that they are going to read and pronounce the sounds *bl, fl, gl, pl* and *sl.* Play the audio.

1 bl black **2** fl flag **3** gl glasses
4 pl plate **5** sl sleep

20 B:38 Listen and blend the sounds.

- Stay silent. Show the group the first letter card for a word, e.g., *glass*, and elicit the phoneme *g.* Place it on the board. Now repeat this for *l*, *a* and *ss.* Now tap your finger under each card to prompt the students to blend the letter-sounds. Finally make a 'What is it? gesture to elicit the word, then look delighted when they get it. Repeat with the rest of the words.
- Turn to the book and do the activity on the page.

1 bl a ck black **2** fl a g year
3 gl a ss glass **4** pl ate plate
5 sl ee p sleep

21 Underline *bl, fl, gl, pl,* and *sl*. Read the sentences aloud.

- Review the high-frequency words from the sample sentences (*I, want, a, of, go, to, on, the, at*) by writing them on the board. Say each word and have students repeat.
- Have students complete the activity. Check answers as a class.

Pop Quiz: Before the end of the lesson, write a giant *l* in the middle of the board. Ask students to tell you as many words as they can that have *l* as the second letter, e.g., *sleep, blue, black, flag, clean, please, glass, flower, slow.*

Materials
Letter cards (Units 1 and 2), large sheets of paper, colored pens or pencils

Homework WB page 65

22 Listen and ✓ or ✗.

I CAN DO IT!

Jake	✓	✓	✓	✗	✓	✓	✗
Tina	✓	✓	✗	✓	✗	✓	✓
Simon	✓	✗	✓	✓	✗	✓	✗
Donna	✗	✓	✗	✗	✓	✓	✓

23 Play a guessing game. Look at Activity 22. Ask and answer.

He can ride a bike, but he can't play baseball.

Can he play soccer?

Yes, he can.

It's Jack.

24 Mime a sport. Ask and answer.

Are you at the basketball court?

Yes, I am.

You can play basketball!

I CAN

I can identify sports and abilities.

I can ask and answer about what people can and can't do.

I can make a healthy living poster.

80 Lesson 9 Can assess what I have learned in Unit 6

Lesson 9 SB page 80 or Poptropica English World

Learning Objective
Can assess what I have learned in Unit 6

Warm-up

- Put all the Picture Cards (83–99; 100–119; 139–146; 147–156) on one side of the board and write the matching words/phrases in a jumbled up column on the other side of the board. Call students to the front to match Cards and words.

Open books and ask students to look at the activities on the page. Explain to students that they are going to review what they have learned in this unit. Write the lesson objective on the board: *We're thinking about our learning adventure.*

Ask students if they can remember the things they learned in this unit, e.g., *How many sports words can you remember?* Put their ideas on the board.

- For each example (e.g., *sports*), ask students, *Where are you on your learning adventure?*

22 Listen and ✓ or ✗.

- Play the audio. Have the students listen and mark a check or a cross in the chart according to whether the child can or cannot do each activity. Then check their charts with a partner.
- Now ask students to work in pairs to help each other remember any of the words they couldn't remember.

I'm Jake. I can run and I can ride a bike. I can play soccer, but I can't play baseball. I can play tennis and I can play basketball. I can't do taekwondo.

I'm Tina. I can run really fast and I can ride a bike. I can play baseball, but I can't play soccer. I can't play tennis, but I can play basketball. I can do taekwondo.

I'm Simon. I can run, but I can't ride a bike. I can play soccer and I can play baseball. I can't play tennis and I can't do taekwondo. I can play basketball.

I'm Donna. I can't run. I'm really slow! I can ride a bike and I can play tennis. I can't play soccer and I can't play baseball. I can do taekwondo and I can play basketball.

23 Play a guessing game. Look at Activity 22. Ask and answer.

- Students work in small groups and take turns to choose a child from Activity 22. Their partner guesses who they have chosen by asking questions about what they can do.

24 Mime a sport. Ask and answer.

- Students work in small groups and take turns to mime a sport for the rest of their group to guess. Encourage them to also ask about the place where the sport takes place.

Ask students how they feel about their learning in this unit. Ask students to tell you what they found easy and what they found the most difficult to learn in the unit.

- Students review the I Can statements at the bottom of the page and color each bar according to how confident they feel about the language point.
- Ask students, *Where are you on your learning adventure?* Students indicate where they think they are on the learning adventure poster. Tell students, *Good job!* to reinforce the progress they are making.

Pop Quiz: In groups of four, students tell the others the answers to the following questions: *Which is your favorite activity in the unit? Why? Which activity don't you like? Why? What is your favorite new word? Which word is the most difficult for you?*

Materials
Picture Cards (83–99; 100–119; 139–146; 147–156), poster

Homework WB page 66

Lesson 10 SB page 81 or Poptropica English World

Learning Objective
Can use what I have learned in Unit 6

Warm-up

- Stick Picture Cards 147–156 on the board. Now divide the class into pairs. Give each student a half sheet of blank paper. Students draw one of the items from the board but keep it hidden. Their partner tries to guess what was drawn by asking questions, e.g., *Is it a (gym)?*

Open books and ask students to look at the activities on the page. Ask, *What are we learning today?* Write the lesson objective on the board: *We're learning to talk about sports and activities.*

Say: *Healthy people are happy people.* Ask learners to agree or disagree and to give reasons, e.g., *you feel good, you eat and sleep well, sports are fun, you do sports with friends*, etc. Give pairs two minutes to think of their reasons. They might like to write their ideas in their notebooks. Write their suggestions on the board.

25 Do the quiz.

- Have students work in pairs. They switch books, take turns to read the quiz questions, and circle their friend's answers.
- Ask students to count the number of *yes* answers given by their partner, and then to read out the appropriate results to their partner. This activity helps build students' confidence as they are using the language they have learned in a different context.

I want to know more

- Ask students to choose anything they enjoyed from the unit and to go and find out more. You might like to set this activity as homework with a quick feedback session at the beginning of the next class, e.g. find out more words for sports, think of more ways to stay fit, find out some more information about different sports and sports facilities.

Are you ready for Unit 7?

- Ask students if they are ready to move onto the next unit. Tell students that it is fine if they do not remember everything as they will continue to practice throughout the level.
- Encourage students to ask if they have any questions about what they learned in Units 5 and 6.

You may wish to give Unit 6 test (see page 198) at this time.

Materials
Picture Cards 147–156, sheets of paper, colored pens or pencils

Homework WB page 67

Unit 6 Story Cards

Review Units 5 and 6

SB pages 82–83 or Poptropica English World

Learning Objective
Can talk about clothes and sports

Warm-up

- Stick some Picture Cards (from 120–156) on the board. Write the vocabulary words next to the incorrect pictures and have students correct your mistakes.

Open books and ask students to look at the activities on the page. Ask, *What are we learning today?* Write the lesson objective on the board: *We're talking about clothes and sports.*

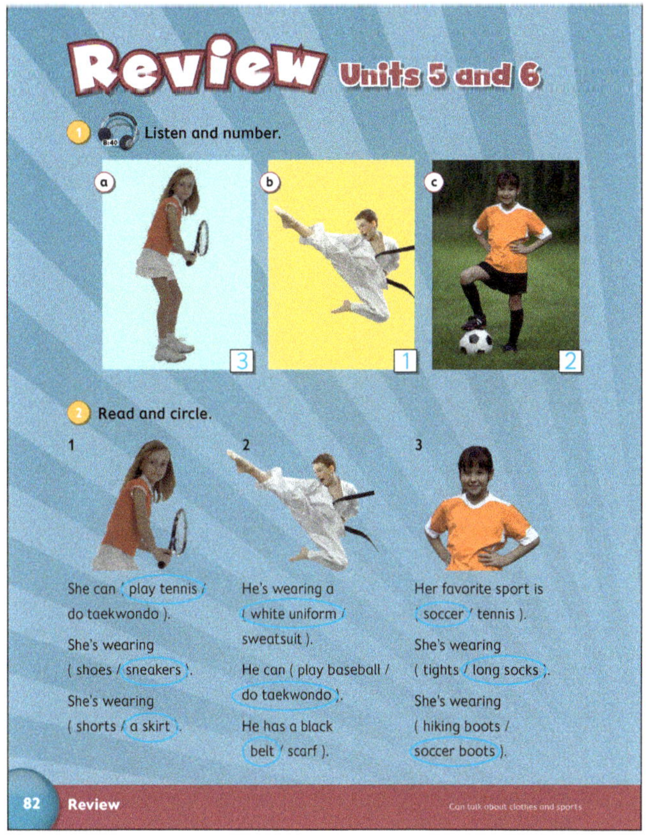
Review Units 5 and 6

1 Listen and number.

a 3 b 1 c 2

2 Read and circle.

1 She can (play tennis / do taekwondo). She's wearing (shoes / sneakers). She's wearing (shorts / a skirt).

2 He's wearing a (white uniform / sweatsuit). He can (play baseball / do taekwondo). He has a black (belt / scarf).

3 Her favorite sport is (soccer / tennis). She's wearing (tights / long socks). She's wearing (hiking boots / soccer boots).

82 Review Can talk about clothes and sports

1 Listen and number.

B:40

- Have students look at the pictures and say which sports they think the children like to do.
- Play the audio, and ask students to listen and write the numbers next to the appropriate pictures.
- Check the answers with the whole class.

1 I'm wearing a white uniform. I have a black belt. I'm not wearing shoes. I can do taekwondo.
2 I'm wearing long black socks and black shorts. I'm wearing an orange T-shirt. I love soccer.
3 I'm wearing a white skirt and a red T-shirt. I'm wearing blue and white sneakers. Tennis is my favorite sport.

2 Read and circle.

- Ask students to look at the children and refer back to the pictures in Activity 1. Then have them circle the correct words in each sentence.
- Have students read out the sentences to check that they have circled the correct words.

Materials
Picture Cards 120–156

3 Play a guessing game.

- Ask students to play the game in pairs. One student chooses a picture from the grid. Their partner asks questions about the clothes and location of the child in the picture. When they have found the correct picture, students switch roles.

Watch the video story *Gardening day* on Poptropica English World. Ask students what happened in the story. Watch again, stopping at key points, and ask them about the language, the images, or the story. Ask the students to role-play the story. Assign the roles of two of the characters to confident speakers and let other students play the other parts. Encourage them to say as much of the dialog as they can and prompt them where necessary.

Point to the learning objective on the board. Ask students, *How many words do you know for sports now?* Give students a minute to tell their partner as many sports words as they can.

- Ask students, *Where are you on your learning adventure?* Ask students which words they find easiest or most difficult to remember. Tell students, *Good job!* to reinforce the progress they are making.

Pop Quiz: Ask students in pairs to take turns to role-play one of the children from the grid in Activity 3. Their partner asks three questions to find out who they are, e.g., *1 Are you wearing (shorts)? 2 Are you at the (soccer field)? 3 Can you (play tennis)?*

You may wish to give Review Test 3 (see page 212) at this time.

7 Food

Unit Overview

Unit Objective

- I can talk about food

Language

Target Vocabulary	Fruit/Vegetables: peas, mangoes, carrots, cucumbers, plums, oranges, peaches, potatoes, tomatoes, strawberries, beans, broccoli, lettuce, spinach, cabbage, pears, apricots, avocados, cherries
Target Structures	Do you like peas? Yes, I do. / No, I don't. Does he/she like peas? Yes, he/she does. / No, he/she doesn't. Is there any broccoli? Yes, there is. / No, there isn't. Are there any pears? Yes, there are. / No, there aren't.
Features	**Values:** Stay healthy. Eat more fruit and vegetables. **Cross-curricular:** Science: Healthy eating plate. **Phonics:** *br, cr, dr, fr, gr, pr, str, tr* (brown, crab, drop, frog, green, press, string, train)

Skills

Reading	• Can understand a simple story • Can understand details of a story	• Can understand a text about food groups
Writing	• Can make a healthy food plate • Can copy food words and write a shopping list • Can complete simple sentences about food people like and don't like (*Workbook*)	• Can complete simple sentences using Is/Are there any...? (*Workbook*) • Can write simple sentences about my favorite healthy and unhealthy foods (*Workbook*)
Listening	• Can identify fruit and vegetables • Can understand a simple story	• Can understand a text about food groups
Speaking	• Can ask and answer about food likes and dislikes • Can ask and answer using *Is there any...?* and *Are there any...?*	• Can role-play a story • Can talk about staying healthy and eating more fruit and vegetables • Can pronounce the sounds *br, cr, dr, fr, gr, pr, str,* and *tr*

Lesson 1 SB page 84 or Poptropica English World

Learning Objective
Can identify fruits and vegetables

Target Language
peas, mangoes, carrots, cucumbers, plums, oranges, peaches, potatoes, tomatoes, strawberries, beans

1 What do you know?

- Open books and ask students to look at the activities on the page. Ask, *What are we learning today?* Write the lesson objective on the board: *We're learning to talk about food.*
- Close books. Ask students what English words they know for food, e.g., *ice cream, pizza.* Write on board.
- Refer to the learning adventure poster and say, *Great! You are already moving along your learning adventure!*

2 Listen and find. What's missing?

B:41

- Use the Picture Cards of foods (157–166) on the board, to teach the new vocabulary. Say the words and have students repeat.
- Play the audio. Students listen to the dialog and check the pictures when they hear the words. Ask, *What's missing?* (*potatoes, peaches*)

BB: Welcome to my restaurant. Are you hungry?
CC: Oh, yes.
BB: Do you like carrots, Kim?
Kim: Yes, I do. I like carrots, but I don't like peas. Katy likes salad with cucumber and tomatoes. She doesn't like green beans.
Katy: Yes, that's right. Can I have cucumbers and tomatoes? No green beans, thank you.
BB: Yes, sure. Do you like fruit, Captain Conrad?
CC: Oh, yes, I do. Mangoes and plums, please.
Katy: I don't like plums.
BB: Really Katy? What about you, PROD 1? Do you like fruit?
PROD 1: I like oranges, but I don't like strawberries.
BBL: You don't like strawberries?
PROD 2: No, I don't. They have spots. Ha, ha!

3 Listen and number.

B:42

- Ask questions about the main picture: *Who's this? Where are they?* Call out food words, and students find them on the page and point at them.
- Ask students to look at their books. Play the audio again and have students find and number.

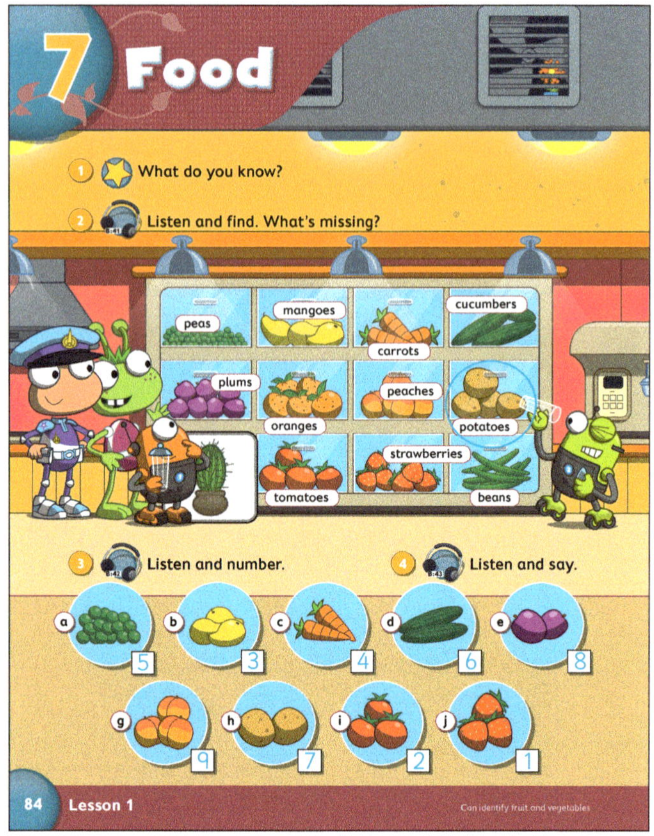

1 Look at the strawberries. Mmmm, I like strawberries.
2 The tomatoes are red. They're next to the strawberries.
3 The mangoes are yellow.
4 I like carrots.
5 I don't like peas. Do you like peas?
6 Cucumbers are long and green.
7 I don't like potatoes.
8 I like these purple plums.
9 Look at the peaches. They're yum!
10 Do you like oranges?
11 She doesn't like beans. Green beans.

4 Listen and say.

B:43

- Play the audio. Pause after each item and have students repeat.

Give students a minute to tell their partner the new words for food they know.

- Ask students to say where they are on their adventure now. Ask students which words they find easiest or most difficult to remember. Tell students, *Good job!* to reinforce the progress they are making.

Pop Quiz: As students are leaving the class, ask them to describe a fruit for the class to guess.

Materials
Poster, Picture Cards 157–166

Homework WB page 68

Lesson 2 SB page 85 or Poptropica English World

Learning Objective
Can ask and answer about food likes and dislikes

Target Language
Do you like peas? Yes, I do. / No, I don't.
Does he/she like peas? Yes, he/she does. / No, he/she doesn't.

Warm-up

- Stick Picture Cards 157–166 on the board and in a separate column write the names of the same items, with a letter missing. Call students to the front to write in the missing letter for the word of their choice, and match it to the Picture Card.

Open books and ask students to look at the chant and the Look! box. Ask, *What are we learning today?* Write the lesson objective on the board: *We're learning to ask and answer about food likes and dislikes.*

5 Listen and chant.

- Play the chant about food. Have students tell you what new words they hear on the chant. Then ask them to point to the items in the main picture.
- Play the audio a few times and have students chant along. If students are confident, use the karaoke version.

6 Listen again. Then ask and answer.

- Read through the Look! box with the students and play the audio (track B:46), then look at the pictures. Ask students which characters they can see in the pictures *(Captain Conrad, Ben Beamaway, Kim, Katy, PROD 1, and PROD 2)*, and have them read the questions and answer choices. Ask them to listen to the audio for the activity.
- Have students listen again, and point to the correct answers.
- Check the answers by asking, e.g., *Look at Katy. Does she like plums? (No, she doesn't.)*
- Pair students and have them practice asking and answering questions about each character.
- Direct students' attention to the cactus card on page 84. Tell students to go online to the Poptropica English Island Adventure Game and find the item. Once students click on it, they are taken to a supplementary language task.

Pop Quiz: Before students leave the class, have them talk to a partner to find two foods they like, and two they don't like. They report back to the class, e.g., *He likes carrots and mangoes. He doesn't like peas and plums.*

Materials
Picture Cards 157–166

Homework WB page 69

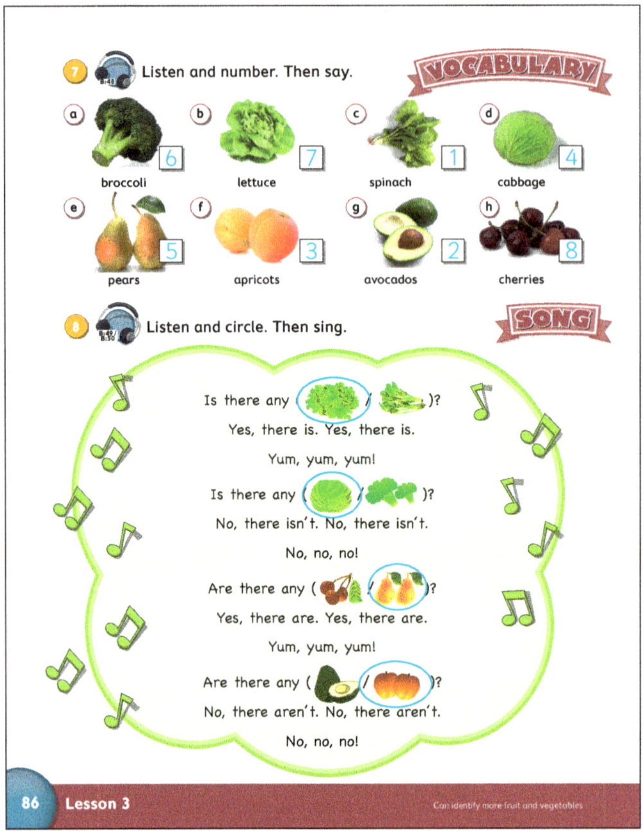
7 Listen and number. Then say. VOCABULARY

a broccoli 6
b lettuce 7
c spinach 1
d cabbage 4
e pears 5
f apricots 3
g avocados 2
h cherries 8

8 Listen and circle. Then sing. SONG

Is there any (/)?
Yes, there is. Yes, there is.
Yum, yum, yum!
Is there any (/)?
No, there isn't. No, there isn't.
No, no, no!
Are there any (/)?
Yes, there are. Yes, there are.
Yum, yum, yum!
Are there any (/)?
No, there aren't. No, there aren't.
No, no, no!

86 Lesson 3 Can identify more fruit and vegetables

Lesson 3 SB page 86 or Poptropica English World

Learning Objective
Can identify more fruit and vegetables

Target Language
broccoli, lettuce, spinach, cabbage, pears, apricots, avocados, cherries

Warm-up

- Ask a student to drill the class on fruit/vegetables by holding up Picture Cards 157–174 one by one, in front of the class, as students call out the item.

Open books and ask students to look at the activities on the page. Ask, *What are we learning today?* Write the lesson objectives on the board: *We're learning more words for fruit and vegetables, and we're following a story.*

- Close books. Ask students what English words they know for food, e.g., *cheese, tomato.* Write on board.
- Refer to the learning adventure poster and say, *Great! You are moving along your learning adventure!*

7 Listen and number. Then say.

B:48

- Play the audio and have students number the pictures as they hear them. Then play the audio again and have students repeat.
- Point to the pictures and have students say the words.

1 spinach	**5** pears
2 avocados	**6** broccoli
3 apricots	**7** lettuce
4 cabbage	**8** cherries

8 Listen and circle. Then sing.

B:49 B:50

- Point to the picture choices in the first line and ask, *What's this? (broccoli)* Ask, *Do you like broccoli?* Repeat for the other lines.
- Play the audio and have students listen.
- Play the audio again and ask students to circle the correct item. Have students check their answers in pairs.
- Play the song again and have students sing along. If students are confident, use the karaoke version.

Ask students, *How many words for food do you know now?* Give students a minute to tell their partner the new words they know.

- Ask students to say where they are on their adventure now. Ask students which words they find easiest or most difficult to remember. Tell students, *Good job!* to reinforce the progress they are making.
- For further practice, give a copy of Activity Sheet 6 (see page 160) to each student. Have students cut out the pictures. Pair students and put a divider between them, so that they cannot see each other's sheets. Have students stick three fruits and three vegetables they like into the first box without telling their partners. Have students guess their partner's favorite food, e.g., *Do you like oranges? (No, I don't. / Yes, I do.)* When a student guesses correctly, he/she writes the word into the second box.

Pop Quiz: Write two headings on the board: *Fruit/Vegetables.* Ask students to think of different foods and to come to the front to write them under the correct heading.

Materials
Picture Cards 157–174, poster, Activity Sheet 6, colored pencils or crayons, scissors, glue

Homework WB page 70

7

LOOK!

Is there any broccoli?	Yes, there is.
	No, there isn't.
Are there any pears?	Yes, there are.
	No, there aren't.

9 Choose five foods and stick. Then ask and answer.

10 Listen and read. Then write.

READING

Lisa Martin Astronaut

Reporter: Hello, Lisa. Do you have breakfast in space?
Lisa: Yes, I do. Breakfast, lunch, and dinner.
Reporter: Is there any fruit?
Lisa: Yes, there is. I eat strawberries for breakfast. They're my favorite! I also eat yogurt.
Reporter: Do you have pears and avocados?
Lisa: We have pears, but we don't have avocados.
Reporter: Are there any vegetables?
Lisa: Yes, there are. I like beans, but I don't like spinach.
Reporter: Thank you, Lisa.

1 Does Lisa like strawberries? Yes
2 Are there any avocadoes? No
3 Does she have any yogurt? Yes
4 Does she like spinach? No

Lesson 4 Can ask and answer using *Is there any...?* and *Are there any...?* 87

Lesson 4 SB page 87 or Poptropica English World

Learning Objective
Can ask and answer using *Is there any...?* and *Are there any...?*

Target Language
Is there any broccoli?
Yes, there is. / No, there isn't.
Are there any pears?
Yes, there are. / No, there aren't.

Warm-up

- Hand out a Picture Card (from 157–174) to several students, but ask them to keep their Card a secret. Explain that each student is going to say a sentence about the Card he/she is holding, but it may or may not be true. Without showing the Card, the student asks, e.g., *Is there any lettuce?* Students who answer, *Yes, there is.* stand up, and students who answer, *No, there isn't.* remain seated. The student then shows the Card. Play this game in teams. Teams win a point for each correct guess.

Open books and ask students to look at the activities on the page. Ask, *What are we learning today?* Write the lesson objective on the board: *We're learning to ask and answer questions using* Is there any...? *and* Are there any...?

9 Choose five foods and stick. Then ask and answer.

- Have students find the stickers at the back of the book and name each food item.
- Ask students to choose five foods and stick them onto the empty circles.
- Refer students to the Look! box. Play the audio (track B:51), and remind students that some food words are countable and others are uncountable. Have them practice using the singular form, *Is there any...?* with uncountable nouns, and *Are there any...?* with countable nouns.
- Pair students and have them ask and answer to find their partner's five foods. Encourage students to say why they have chosen the foods, e.g., *I like carrots. Carrots are healthy.*

10 Listen and read. Then write.

- Focus students' attention on the picture and pre-teach the word *astronaut*.
- Play the audio and have students follow.
- Pair students and have them read the interview. Explain any unfamiliar words.
- Check the answers as a class. Ask each question and have individual students answer.

Pop Quiz: Before the end of the lesson, show students several different foods – either stick several Picture Cards on the board, or show them a picture of a shopping trolley full of food. Students look for one minute. Then hide the Cards/pictures. Students try to remember what was there by asking, e.g., *Is there any spinach? / Are there any pears?* They get a point for each item they remember.

Materials
Picture Cards 157–174, stickers, picture of a shopping trolley full of food (cut from magazines)

Homework WB page 71

Lesson 5 SB page 88 or Poptropica English World

Learning Objectives
Can understand a simple story
Can role-play a story

Functional Language
Wow! That's amazing! Yuck! Be careful!

Warm-up

- Put the fruit/vegetables Picture Cards (157–174) in a pile. Choose a Picture Card at random and say, e.g., *I like spinach.* Students who like that fruit or vegetable clap their hands and repeat the sentence. Continue with the other Cards.

Open books and ask students to look at the story. Ask, *What are we learning today?* Write the lesson objectives on the board. *We're reading a story and we're role-playing a story.*

11 Talk about the pictures. Then listen and read.

B:53

- Direct students' attention to the story and ask questions about the characters and the scene: *Who can you see? Where are they? What are they doing? Can you see the tifftiff plant?*
- Play the audio and have students listen and follow. Check understanding by pointing at the pictures and asking questions: *Does Kim like strawberries? Is the strawberry big? Does Katy like eggs? Where's the egg? Where's the tifftiff plant?*
- Play the recording again, stopping after each line to have students repeat.
- Play the audio again. Have students speak along and mime the actions.

Ask the students to think about which foods they would put on the Yum machine, and which they would put on the Yuck machine. Ask them why they chose these foods.

12 Role-play the story.

- See the "How to use stories" section on page 22 for more ideas on how to build your students' confidence with role-plays.
- Divide students into groups of five. Give each group a set of cut-up Story Cards and have students place them in order.
- Divide students into groups and have them role-play the story. When you say, *change*, they should change character and role-play a new character. Rotate through the characters, giving students the chance to play each one.

You might like to give the students feedback on their role-play.

Pop Quiz: Before the end of the lesson, make statements about the story and have students say whether they are true or false, e.g., *Kim loves strawberries. (true) PROD 1 doesn't like tifftiff plants. (false)*, etc.

Materials
Picture Cards 157–174, Story Cards

Homework WB page 72

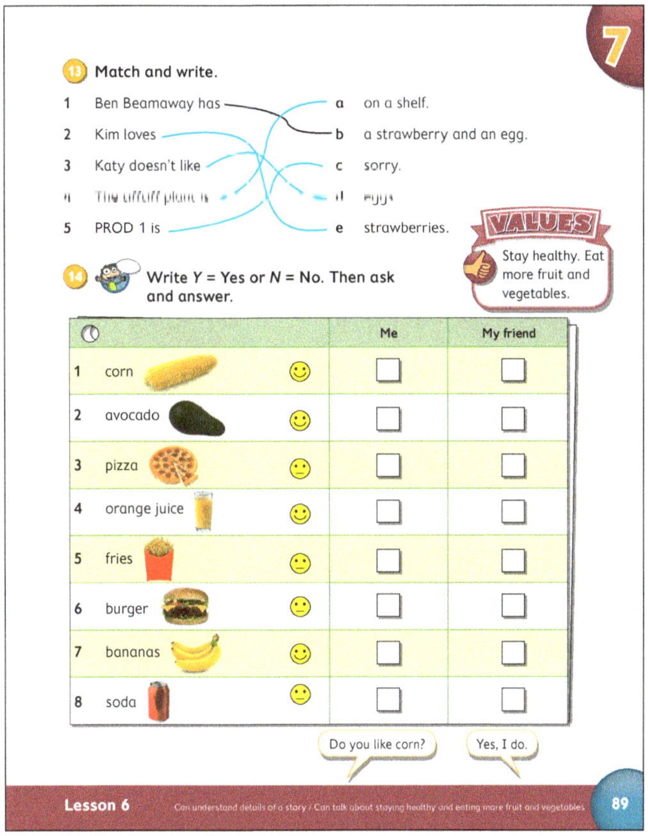

7

13 Match and write.

1 Ben Beamaway has — a on a shelf.
2 Kim loves — b a strawberry and an egg.
3 Katy doesn't like — c sorry.
4 [illegible] — d [illegible]
5 PROD 1 is — e strawberries.

VALUES
Stay healthy. Eat more fruit and vegetables.

14 Write *Y* = Yes or *N* = No. Then ask and answer.

		Me	My friend
1	corn	☐	☐
2	avocado	☐	☐
3	pizza	☐	☐
4	orange juice	☐	☐
5	fries	☐	☐
6	burger	☐	☐
7	bananas	☐	☐
8	soda	☐	☐

Do you like corn?
Yes, I do.

Lesson 6 Can understand details of a story / Can talk about staying healthy and eating more fruit and vegetables 89

Lesson 6 SB page 89 or Poptropica English World

Learning Objectives
Can understand details of a story
Can talk about staying healthy and eating more fruit and vegetables

Additional Language
corn, avocado, pizza, orange juice, fries, burger, bananas, soda

Values
Stay healthy. Eat more fruit and vegetables.

Open books and ask students to look at the activities on the page. Ask, *What are we learning today?* Write the lesson objectives on the board: *We're understanding details of a story and we're learning how to stay healthy.*

Warm-up

- Put students in groups of five. Write five words from the unit on the board. Each student in a group writes a different word from the list on a card. Next, say one of the words. The student in each group who has this word must raise his/her card as quickly as possible and say the word. The first student to hold up his/her card gets to choose and say the next word. Repeat. Then choose five new words from another unit and play the game again.

13 Match and write.

- Have students work in pairs. They look carefully at the story frames and match the two halves of the sentences. Then they write the sentences out in full.
- Have students work with a partner. They read the sentences out loud and check that they are correct.

14 Write Y = Yes or N = No. Then ask and answer.

- Read the value, *Stay healthy. Eat more fruit and vegetables.* Remind students of the discussion you had about doing exercise (Unit 6). Explain that they are going to learn about healthy eating. Introduce *healthy = it's good for you, unhealthy = it's not good for you.* Write both words on the board and give an example of food for each category. Brainstorm more examples with the class. Explain why fruit and vegetables are good for them.
- Have students look at the pictures and the faces in their books. Point and ask if the items are good for us, e.g., *Is corn good for us? Is it healthy? (Yes, it is.)*
- Ask students to write *Y* in the boxes if they like to eat these foods.
- Pair students and have them ask their partners if they like the foods and complete the "My friend" column.

Write the following questions on the board: *Why is it good to eat more fruit and vegetables? (It helps us to stay healthy.) What other things can we do to stay healthy? (Exercise every day. Walk more. Drink plenty of water.)*

- Tell students to work with a partner. Give pairs two minutes to discuss and note down their answers. Ask students to share their answers with the class.

Pop Quiz: Play a guessing game. Describe a food. Say, e.g., *It's a vegetable, it's green, it's long. It's healthy. I like it in my salad! (cucumber).* Once a student has guessed, they describe the next food.

Materials
Cards

Homework WB page 73

Lesson 7 SB page 90 or Poptropica English World

Learning Objective
Can understand a text about food groups

Additional Language
healthy food, food groups, pasta, bread, cereal, grains, protein, yogurt, dairy, cakes, candy, cheese, meat, fats, sugars

Warm-up

- Select a fruit/vegetable Picture Card (from 157–174) without looking at it, then hold it over your head so that students can see it, but you can't. Try to guess what it is. Ask, e.g., *Is there any broccoli?* Students answer your questions to help you guess.

15 What do you know?

- Open books and ask students to look at the activities on the page. Ask, *What are we learning today?* Write the lesson objective on the board: *We're learning about different food groups.*
- Close books. Ask students what they know about different food groups. Write their ideas on the board.
- Refer to the learning adventure poster and say, *Great! You are moving along your learning adventure!*

16 Listen and read. Then put these foods in the correct place.

B:54

- Have students read the text and put the six foods in the correct section on the plate.
- Check that they have put chicken in the protein section, bananas and cucumbers in the fruit and vegetables section, cereal in the grains section, milk in the dairy section, and chocolate in fats and sugars.

17 Say the word. Find the food group.

- Pair students and have them look at each food item on the healthy eating plate and say the name of a type of food. Their partner finds the food and names the food group. They switch roles.

Ask the students: *What do you now know about different food groups? How could you change your diet to make it more balanced? Could you eat more vegetables or cut out some fats and sugars?* Give students a minute to tell their partner the new ideas and words they can remember. Ask students, *Where are you on your learning adventure?* Tell students, *Good job!* to reinforce the progress they are making.

Pop Quiz: Before the end of the lesson, write the food groups on the board and have students brainstorm different foods to put under each heading.

Materials
Picture Cards 157–174, poster, a coin

Homework WB page 74

7

PROJECT

18 Make a healthy food plate. Talk to a friend.

1 **Think** about healthy food.
2 **Draw** or find examples of healthy food.
3 **Make** a healthy food plate.
4 **Talk** about your food plate.

HOME SCHOOL LINK
Show your healthy food plate to your family.

I like to eat a lot of fruit and vegetables.

19 Listen.

PHONICS

1 brown 2 crab 3 drop 4 frog
5 green 6 press 7 string 8 train

20 Listen and blend the sounds.

21 Underline *br, cr, dr, fr, gr, pr, str,* and *tr.* Read the sentences aloud.

1 Press to go up.
2 Look at the green frog.
3 The crab is brown.
4 Pull the train with the string.

Lesson 8 Can make a healthy food plate / Can pronounce the sounds *br, cr, dr, fr, gr, pr, str,* and *tr* 91

Lesson 8 SB page 91 or Poptropica English World

Learning Objectives
Can make a healthy food plate
Can pronounce the sounds *br, cr, dr, fr, gr, pr, str,* and *tr*

Warm-up

- Prepare large letter cards to review the sounds and letters. Show the cards in random order and have the students chorus the letter-sounds. Start slowly and then increase the speed.

Open books and ask students to look at the activities on the page. Ask, *What are we learning today?* Write the lesson objectives on the board: *We're learning to make a healthy food plate, and we're learning to pronounce the sounds* br, cr, dr, fr, gr, pr, str, *and* tr.

18 Make a healthy food plate. Talk to a friend.

Look at the healthy food plate in the Student Book. Ask, *Is it good? Why?* Write students' ideas on the board.

- Tell the students they are going to make their own healthy food plates.
- Provide the materials they need and give students time to draw or cut out food pictures. Distribute the paper plates for students to stick their pictures onto.
- Invite students to the front to talk about their healthy food plates.
- Display the food plates in the classroom.

You may also wish to give students feedback on their projects.

- **Home-School link:** Read the instruction with the class: *Show your healthy food plate to your family.* Ask students to do this at home.

19 Listen.

- Have students open their books and look at the eight words, *brown, crab, drop, frog, green, press, string,* and *train.* Explain to students that they are going to read and pronounce the sounds *br, cr, dr, fr, gr, pr, str,* and *tr.* Play the audio.

1 br brown **2** cr crab **3** dr drop
4 fr frog **5** gr green **6** pr press
7 str string **8** tr train

20 Listen and blend the sounds.

- Write a word on the board. Underline each phoneme in the word, e.g., *s – t – r – i – ng* as you sound it out, *s-t-r-i-ng.* Ask for a volunteer to say the word and encourage the students to cheer if they got it right.
- As a class, chorus the sounding out and word one more time. Repeat with the other words.
- Turn to the book and do the activity on the page.

1 br ow n brown **2** cr a b crab
3 dr o p drop **4** fr o g frog
5 gr ee n green **6** pr e ss press
7 str i ng string **8** tr ai n train

21 Underline *br, cr, dr, fr, gr, pr, str,* and *tr.* Read the sentences aloud.

- Have the students underline the graphemes and read the line of sentences aloud. In pairs, have students take turns to read the sentences to each other.

Pop Quiz: Before the end of the lesson, write a giant *r* in the middle of the board. Ask students to tell you as many words as they can that have *r* as the second letter, and write these on the board. Examples they know include: *brown, drop, dress, green, gray, string, strong, crab,* and *frog.*

Materials
A selection of pictures of healthy food (cut from magazines), scissors, glue, colored pens or pencils, paper plates, letter cards (Units 1 and 2)

Homework WB page 75

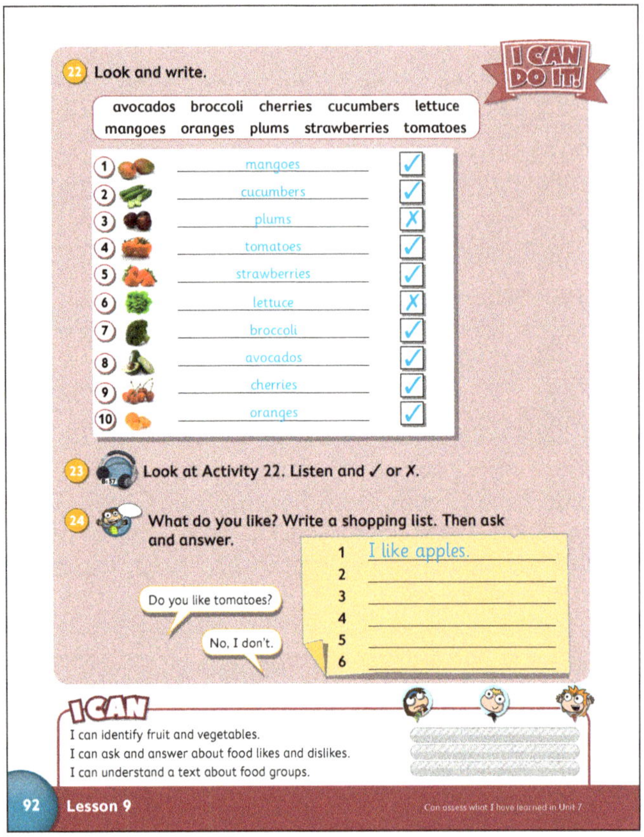

22 Look and write.

avocados broccoli cherries cucumbers lettuce mangoes oranges plums strawberries tomatoes

1 mangoes ✓
2 cucumbers ✓
3 plums ✗
4 tomatoes ✓
5 strawberries ✓
6 lettuce ✗
7 broccoli ✓
8 avocados ✓
9 cherries ✓
10 oranges ✓

23 Look at Activity 22. Listen and ✓ or ✗.

24 What do you like? Write a shopping list. Then ask and answer.

1 I like apples.
2
3
4
5
6

I CAN

I can identify fruit and vegetables.

I can ask and answer about food likes and dislikes.

I can understand a text about food groups.

92 Lesson 9 Can assess what I have learned in Unit 7

Lesson 9 SB page 92 or Poptropica English World

Learning Objective
Can assess what I have learned in Unit 7

Warm-up

- Hold up a Picture Card (from Units 1–6), and have students call out the word.

Open books and ask students to look at the activities on the page. Explain to students that they are going to review what they have learned in this unit. Write the lesson objective on the board: *We're thinking about our learning adventure.*

- Ask students if they can remember the things they have been learning in this unit, e.g., *How many food words can you remember?* Put their ideas on the board.
- For each example (e.g., *strawberries*), ask students, *Where are you on your learning adventure?*

22 Look and write.

- Have students look at the pictures and write the words on the shopping list. They can check their answers with a partner.

23 Look at Activity 22. Listen and ✓ or ✗.

- Ask students to listen and check the items that are available at the market, and cross those that aren't. Have them check answers with a partner.

Woman: Good morning. Is there any broccoli?
Stall holder: Yes, there is. Here you are.
Woman: Thank you. Are there any tomatoes?
Stallholder: Yes, there are lots of tomatoes.
Woman: Is there any lettuce?
Stallholder: Sorry! I don't have any lettuce. Do you like cucumbers? There are cucumbers and there are avocados.
Woman: Oh, yes please. Are there any mangoes?
Stallholder: Yes, there are mangoes and oranges. There aren't any plums.
Woman: OK, some mangoes and some strawberries, please.
Stallholder: Do you like cherries?
Woman: Oh, yes, I do. Thank you.

24 What do you like? Write a shopping list. Then ask and answer.

- Have students think of six food items that they like and write their own shopping lists. Then in pairs, have them find out which items their partner has chosen by asking: *Do you like (tomatoes)? (Yes, I do. / No, I don't.)*

Ask students how they feel about their learning in this unit. Ask students to tell you what they found easy and what they found the most difficult to learn in the unit.

- Students review the I Can statements at the bottom of the page and color each bar according to how confident they feel about the language point.
- Ask students, *Where are you on your learning adventure?* Students indicate where they think they are on the learning adventure poster. Tell students, *Good job!* to reinforce the progress they are making.

Pop Quiz: In groups of four, students tell the others the answers to the following questions: *Which is your favorite activity in the unit? Why? Which activity don't you like? Why? What is your favorite new word? Which word is the most difficult for you?*

Materials
Picture Cards (Units 1–6), poster

Homework WB page 76

Lesson 10 SB page 93 or Poptropica English World

Learning Objective
Can use what I have learned in Unit 7

Warm-up

- Start the lesson by playing a chain game of *I like to eat….* The first student says, e.g., *I like to eat (cherries).* The next student repeats and adds another food item, e.g., *I like to eat (cherries and bananas).* The chain continues until they've run out of food items.

Open books and ask students to look at the activities on the page. Ask, *What are we learning today?* Write the lesson objective on the board: *We're learning to talk about food.*

Ask students to write a list of 10 fruits and vegetables, with number 1 as their favorite and number 10 as their least favorite. Give pairs two minutes to prepare their lists. They might like to write their ideas in their notebooks. Write their suggestions on the board and compare different lists to show that everybody has different preferences.

25 Spot the differences. Ask and answer.

- Have students work in pairs. They choose one picture each and cover the other picture. The aim is to find six differences between the pictures by asking their partner what fruits and vegetables are in their picture. Once they have found six differences, they can look at both pictures and check whether they were right.
- Ask students to work in pairs to make sentences and questions with the target language. Then ask students if they can make sentences and questions using vocabulary from other topics. Give pairs a minute to think of one example. This activity helps build students' confidence as they are using the language they have learned in a different context.

I want to know more

- Ask students to choose anything they enjoyed from the unit and to go and find out more. You might like to set this activity as homework with a quick feedback session at the beginning of the next class, e.g. find out more words for food, think of more ways to stay healthy, find out some more information about different categories of food.

Are you ready for Unit 8?

- Ask students if they are ready to move onto the next unit. Tell students that it is fine if they do not remember everything as they will continue to practice throughout the level.
- Encourage students to ask if they have any questions about what they learned in Unit 7.

You may wish to give Unit 7 test (see page 200) at this time.

Unit 7 Story Cards

SB pages 94–95 or Poptropica English World

Learning Objectives
Can understand texts about food likes and dislikes
Can talk about food likes and dislikes

Recycled/Additional Language
I'm from (Argentina/Turkey/Jamaica/Italy).
dinner, barbecue, chocolate sandwiches, fantastic, pastries, nuts, chicken, lunch, jerk chicken, rice, traditional dish, patties, pumpkin soup, pasta

1 What do you know?

- Ask students about the typical dishes of their country or region. Ask them if the dishes include any of the food they have learned in this unit.
- Bring a map of the world, or globe, and show it to the class. Locate your country on the map and say, *I'm from (Japan).*

Open books and ask students to look at the activities on the page. Ask, *What are we learning today?* Write the lesson objective on the board: *We're learning about food from around the world.*

2 Listen and read.

B:58

- Tell students they are going to hear about the children's favorite dishes.
- Play the audio once for students to follow. Then play each part separately and ask questions to check comprehension, e.g., *What's the child's name? What does he/she like to eat? What does he/she not like?*
- Discuss with the class which of the dishes they like, and which they think are healthy.

3 Match.

- Have students cover the four texts. Pair them and ask them to match each child's name to his/her favorite food.
- Have students uncover the texts and check the answers with the whole class by asking them to read the completed sentences.

Materials
World map

3

My name's Kay. I'm from Jamaica. My favorite lunch is jerk chicken with rice and peas. It's a traditional dish. Yum! I also like meat patties. I like vegetables, but I don't like pumpkin soup.

jerk chicken

meat patties

4

I'm Berta, and I'm from Italy. My favorite dinner is pasta or pizza with cheese and tomatoes. I also like ice cream. Chocolate ice cream is my favorite!

ice cream

4 Ask and answer.

1 Does Andrea like *asado*?
Yes, she does.

2 Does Zeki like pastries?
Yes, he does.

3 Does Kay like pumpkin soup?
No, she doesn't.

4 Does Berta like ice cream?
Yes, she does.

5 What's your favorite food?

Tell the Class

Wider World 4 Can talk about food likes and dislikes 95

Tell the Class

4 Ask and answer.

- Have students work in pairs. They take turns to ask and answer the questions. Check answers as a class.
- Ask the children to think about how their food is similar to the food from around the world, and how it is different.

Point at the learning objective on the board. Ask students, *How many words do you know for food now?* Give students a minute to tell their partner as many food words as they can.

- Ask students, *Where are you on your learning adventure?* Ask students which words they find easiest and most difficult to remember. Tell students, *Good job!* to reinforce the progress they are making.

Pop Quiz: As students are leaving the class, ask them to make two statements about food from their country, one positive and one negative, e.g., *I like (tacos). I don't like (soup).*

8 Things we do

Unit Overview

Unit Objective

- I can talk about things we do

Language

Target Vocabulary	Actions: listening to music, walking, sleeping, reading, doing homework, drinking, eating, cleaning, dancing, playing the piano, playing the trumpet, playing the flute, playing the violin, singing Adverbs of manner: quickly, quietly, terribly, loudly, slowly
Target Structures	What are you doing? I'm sleeping. What are they doing? They're sleeping. What's he/she doing? He's/She's sleeping. Are you singing? Yes, I am. / No, I'm not. Is he/she singing? Yes, he/she is. / No, he/she isn't. Is he/she singing quietly? Yes, he/she is / No, he/she isn't. He's/She's singing loudly.
Features	**Values:** Learn new things. Develop your talents. **Cross-curricular:** Science: Flying machines **Phonics:** *ft, mp, nd, nt, sk, sp, st* (left, bump, wind, paint, ask, wisp, nest)

Skills

Reading	• Can understand a simple story • Can understand details of a story • Can understand short texts about flying machines
Writing	• Can complete simple sentences about what people are doing • Can copy simple words for actions and activities (*Workbook*) • Can complete simple sentences about learning new things (*Workbook*) • Can write simple sentences about what people are doing (*Workbook*)
Listening	• Can identify actions and activities • Can identify more activities and words that describe how you do them • Can understand a simple story • Can understand short texts about flying machines
Speaking	• Can ask and answer about what people are doing • Can talk about how people are doing activities • Can role-play a story • Can talk about learning new things and developing my talents • Can pronounce the sounds *ft, mp, nd, nt, sk, sp,* and *st*

Lesson 1 SB page 96 or Poptropica English World

Learning Objective
Can identify actions and activities

Target Language
listening to music, walking, sleeping, reading, doing homework, drinking, eating, cleaning, dancing

1 What do you know?

- Open books and ask students to look at the activities on the page. Ask, *What are we learning today?* Write the lesson objective on the board: *We're learning to talk about actions and activities.*
- Close books. Ask students what English words they know for actions, e.g., *swim, tennis,* etc. Write on board. Refer to the learning adventure poster and say, *Great! You are already moving along your learning adventure!*

2 C:02 Listen and find. What's missing?

- Play the audio. Students listen to the dialog and check the pictures when they hear the related words. Ask, *What's missing?* (*walking, listening to music, cleaning*).

CC: What are you doing, Kim?
Kim: I'm looking for a tifftiff plant.
CC: What can you see?
Kim: I can see a girl. She's dancing in her bedroom.
Katy: There's a boy in his bedroom.
CC: What's he doing?
Katy: He's doing homework.
Kim: I can see two people in the kitchen.
CC: What are they doing?
Katy: He's eating and she's drinking.
Kim: There's a boy in the living room.
CC: What's he doing?
Kim: He's reading.
Kim: What are PROD 1 and PROD 2 doing?
CC: They're sleeping. Wake up!

3 C:03 Listen and number.

- Use Picture Cards 175–183 to teach the new vocabulary. Say the words and have students repeat.
- Ask questions about the main scene: *Who's this? Where are they?* Call out the new words and have students find and point.
- Ask students to look at the scene in their books and listen as you play the audio.
- Play the audio again and ask them to find the items and number them.

1 He's walking in the yard...
2 They're sleeping under a tree.
3 She's dancing in her bedroom.
4 He's reading. He's on the sofa.
5 He's doing homework in his bedroom.
6 He's eating in the kitchen.
7 She's drinking in the kitchen.
8 ...and he's listening to music.
9 She's cleaning.

4 C:04 Listen and say.

- Play the audio. Students listen, point to the actions, and repeat the words.

Ask students how many words for actions they know now. Give students a minute to tell their partner the new words they know.

- Ask students to say where they are on their adventure now. Ask students which words they find easiest or most difficult to remember. Tell students, *Good job!* to reinforce the progress they are making.

Pop Quiz: As students are leaving the class, ask them to mime an action from the lesson.

Materials
Poster, Picture Cards 175–183

Homework WB page 78

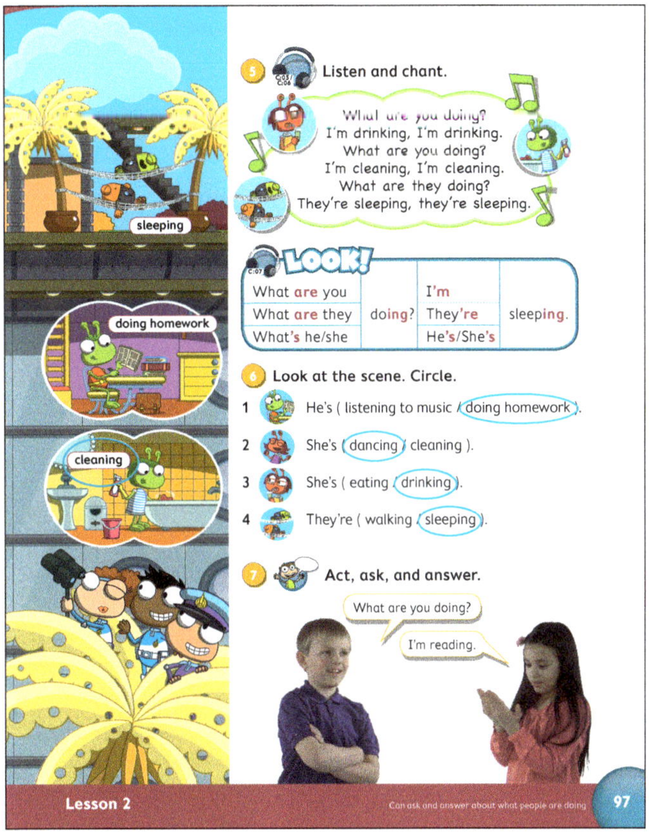
5 Listen and chant. C:05 C:06

What are you doing?
I'm drinking, I'm drinking.
What are you doing?
I'm cleaning, I'm cleaning.
What are they doing?
They're sleeping, they're sleeping.

LOOK! C:07

What are you	doing?	I'm	sleeping.
What are they		They're	
What's he/she		He's/She's	

6 Look at the scene. Circle.

1 He's (listening to music / doing homework).
2 She's (dancing / cleaning).
3 She's (eating / drinking).
4 They're (walking / sleeping).

7 Act, ask, and answer.

Lesson 2 Can ask and answer about what people are doing 97

Lesson 2 SB page 97 or Poptropica English World

Learning Objective
Can ask and answer about what people are doing

Target Language
What are you/they doing? I'm/They're sleeping.
What's he/she doing? He's/She's sleeping.

Warm-up

- Show Picture Cards 175–183 in turn and say a wrong sentence, e.g., show *eating* and say, *I'm listening to music.* Have students correct you, e.g., *No, eating!*

Open books and ask students to look at the book and the Look! box. Ask, *What are we learning today?* Write the lesson objective on the board: *We're learning to ask and answer about what people are doing.*

5 Listen and chant. C:05 C:06

- Read through the Look! box with the students, and play the audio (track C:07), then play the chant. Ask students to tell you what new words they hear on the chant. Then ask them to point to the actions in the main picture.
- Play the chant a few times and have students chant along. If students are confident, use the karaoke version.

6 Look at the scene. Circle.

- In pairs, have students find the four characters in the main scene and say what they are doing. They circle the sentence that describes the action of each character.
- Have students find the tifftiff plant in the main illustration.

7 Act, ask, and answer.

- Display Picture cards 175–183 on the board. Pair students and have one student choose a card and mime the action while the other student asks the question.
- Direct students' attention to the mailbox card on page 96. Tell students to go online to the Poptropica English Island Adventure Game and find the item. Once students click on it, they are taken to a supplementary language task.

Pop Quiz: As students are leaving the class, show them Picture Cards of people doing different actions (from 175–183). Ask, *What's he/she doing?* Students respond, e.g., *He's/She's eating/cleaning/listening to music.*

Materials
Picture Cards 175–183

Homework WB page 79

Lesson 3 SB pages 98 or Poptropica English World

Learning Objective
Can identify more activities and words that describe how you do them

Target Language
singing, playing the piano, playing the violin, playing the trumpet, playing the flute, quietly, loudly, quickly, slowly, terribly

Warm-up

- Review action words with Picture Cards 175–183. Reveal each Card slowly and have students guess the words.

Open books and ask students to look at the activities on the page. Ask, *What are we learning today?* Write the lesson objective on the board: *We're learning more activities and words that describe them.*

8 Listen and number. Then say.

- Introduce the new words with Picture Cards 184–194. Hold them up one by one and ask students to repeat the words after you. Then ask students to look in their books and point at the words as you say them.
- Play the audio and have students number the words as they hear them.
- Point to individual pictures and ask students to tell you the word.

1 singing	**6** quietly
2 playing the piano	**7** loudly
3 playing the violin	**8** quickly
4 playing the trumpet	**9** slowly
5 playing the flute	**10** terribly

9 Listen and stick. Then sing.

- Pair students and have them go through the lyrics on the page. Have them predict some actions for the empty spaces. If necessary, pre-teach, *Can you hear me? Doing homework.* and, *Now she's finished.*
- Play the song audio and have students listen.
- Have students find the stickers at the back of the book. Play the audio again and ask them to stick them into the correct spaces. Check the answers by asking different students to read the lines with the stickers.
- Play the audio again and have students sing along and mime. If students are confident, use the karaoke version.

Ask students, *How many words for actions, and adverbs do you know now?* Give students a minute to tell their partner the new words they know.

- Ask students to say where they are on their adventure now. Ask students which words they find easiest or most difficult to remember. Tell students, *Good job!* to reinforce the progress they are making.
- Pair students and give each pair a copy of Activity Sheet 7 (see page 161). Have students first unscramble the actions and adverbs. Then students cut out the cards and place them face down in two piles (*actions* and *adverbs*) in front of them. Students take turns taking a card from each pile and asking their partners questions about their cards, e.g., *What are you doing? (I'm singing.) Are you singing terribly? (No, I'm singing loudly.)* If students can't ask a question, they put the card back. If they ask the right questions and answer correctly, they keep the card. The winner is the student with the most cards.

Pop Quiz: Before the end of the lesson, write two headings on the board: *actions* and *adverbs.* Ask students to brainstorm different actions and adverbs. Ask them to make sentences using one word from each group, e.g., *He's playing the piano loudly.*

Materials
Picture Cards 175–183; 184–194, stickers, Activity Sheet 7

Homework WB page 80

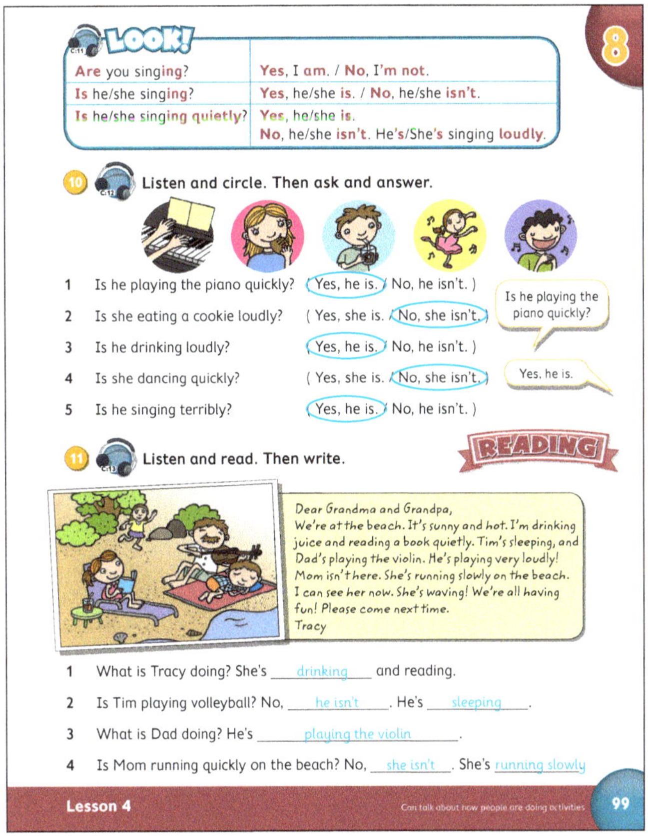

Lesson 4 SB page 99 or Poptropica English World

Learning Objective
Can talk about how people are doing activities

Target Language
Are you singing? Yes, I am. / No, I'm not.
Is he/she singing? Yes, he/she is. / No, he/she isn't.
Is he/she singing quietly? Yes, he/she is. / No, he/she isn't. He's/She's singing loudly.

Warm-up

- Display some of the Picture Cards (from 157–194). Put students into two or more teams. Teams take turns throwing a soft ball into a box or basket. If the ball goes in, the team gets five points. Before throwing the ball, a student or the team answers a question, e.g., *Is he singing loudly? Are these peaches?*

Open books and ask students to look at the chant and the Look! box. Ask, *What are we learning today?* Write the lesson objective on the board: *We're learning to talk about how people are doing activities.*

10 Listen and circle. Then ask and answer.

- Read through the Look! box with students and play the audio (track C:11). Then point to each picture and have students name the action. Then play the audio for the activity and have students circle the correct answer.
- Have students check their answers in pairs, by pointing to the pictures and reading the questions and answers.

11 Listen and read. Then write.

- Play the audio and have students listen and follow in their books.
- Ask students to look at the questions. Read them aloud and elicit some answers. Have each student fill in the blanks.
- Invite individual students to read the completed sentences. If necessary, write them on the board.
- Further practice (if not already used in lesson 3): Pair students and give each pair a copy of Activity Sheet 7 (page 161). Have students first unscramble the actions and adverbs. Then students cut out the cards, and place them face down in two piles in front of them. Students take turns taking two cards while their partners try to guess the action and adverb by asking questions, e.g., *Are you singing loudly? Are you playing he flute quietly?* Students can only ask three questions and their partners should only answer *yes* or *no*. If they guess, they can keep their partner's cards. The winner is the student with the most cards.

Pop Quiz: Before the end of the lesson, place a selection of Picture Cards of people doing activities (from 157–194) face down at the front of the class. Students take turns to pick up a Card and look at it, without showing the rest of the class. The class guesses the action by asking questions, e.g., *Is he/she sleeping/singing loudly/eating?*

Materials
Picture Cards 157–194, soft ball, box or basket, Activity Sheet 7

Homework WB page 81

Lesson 5 SB page 100 or Poptropica English World

Learning Objectives
Can understand a simple story
Can role-play a story

Additional Language
gardening, pull up, weeds, Earth, anti-trickster pack

Functional Language
Can I help? Fantastic! Good luck! We're safe.

Warm-up

- Have students build a tower. Divide the class into two teams. Get a set of building blocks and give each team an equal number of blocks. Ask a vocabulary or comprehension question, using the Student Book or the Picture Cards. The first team to answer correctly gets to start building a tower with its blocks, one block at a time. The aim is to have the highest tower at the end of the game. If the tower falls over during the game, the team has to start building it again.

Open books and ask students to look at the story. Ask, *What are we learning today?* Write the lesson objectives on the board: *We're reading a story and we're role-playing a story.*

12 Talk about the pictures. Then listen and read.

- Direct students' attention to the story and ask questions about the characters and the scene.
- Play the audio and have students listen and follow. Check understanding by pointing at the pictures and asking questions: *What's the Space Island character doing? What can PROD 2 see? Who is running? Why are they happy?*
- Play the recording again, pausing after each line. Have students repeat.
- Play the audio again. Have students speak along and mime.

Ask students to think about what's going to happen next. Ask: *Where are they going? What are they going to do when they get to Earth? What are they going to do with the tifftiff plant?*

13 Role-play the story.

See the "How to use stories" section on page 22 for more ideas on how to build your students' confidence with role-plays.

- Divide students into groups of seven. Give each group a set of cut-up Story Cards and have students place them in order.
- Divide students into groups and have them role-play the story. When you say, *change*, they should change character and role-play a new character. Rotate through the characters giving students the chance to play each one.

You might like to give the students feedback on their role-play.

Pop Quiz: As students are leaving the class, make statements about the story and have students say whether they are *true* or *false*.

Materials
Building blocks, Picture Cards (various), Story Cards, scissors

Homework WB page 82

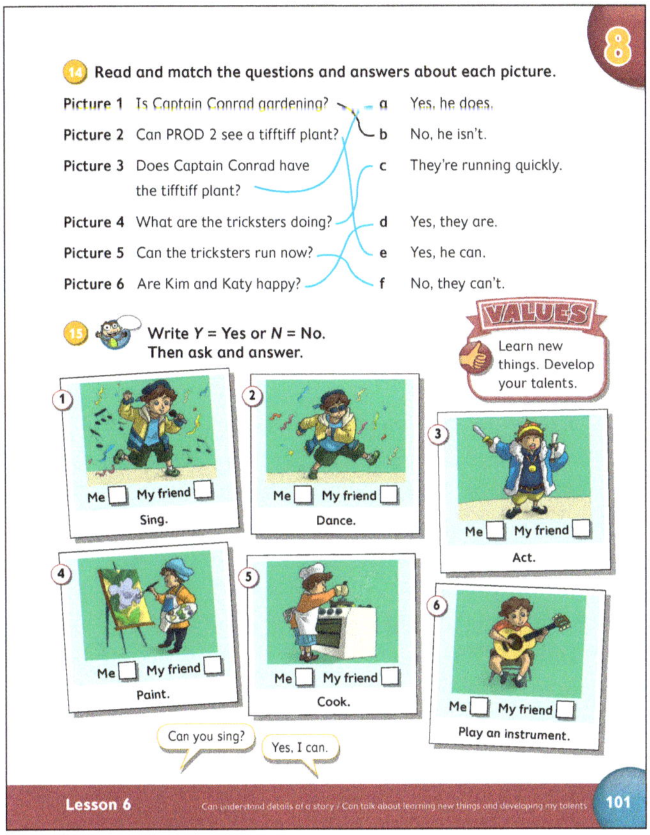
8

14 Read and match the questions and answers about each picture.

Picture 1	Is Captain Conrad gardening?	a	Yes, he does.
Picture 2	Can PROD 2 see a tifftiff plant?	b	No, he isn't.
Picture 3	Does Captain Conrad have the tifftiff plant?	c	They're running quickly.
Picture 4	What are the tricksters doing?	d	Yes, they are.
Picture 5	Can the tricksters run now?	e	Yes, he can.
Picture 6	Are Kim and Katy happy?	f	No, they can't.

15 Write *Y* = Yes or *N* = No. Then ask and answer.

VALUES Learn new things. Develop your talents.

Lesson 6 Can understand details of a story / Can talk about learning new things and developing my talents 101

Lesson 6 SB page 101 or Poptropica English World

Learning Objectives
Can understand details of a story
Can talk about learning new things and developing my talents

Additional Language
sing, dance, act, paint, cook, play an instrument

Value
Learn new things. Develop your talents.

Warm-up

- Read the story frame by frame in jumbled order. Have students find the correct frame and call out the number written in the top left corner. Make the activity more challenging by having students call out the names of the characters saying the lines.

Open books and ask students to look at the activities on the page. Ask, *What are we learning today?* Write the lesson objectives on the board: *We're understanding details of a story, and we're learning how to develop our talents.*

14 Read and match the questions and answers about each picture.

- Have students work in pairs. They look carefully at the story frames and match the questions to the answers.
- Have students work in new pairs to read the questions and answers and check that they are correct.

15 Write Y = Yes or N = No. Then ask and answer.

- Read the value, *Learn new things. Develop your talents.* Explain the concept of *talent* to students and say, *Everybody has a talent, but you need to develop it.* Ask students to look at the pictures and name each activity, e.g., *sing*, *dance*, etc.
- Have students write *Y* for the things they can do and *N* for things they can't do. Then pair students and have them ask each other questions to find out if their partners can do these activities.
- Invite individual students to tell the class what they or their friends can do, e.g., *I can sing, but my friend can't. I can't dance, but my friend can.*

Ask students to look at the six pictures again and to consider how easy or difficult it would be to develop the talents shown. Ask, *Do they think anyone can learn to sing or dance (in their own way)? Is cooking easy or difficult? Does it take a long time to learn to play an instrument?* There is no correct answer, but this will extend student thinking on the value.

Pop Quiz: As students are leaving the class, ask them to think of one thing they can do well and another that they can't do. Ask them to make sentences, e.g., *I can paint, but I can't cook.*

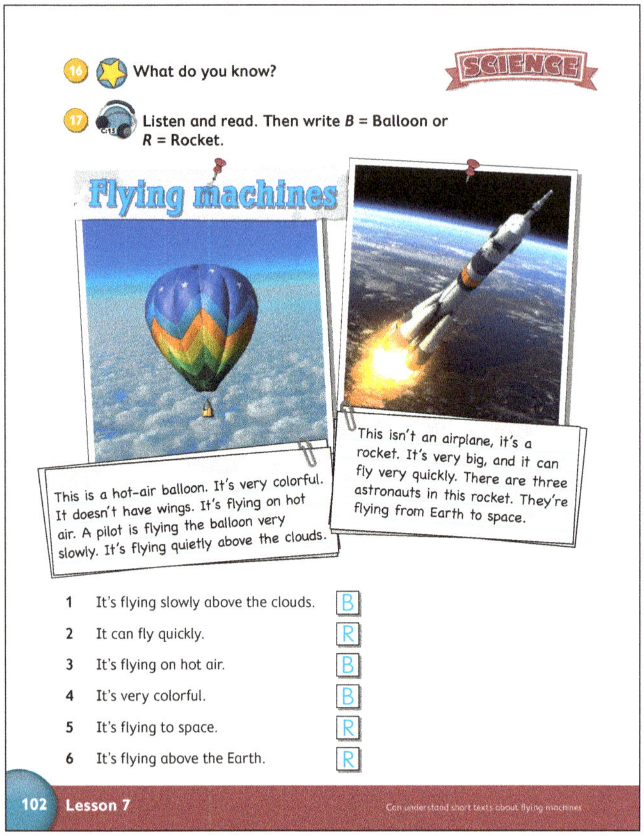
16 What do you know?

SCIENCE

17 Listen and read. Then write *B* = Balloon or *R* = Rocket.

Flying machines

This is a hot-air balloon. It's very colorful. It doesn't have wings. It's flying on hot air. A pilot is flying the balloon very slowly. It's flying quietly above the clouds.

This isn't an airplane, it's a rocket. It's very big, and it can fly very quickly. There are three astronauts in this rocket. They're flying from Earth to space.

1 It's flying slowly above the clouds. B
2 It can fly quickly. R
3 It's flying on hot air. B
4 It's very colorful. B
5 It's flying to space. R
6 It's flying above the Earth. R

102 Lesson 7 Can understand short texts about flying machines

Lesson 7 SB page 102 or Poptropica English World

Learning Objective
Can understand short texts about flying machines

Additional Language
flying machines, hot-air balloon, pilot, rocket, astronaut, space

Warm-up

- Show students pictures of different flying machines, old and modern, and ask if they know what they are and what they have in common. (*They fly.*)
- Show a picture of a modern plane. Point at the wings and say, e.g., *It's got two wings.* Ask, *What else has wings?* Explain that the person who flies a plane is a *pilot*.

16 What do you know?

- Open books and ask students to look at the activities on the page. Ask, *What are we learning today?* Write the lesson objective on the board: *We're learning about some flying machines.*
- Close books. Ask students what they know about flying machines. Write their ideas on the board.
- Refer to the learning adventure poster and say, *Great! You are moving along your learning adventure!*

17 Listen and read. Then write B = Balloon or R = Rocket.

C:13

- Have students look at the pictures of the balloon and the rocket. Introduce the words. Explain that the person who flies a rocket is an *astronaut*.
- Play the audio. Students listen and follow. Play the audio again, pausing after each sentence to check comprehension.
- Have students close their books. Read the sentences in turn and ask them to call out *balloon* or *rocket*.
- Ask students to open their books and write *B* or *R* next to the sentences.

Ask students, *What do you know about flying machines? Would you prefer to fly in a balloon or in a rocket? Where would you like to go? How would you feel?*, etc. There is no correct answer. Give students a minute to tell their partner the new ideas and words they can remember.

- Ask students, *Where are you on your learning adventure?* Tell students, *Good job!* to reinforce the progress they are making.

Pop Quiz: Before the end of the lesson, draw a line horizontally across the board to represent the ground. Ask students to give you the names of different means of transport and write them either along the line on the ground or above the line, in the air, e.g., (ground) *car, bus, bike,* (sky) *airplane, rocket, balloon.*

Materials
Pictures of flying machines including plane, hot-air balloon, rocket, poster

Homework WB page 84

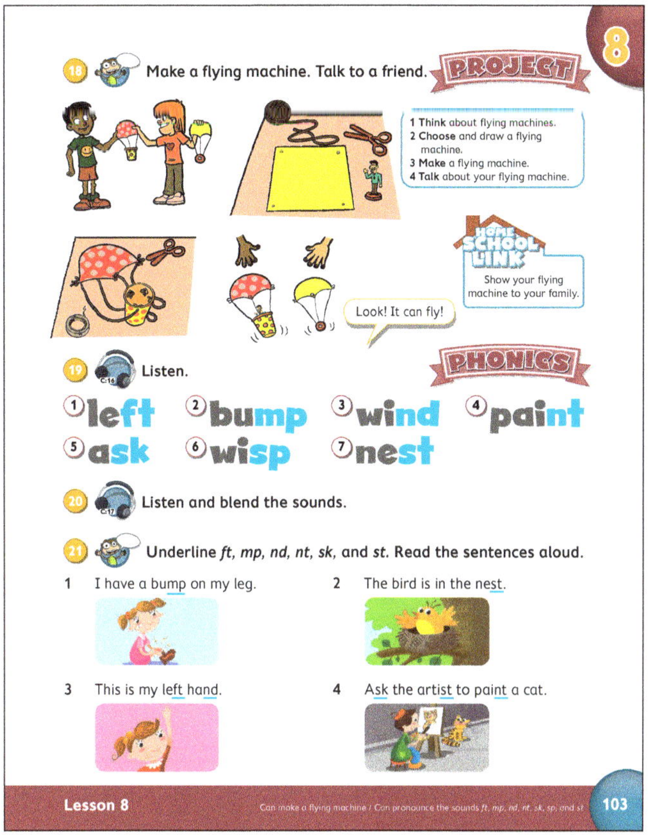

8

18 Make a flying machine. Talk to a friend. PROJECT

1 Think about flying machines.
2 Choose and draw a flying machine.
3 Make a flying machine.
4 Talk about your flying machine.

HOME SCHOOL LINK
Show your flying machine to your family.

Look! It can fly!

19 Listen. PHONICS

1 left 2 bump 3 wind 4 paint
5 ask 6 wisp 7 nest

20 Listen and blend the sounds.

21 Underline *ft, mp, nd, nt, sk,* and *st.* Read the sentences aloud.

1 I have a bump on my leg.
2 The bird is in the nest.
3 This is my left hand.
4 Ask the artist to paint a cat.

Lesson 8 Can make a flying machine / Can pronounce the sounds *ft, mp, nd, nt, sk, sp,* and *st* 103

Lesson 8 SB page 103 or Poptropica English World

Learning Objectives
Can make a flying machine
Can pronounce the sounds *ft, mp, nd, nt, sk, sp,* and *st*

Warm-up

- Put the letter cards on the board. Say a letter-sound and choose a student to come forward and touch the correct letter. Repeat until everyone has had a go.

Open books and ask students to look at the activities on the page. Ask, *What are we learning today?* Write the lesson objectives on the board: *We're learning to make a flying machine and we're learning to pronounce the sounds* ft, mp, nd, nt, sk, *and* st.

18 Make a flying machine. Talk to a friend.

- Show students the example of a flying machine in their books. Ask students to think about flying machines and to talk to a friend about what they know about them. Then have them look at the instructions.
- Provide the materials they need and give students time to punch holes in the corners of the parachute and in the cup. Show them how to thread even lengths of wool through the holes and tie them.
- Have the students practice dropping their parachutes from a height and talk to a partner about their flying machines. Have them put different objects in the cups.
- Display the flying machines in the classroom and ask students to choose their favorite.

You may also wish to give students feedback on their projects.

- **Home-School link:** Read the instruction with the class: *Show your flying machine to your family.* Ask students to do this at home.

19 Listen.

- Have students open their books and look at the seven words, *left, bump, wind, paint, ask, wisp,* and *nest.* Explain to students that they are going to read and pronounce the sounds *ft, mp, nd, nt, sk, sp,* and *st.* Play the audio.

1 ft left **2** mp bump **3** nd wind
4 nt paint **5** sk ask **6** sp wisp
7 st nest

20 Listen and blend the sounds.

- Blend the sample words one by one in a different order to the one in the book, by writing them up on the board. Model the blending yourself. Now have students turn to their books and do the same blending activity in pairs. Then play the audio for students to check.

1 l e ft left **2** b u mp bump
3 w i nd wind **4** p ai nt paint **5** a sk ask
6 w i sp wisp **7** n e st nest

21 Underline *ft, mp, nd, nt, sk,* and *st.* Read the sentences aloud.

- Write one of the sentences on the board. Run your finger under the sentence, sound out and read. Put three pictures on the board and ask students which picture matches the sentence. Repeat with the other sentences and then have students work through the activity individually.
- Have students read the sentences aloud.

Pop Quiz: Before the end of the lesson, write these letters on the board: *ft, mp, nd, nt, sk,* and *st.*

- Invite students to come to the front, add letters before these to make words, and say the words.

Materials
Letter cards (Units 1 and 2), sheets of paper, scissors, colored pens or pencils, wool, adhesive tape

Homework WB page 85

22 Match. Then write a sentence.

I CAN DO IT!

1	eat	a	to music	She is listening to music.
2	drink	b	homework	They are doing homework.
3	listen	c	the tub	Are you cleaning the tub?
4	play	d	juice	He is drinking juice.
5	read	e	a book	Is he reading a book?
6	do	f	to school	They are walking to school.
7	walk	g	lunch	He's eating lunch.
8	clean	h	the trumpet	She is playing the trumpet.

23 Choose actions from Activity 22 and an adverb. Then ask and answer.

loudly quickly quietly slowly terribly

Are you eating lunch quickly?

Yes, I am.

24 Draw a picture of you or a friend doing an action. Write.

This is ______.

I'm/He's/She's ______.

I CAN

I can ask and answer about what people are doing.

I can talk about how people are doing activities.

I can understand short texts about flying machines.

104 Lesson 9 Can assess what I have learned in Unit 8

Lesson 9 SB page 104 or Poptropica English World

Learning Objective
Can assess what I have learned in Unit 8

Warm-up

- Display a selection of Picture Cards (from 120–138; 157–194). Tell students to look closely and try to remember what they see. Ask them to turn around so that they cannot see the cards. Take one card away. Tell students to look and tell you the missing item. Allow students to act out the item if they can't remember the name.

Open books and ask students to look at the activities on the page. Explain to students that they are going to review what they have learned in this unit. Write the lesson objective on the board: *We're thinking about our learning adventure.*

- Ask students if they can remember the things they learned in this unit, e.g., *How many action words can you remember?* Put their ideas on the board.
- For each example (e.g., *actions*), ask students, *Where are you on your learning adventure?*

22 Match. Then write a sentence.

- Ask the students to look at the lists and make collocations by joining a word from the first column to a word from the second column. Then they complete the sentences.

23 Choose actions from Activity 22 and an adverb. Then ask and answer.

- Ask students to work in pairs. They take turns to choose an activity from Activity 22 and match it to an adverb, e.g. *eating lunch quickly / playing the trumpet loudly / walking to school slowly,* etc. Their partner asks questions in order to guess the activity. When they guess correctly, they switch roles.

24 Draw a picture of you or a friend doing an action. Write.

- Ask students to draw somebody doing an action then complete the sentences below their picture, e.g., *This is my friend. She's reading a book quietly.*

Ask students how they feel about their learning in this unit. Ask students to tell you what they found easy and what they found the most difficult to learn in the unit.

- Students review the I Can statements at the bottom of the page and color each bar according to how confident they feel about the language point.
- Ask students, *Where are you on your learning adventure?* Students indicate where they think they are on the learning adventure poster. Tell students, *Good job!* to reinforce the progress they are making.

Pop Quiz: In groups of four, students tell the others the answers to the following questions: *Which is your favorite activity in the unit? Why? Which activity don't you like? Why? What is your favorite new word? Which word is the most difficult for you?*

Materials
Picture Cards 120–138; 157–194, poster, colored pens or pencils

Homework WB page 86

Lesson 10 SB page 105 or Poptropica English World

Learning Objective
Can use what I have learned in Unit 8

Warm-up

- Prepare some word cards with the target vocabulary on them. Divide the class into teams. Invite a student from one team to the front and stick a word card to his/her back without him/her seeing it. The student turns to show the class, then tries to guess the word. *(Is it reading? Is it terribly?)* If the student guesses the correct category, have the rest of the class indicate this by calling out, *warm*. When the student guesses correctly, he/she wins a point for his/her team. Continue with students from each team.

Open books and ask students to look at the activities on the page. Ask, *What are we learning today?* Write the lesson objective on the board: *We're learning to talk about the things we do.*

Think of a question to which you can answer, *No, I'm not.*, e.g., *Are you playing the trumpet?* Say the answer, *No, I'm not.* Students need to find the correct question for each of your answers. Students prepare a list of questions in pairs. Give pairs two minutes to prepare their lists. They might like to write their ideas in their notebooks. Write their suggestions on the board. Students ask you the questions. Shake your head but remain silent until they ask your chosen question, then say, *No I'm not!* when they get it right.

25 How many sentences can you make in five minutes? Look and write. Then say.

- Have students look at the picture of the house and say what they can see. Then have them make some example sentences using a person, an activity from the box, and a room in the house, e.g., *I'm cleaning in the bathroom.*
- Pair the students and give them five minutes to write down as many sentences as they can.
- After five minutes, students count up their sentences. The pair with the most sentences reads out their sentences and the rest of the class crosses these off their list. When they have finished, other pairs read out any other sentences from their own lists. This activity helps build students' confidence as they are using the language they have learned in a different context.

I want to know more

- Ask students to choose anything they enjoyed from the unit and to go and find out more. You might like to set this activity as homework with a quick feedback session at the beginning of the next class, e.g. find out more words to describe activities, or find out more about flying machines.

Are you ready for the End of Level Test?

- Ask students if they are ready to take the End of Level Test (see page 220).
- Encourage students to ask if they have any questions about what they learned in Units 7 and 8.

You may wish to give Unit 8 test (see page 202) at this time.

Materials
Word cards, double-sided tape

Homework WB page 87

Unit 8 Story Cards

Review Units 7 and 8

SB pages 106–107 or Poptropica English World

Learning Objectives
Can talk about food and actions
Can talk about actions

Warm-up

- Place some Picture Cards (from 157–174) on a table. Invite a student to come and pick a card. Have the class ask questions to guess the object, e.g., *Are you (eating strawberries)?* If the answer is *yes*, the student who guessed has the next turn. If not, the class continues asking questions until a student guesses. Have students play the game until they have asked about all the cards.

Open books and ask students to look at the activities on the page. Ask, *What are we learning today?* Write the lesson objective on the board: *We're talking about food and actions.*

1 Circle the one that doesn't belong.

- Focus students' attention on each list of words. Ask the class to find the odd word in each list and to give the reason for their choice.
- Divide the class into pairs. Ask them to look through all the units in their books and write two similar sets of words. Remind them to include one word that does not belong in each group.
- Have students exchange their lists with another pair and find the odd-one-out. Then they read their sets and solutions to the class, giving reasons for their choices.

2 C:18 Listen and match.

- Ask students to look at the bowls of salad and to identify what is in each of them, saying, *There's...*
- Play the audio and have students listen.

Tracy likes vegetables in her salads. She likes carrots, tomatoes, and peas. She also likes eggs. She doesn't like strawberries.

Tim likes carrots and beans in his salads. He likes tomatoes, cucumbers, and potatoes. He doesn't like peas.

- Play the audio again for students to decide which salad Tim and Tracy like. Ask, *What does (Tim) like?* Have students answer.

Materials
Picture Cards 157–174

Act, ask, and answer.

- Point to the first pictures and role-play the activity with a student, using the model language on the page.
- Pair students and have them take turns to act and answer questions about the pictures. Encourage them to use gestures and body language to act out each action or activity.
- Have pairs spend a few minutes asking and answering questions until they remember the six pictures.
- Invite a pair to the front. Have the class call out a number frame, e.g., *Number 4*. The pair should try to remember the picture and act out the mini-conversation, e.g., *What are you doing, Tim? I'm drinking water.* Continue until most pairs have had a chance to act, ask, and answer in front of the class.

Watch the video story *The machine* on Poptropica English World. Ask students what happened in the story. Watch again, stopping at key points, and ask them about the language, the images, or the story. Ask the students to role-play the story. Assign the roles of two of the characters to confident speakers and let other students play the other parts. Encourage them to say as much of the dialog as they can and prompt them where necessary.

Point at the learning objective on the board. Ask students, *How many words do you know for things we do now?* Give students a minute to tell their partner as many words for things we do as they can.

- Ask students, *Where are you on your learning adventure?* Ask students which words they find easiest or most difficult to remember. Tell students, *Good job!* to reinforce the progress they are making.

Pop Quiz: Before the end of the lesson, ask a student to come to the front and choose a page from Unit 7 or Unit 8, without showing their classmates. They describe two images from that page, e.g., *A girl is eating a cookie and a boy is drinking.* (page 99) *A girl is dancing and a boy is reading.* (page 96) The rest of the class looks through their books to find the relevant page. The first student to guess correctly then comes to the front and chooses different images from another page to describe.

You may wish to give Review Test 4 (see page 216) at this time.

Goodbye

Unit Overview

Unit Objective

- I can review what I have learned

Skills

Writing	• Can write about what I have learned • Can complete simple sentences about where the tifftiff plant is (*Workbook*) • Can complete simple sentences about my favorite character, nature, pets, what somebody can and can't do, and food likes and dislikes (*Workbook*)
Listening	• Can identify the story characters
Speaking	• Can ask and answer about favorite things

Lesson 1 SB page 108 or Poptropica English World

Learning Objective
Can identify the story characters

Warm-up

- Review different structures learned throughout the course. Show various Picture Cards and ask, e.g., *Do you like oranges? Is there any broccoli? Where's the mirror? Does he have gray hair?* etc.

Open books and ask students to look at the activities on the page. Ask, *What are we learning today?* Write the lesson objective on the board: *We're identifying the story characters.*

1 Listen, find, and number.

C:19

- Ask questions about the main scene. Ask, *Who's this? Where are they? What are they doing?*
- Ask students to look at the scene and listen as you play the audio. Play the audio again and ask students to find and number the items.

1 There are three insects.
2 He has red hair and glasses.
3 It has a hard shell, and it's very slow.
4 She's wearing a purple uniform.
5 He's behind the tree.
6 He can jump really high.
7 He likes strawberries.
8 He's sleeping.

2 Listen. Who is missing?

C:20

- Play the audio. Students listen to the dialog. Ask, *Who's missing? (Arnold jumping)*

Kim:	Goodbye Space Island.
Katy:	Look! I can see Ben. He's eating strawberries.
Captain C:	And look! There's a yellow trickster. He can climb a tree.
Kim:	Can you see Shirley Homeland? She's wearing a purple uniform.
Katy:	Yes, And look! There's a space island animal.
Captain C:	It's a wabberjock. It's pink and it has spots.
Kim:	I can see Fid. He has red hair and glasses. He's waving. Goodbye, Fid! Thank you!
Katy:	Look! The green trickster is in the pond. He can't swim. Ha, ha, ha, ha!
Captain C:	And there's President Pop! I like president Pop. Goodbye!

Pop Quiz: Hide pictures of characters from the course around the room. Describe their positions for students to find them.

Materials
Picture Cards (various), pictures of the characters

Homework WB
page 88

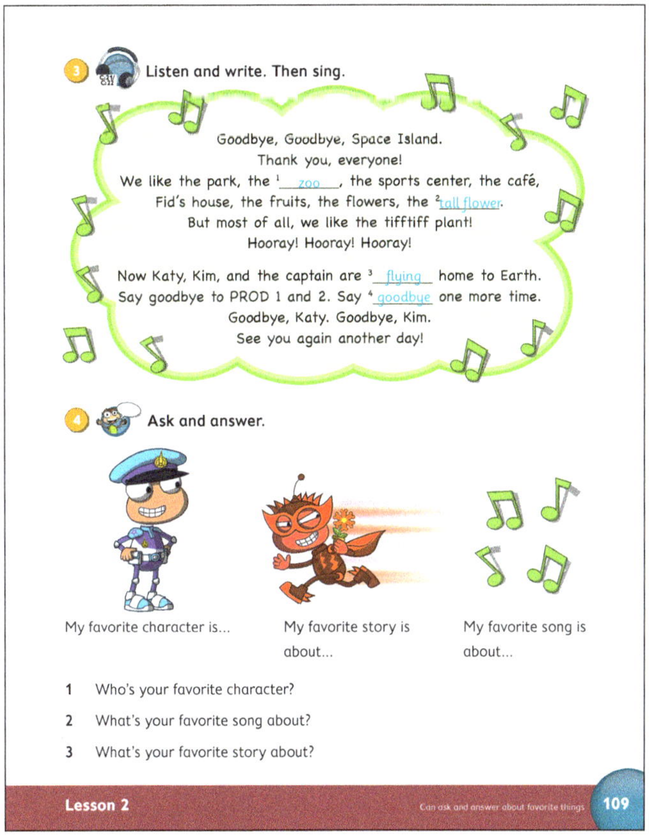

3 Listen and write. Then sing.

Goodbye, Goodbye, Space Island.
Thank you, everyone!
We like the park, the [1] zoo, the sports center, the café,
Fid's house, the fruits, the flowers, the [2] tall flower.
But most of all, we like the tifftiff plant!
Hooray! Hooray! Hooray!

Now Katy, Kim, and the captain are [3] flying home to Earth.
Say goodbye to PROD 1 and 2. Say [4] goodbye one more time.
Goodbye, Katy. Goodbye, Kim.
See you again another day!

4 Ask and answer.

My favorite character is... | My favorite story is about... | My favorite song is about...

1 Who's your favorite character?
2 What's your favorite song about?
3 What's your favorite story about?

Lesson 2 Can ask and answer about favorite things 109

Lesson 2 SB page 109 or Poptropica English World

Learning Objective
Can ask and answer about favorite things

Warm-up

- Stick various Picture Cards on the board and divide the class into two teams. One student from each team chooses a Picture Card and uses the word correctly in a sentence. Teams can repeat items, but they cannot repeat the sentence. Give a point for each correct sentence.

Open books and ask students to look at the activities on the page. Ask, *What are we learning today?* Write the lesson objective on the board: *We're asking and answering about favorite things.*

3 Listen and write. Then sing.

C:21 C:22

- Pair students and have them read through the lyrics and guess the missing words.
- Play the audio and ask students to check any correct guesses/predictions. Praise pairs with the highest number of guesses.
- Play the audio again, pausing after each missing word to allow students enough time to write it down on the line.
- Play the audio a few times and have students sing along. If students are confident, use the karaoke version.

Goodbye, Goodbye, Space Island.
Thank you, everyone!
We like the park, the zoo, the sports centre, the café, Fid's house, the fruits, the flowers, the tall tower.
But most of all, we like the tifftiff plant!
Hooray! Hooray! Hooray!

Now Katy, Kim, and the Captain are flying home to Earth.
Say goodbye to PROD 1 and 2. Say goodbye one more time.
Goodbye, Katy. Goodbye, Kim.
See you again another day!

4 Ask and answer.

- Point to the three pictures on the page and say, e.g., *My favorite character is Captain Conrad. I like him because he is clever / he helps the children.*
- Read the questions and have students answer them.
- Put students in pairs and have them ask and answer the questions. Encourage them to provide reasons for their answers. They can flip through the pages of the book if they need to find any songs or games, or pictures they want to refer to.

Pop Quiz: As students are leaving the class, ask them to mime being their favorite character in the course. The other students guess the character.

Materials
Picture Cards (various)

Homework WB page 89

5 Draw or stick pictures. Then write.

VOCABULARY

My favorite nature scene

There is ______.

There are ______

______.

There aren't any ______.

My pet

My pet is a ______.

It has ______.

It doesn't have ______.

It is so ______.

I love my pet.

6 Draw or stick a picture of you in your home. Then write.

This is me in my ______

______ (room).

I have ______ hair

and ______ eyes.

I'm wearing ______

and ______. These are

my favorite clothes.

My ______ (room) is great.

There is ______.

There are ______.

110 Lesson 3 Can write about what I have learned

Lesson 3 SB page 110 or Poptropica English World

Learning Objective
Can write about what I have learned

Warm-up

- Place several objects or toys around the classroom, e.g. on/under tables or chairs, or in boxes or bags. Ask about each object, e.g., *Where's the pencil? (It's under the table.) Where's the doll? (It's next to the chair.) Where are the books? (They're in the box.)* Then have students ask and answer in pairs.

Open books and ask students to look at the activities on the page. Ask, *What are we learning today?* Write the lesson objective on the board: *We're writing about what we have learned.*

5 Draw or stick pictures. Then write.

- Display Picture Cards 50–67 and 83–92 (nature, animal body parts) to review language learned. Ask questions, e.g., *Are there any ants? Does it have a tail?*.
- Focus students' attention on the two picture frames. Read the headings and explain the task. Students can either bring pictures from home or draw in class.
- Students draw or stick their pictures and complete the descriptions.
- Pair students and have them read their descriptions to each other. Encourage them to check and correct any mistakes.
- Invite individual students to show their pictures and read their descriptions to the class.

6 Draw or stick a picture of you in your home. Then write.

- Display Picture Cards 100–106 and 112–119 (furnishings, household items) on the board. Point to each one to review the vocabulary. Have students say the words.
- Invite students to come to the front and point to the items they have in their rooms and say, e.g., *There is a mirror in my room. It's above my desk.*
- Display Picture Cards 120–135 (clothing). Call out a sentence, e.g., *He's wearing a polo shirt.* and have students repeat and point to the corresponding card. Invite individual students to take on your role.
- Explain the activity. Pair students and have them work together. Encourage them to help each other as they draw or stick their pictures and write about themselves in their homes.
- Invite students to come to the front, show their pictures, and talk about them.

Pop Quiz: Before the end of the lesson, think of a household item or piece of furniture (e.g. shower) and have students guess what you are thinking of by asking, e.g., *Is it in the bedroom? (no) Is it in the bathroom? (yes) Is it the sink? (no) Is it the shower? (yes)*

Materials
Classroom objects or toys, Picture Cards 50–67; 83–92; 100–106; 112–119; 120–135, colored pens or pencils, glue

Homework WB page 90

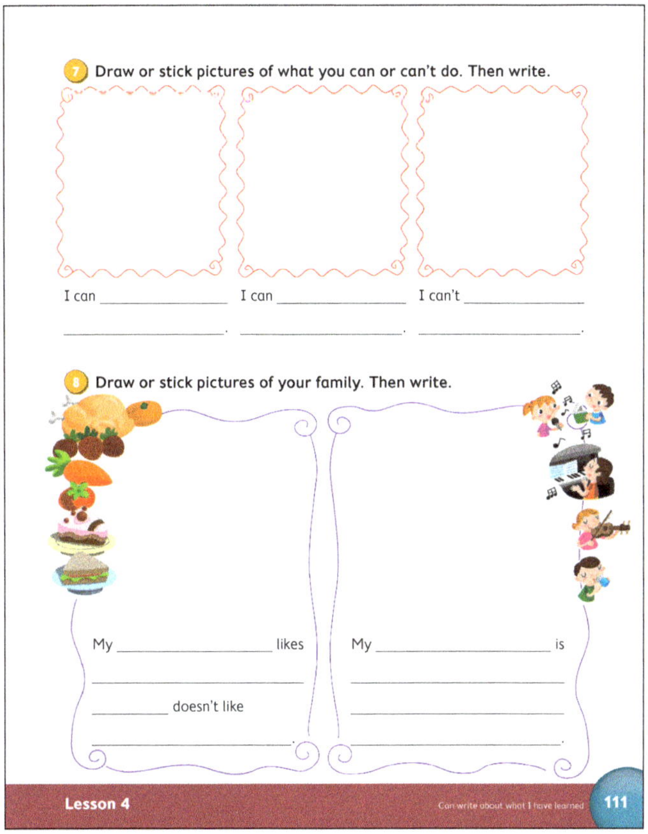

Lesson 4 SB page 111 or Poptropica English World

Learning Objective
Can write about what I have learned

Warm-up

- Play *Simon says* to review vocabulary for sports and actions. Give the class instructions, but explain that they should only mime them as told when you say, *Simon says*, e.g., *Simon says dance.* When a student makes a mistake, he/she must sit out until the next round.
- Divide the class into two groups. Ask a group, e.g., *Can you jump three times?* If the group replies, *Yes, I can.*, say, *OK, go!* They do the action and get a point. If the group says, *No, I can't.*, say, *Too bad!*, and they get no points. Proceed to the next group.

Open books and ask students to look at the activities on the page. Ask, *What are we learning today?* Write the lesson objective on the board: *We're writing about what we have learned.*

7 Draw or stick pictures of what you can or can't do. Then write.

- Display Picture Cards 139–146 (abilities). Invite individual students to mime a Card for the class to guess and call out, e.g., *You're playing basketball.*
- Point to each card, and ask students if they can do the sports or activities.
- Explain the activity. If students have brought pictures of things they can do or can't do, invite them to show them to the class, and have the other students name the activities.
- Have students draw or stick the pictures, and write a sentence for each one.
- Alternatively, you can ask students to work individually without showing their pictures to their classmates. Then pair students and have them play a guessing game. Student A asks until he/she guesses the two things his/her partner can do.

8 Draw or stick pictures of your family. Then write.

- Display Picture Cards 175–189 (fruit/vegetables, actions). Say a sentence about each one, e.g., *My favorite fruit is cherries. I'm playing the violin.* Have students point to the correct Card. Invite individual students to take on your role.
- Show a Picture Card of a fruit or vegetable and say, e.g., *My brother likes strawberries. He doesn't like broccoli.* Invite students to pick a Card and do the same.
- Bring some pictures of people doing different activities, and describe them, e.g., *This is my sister. She's reading. This is my uncle. He's playing the piano.*
- Explain the activity, and have students work individually as they draw or stick their pictures and write.
- Invite students to come to the front of the class to show their drawings or pictures and read their sentences.

Ask students if they can remember the things they learned in this level. Put their ideas on the board. Ask students to choose two or three ideas and write the words or sentences to show they understand the topic or language. Ask students to say where they are on their adventure and say, *Good job! Good luck with your new learning adventure!*

Pop Quiz: Before the end of the lesson, ask a student to describe another student in the class they know well. Talk about what he/she is doing, what he/she likes and what he/she can/can't do. The other students guess who is being described.

Materials
Picture Cards 139–146; 175–189, colored pens or pencils, glue, pictures of people doing activities

Homework WB page 91

Halloween

SB pages 112–113 or Poptropica English World

Learning Objective
Can sing a song about Halloween

Target Language
ghost, witch, broom, bat, pumpkin, spider, hat

Cultural note: Halloween in Britain

- Halloween is on October 31st. On Halloween, children carve faces out of pumpkins, place a candle in the middle, and put them outside their front door. They enjoy dressing up as ghosts, skeletons, and witches, and going trick or treating. They knock at their neighbors' doors and ask, *Trick or treat?* Anyone choosing *treat* has to give the children candies or chocolate. Anyone choosing *trick* will get a nasty surprise, such as a squirt of water in the face.

Open books and ask students to look at the activities on the page. Ask, *What are we learning today?* Write the lesson objective on the board: *We're learning to sing a song about Halloween.*

Warm-up

- Discuss Halloween as a class. Ask questions such as, *When is Halloween? How do people celebrate it?*

1 Listen, find, and say. (C:23)

- Play the recording, pausing after each word for students to find the object, point to it, and say the word.
- Play the recording and repeat.
- Play the recording a third time and have individual students say the words.
- Hold up the Student Book, point to an object, and ask, *What's this?* Repeat with all of the Halloween objects. Write the words on the board and point to them one at a time for students to repeat. Move from one word to the next and increase the pace a couple of times to make the activity more fun.

hat	broom
ghost	bat
pumpkin	witch
spider	

2 Listen and sing. (C:24)

- Play the recording once for students to listen and follow. Students point to the items as they hear them.
- Play the song a second time for students to chant along and do actions.

3 Look and answer.

- Ask students to read the questions.
- Students look at the main illustration. They count up the number of each item and write the answers in their notebooks.
- Check the answers with the whole class.

Ask students, *how many Halloween words do you know now?* Give students a minute to tell their partner the new words they know.

Pop Quiz: Ask students to work in groups of four or five. They draw bats, spiders and other Halloween items on coloured card, cut them out and decorate the class. Students write labels and stick them on.

Materials
Colored card (orange and black, especially), colored pens or pencils, scissors, glue

April Fools' Day

SB page 114 or Poptropica English World

Learning Objective
Can sing a song about April Fools' Day

Target Language
April, fool, fun, surprise, joke

Cultural note: April Fools' Day in Britain

- April Fools' Day is on April 1st. On this day, it's traditional to play jokes on family and friends. People who fall for the jokes are called an *April Fool.* Newspapers, television stations, and radio stations often have fake news items to fool the public. Anyone who wants to play an April Fools' joke must do so before 12 noon, or they themselves will become the fool.

Open books and ask students to look at the activities on the page. Ask, *What are we learning today?* Write the lesson objective on the board: *We're singing a song about April Fools' Day.*

Warm-up

- Tell students when April Fools' Day is celebrated. Ask students if they have a similar celebration in their country. Ask, *What do people do?*
- Discuss jokes and tricks with the class. Ask, *Have you ever played a trick on anyone? What happened?*
- Focus on the pictures. Ask students if they think April Fools' Day is fun. Ask them to say why or why not.

1 C:25 Read. Then listen and say.

- Ask students to read the text about April Fools' Day and the words around the pictures. Check understanding.
- Play the recording, pausing for students to repeat.

2 C:26 Listen and sing.

- Tell students that you are going to play the April Fools' Day song. Play the recording once and have students listen and follow.
- Play the song again and ask students to point at the labelled objects in the picture.
- Play the song a third time for students to sing along.

3 Read the jokes and find the answer.

- Explain to the class that they are going to read jokes in the form of questions and answers. They have to find the answers to the questions to make the jokes.
- Read out the questions and check that they understand. Students find the answers individually, then compare in pairs.
- Check answers with the whole class.

Ask students, *how many April Fools' Day words do you know now?* Give students a minute to tell their partner the new words they know.

Pop Quiz: Ask students if they know any good jokes. They share their jokes with the class. Ask students if they know any jokes in English. Encourage them to tell any jokes they know. If they don't know any, tell a few yourself.

Earth Day

SB page 115 or Poptropica English World

Learning Objective
Can talk about ways to protect the environment

Target Language
plant a tree, turn off the lights, recycle, ride your bike

Cultural note: Earth Day in the UK

- Earth Day is on April 22nd. The purpose of the day is to raise awareness about environmental issues, and encourage people to do what they can to help protect the planet.

Open books and ask students to look at the activities on the page. Ask, *What are we learning today?* Write the lesson objective on the board: *We're learning about ways to protect the environment.*

Warm-up

- Introduce the concept of Earth Day, and explain what it is for. Ask students if they have a similar day in their country. Ask, *What do you do?*
- Discuss with students what the children in the pictures are doing. Ask for other suggestions of how we can protect the planet.

1 Read.

- Read out the text about Earth Day and check understanding. Then ask questions: *When is Earth Day? What do people think about on Earth Day?*

2 Listen and point.

C:27

- Tell students they are going to listen to a recording describing what the people in the pictures are doing.
- Play the recording and have students listen and point to each picture as it is described.
- Play the recording a second time, pausing after each sentence for students to repeat.

1 Ride your bike.	**3** Plant a tree.
2 Recycle.	**4** Turn off the lights.

3 Ask and answer.

- Ask students to work in pairs. Explain to the class that they are going to take turns to ask and answer questions about which of the things in Activity 2 they do.
- Ask a pair of students to read the question and answer in speech bubbles to the class.
- Students take turns to ask and answer with their partners.
- Read out different actions, e.g., *Plant a tree. Eat lots of food. Drive a car. Ride your bike.*
- If the actions are things people can do to protect the planet, students call out, *Earth Day.* If not, students remain silent.

Ask students, *how many Earth Day words do you know now?* Give students a minute to tell their partner the new words they know.

Pop Quiz: Have students work in pairs. They make an information leaflet for Earth Day. They draw pictures of people doing different actions to protect the Earth. They label their pictures with the words from the lesson.

Materials
Optional activity materials: A sheet of paper for each group; colored pens or pencils

Activity Sheet 1

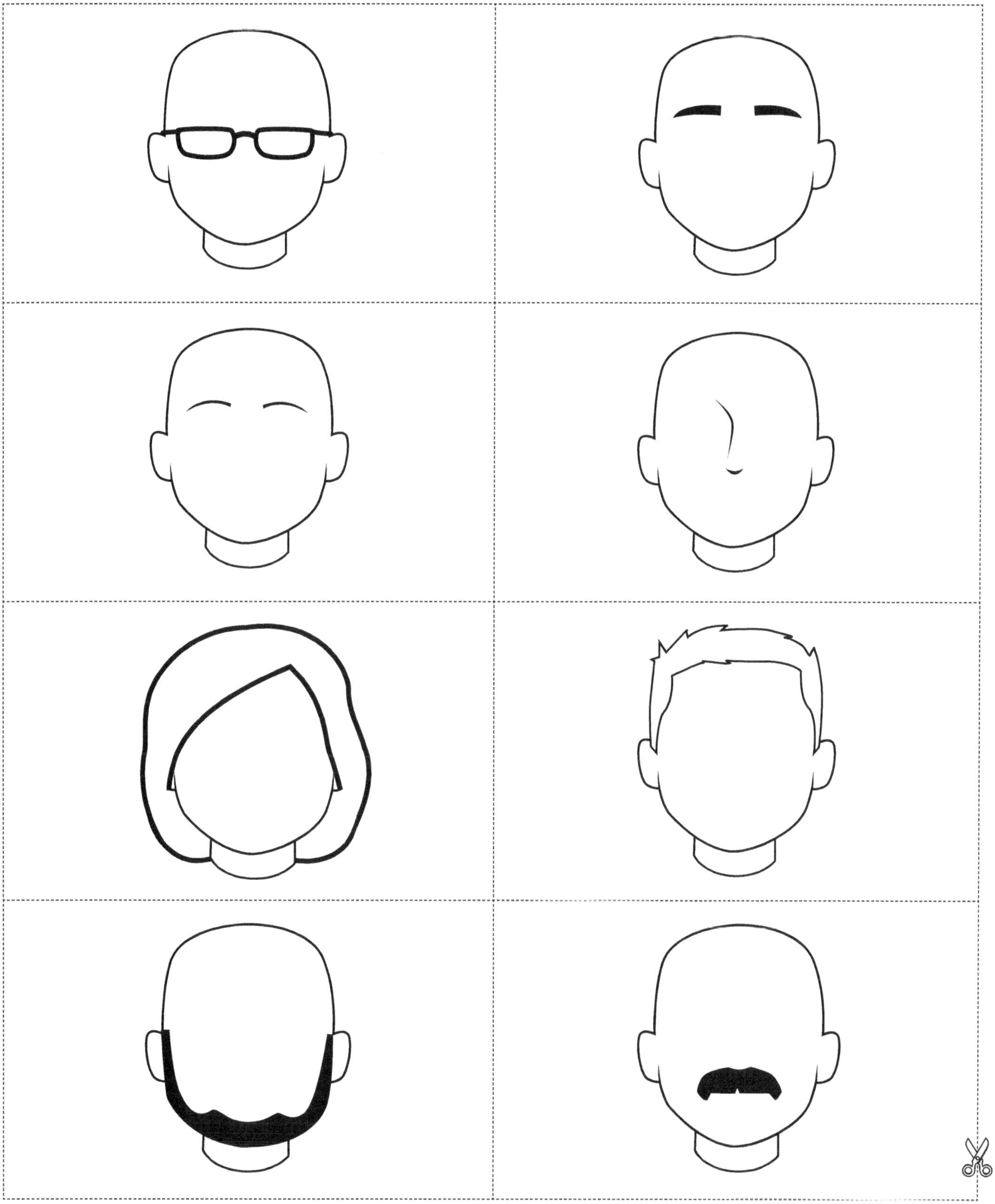

Activity Sheet 2

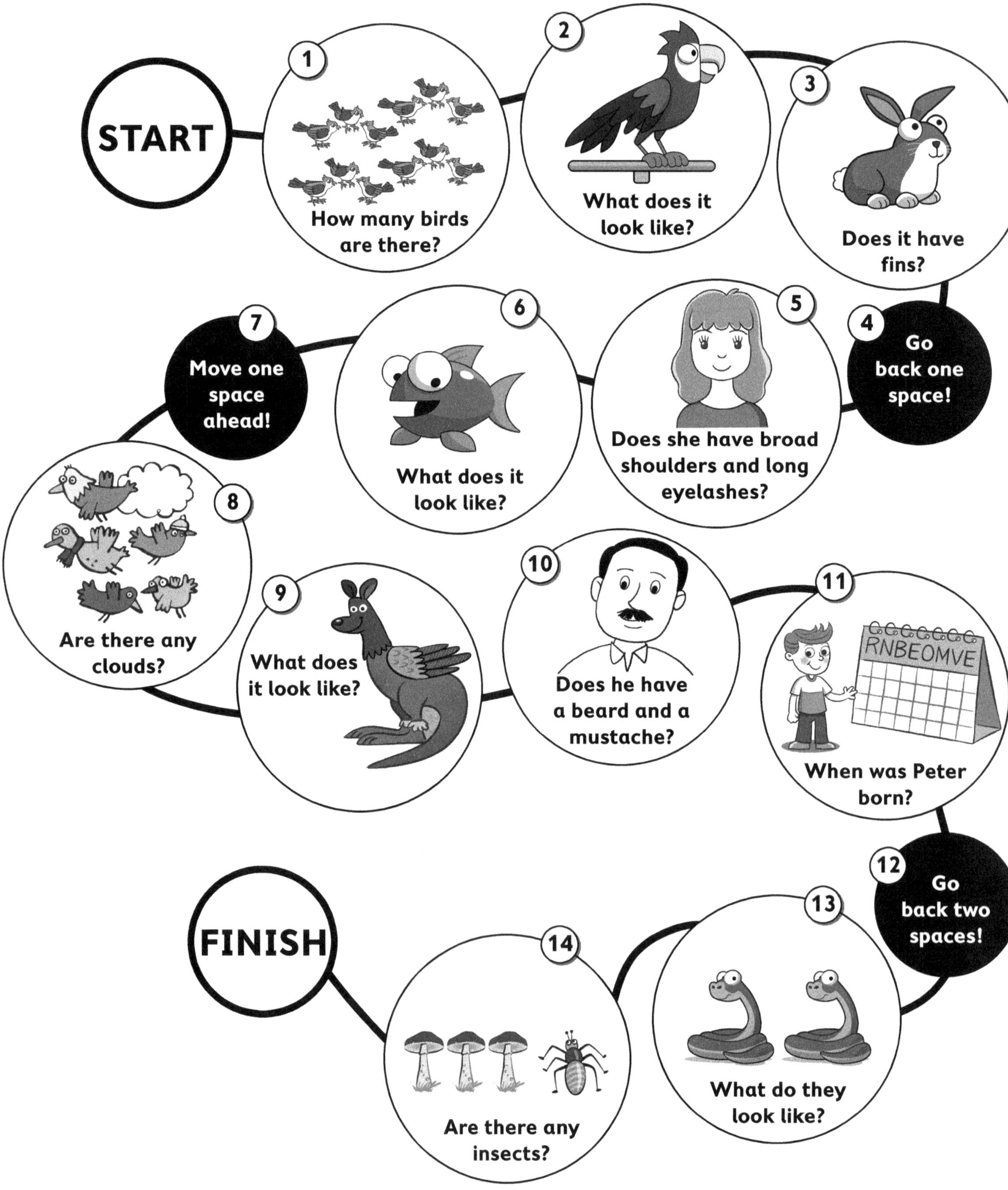

Activity Sheet 3

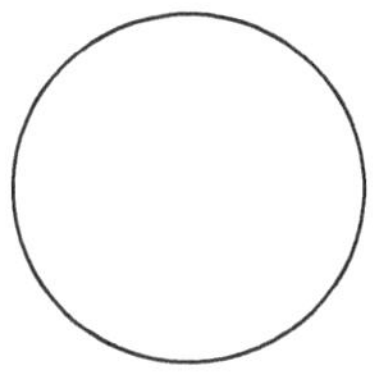

sun

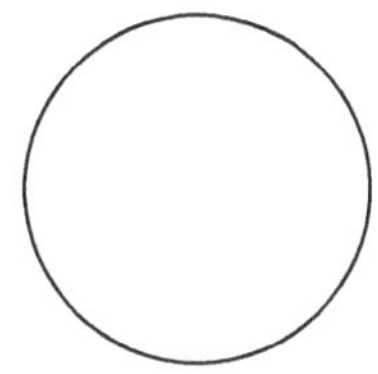

face

house

closet

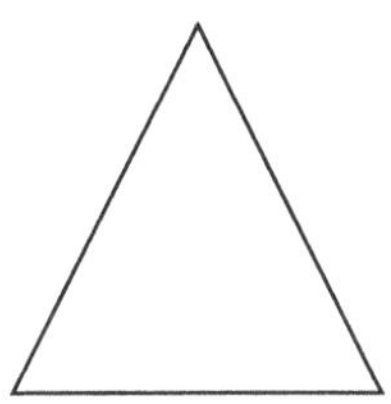

fish

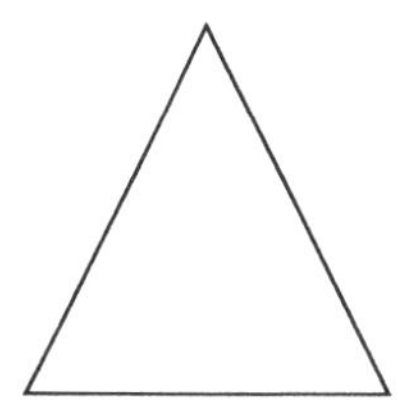

bird

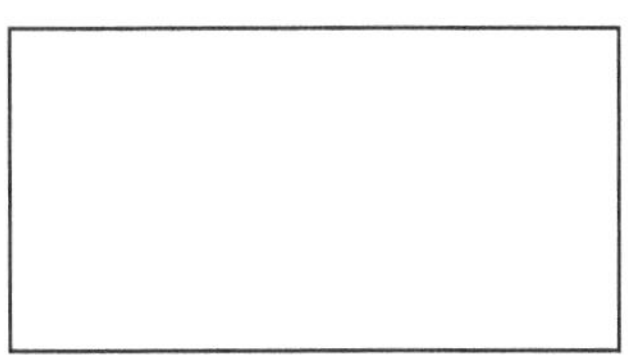

blanket

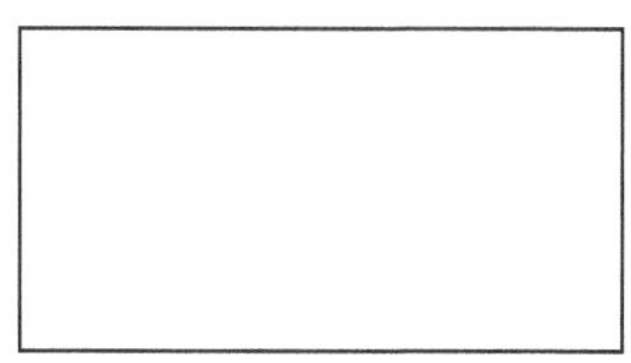

cupboard

Activity Sheet 4

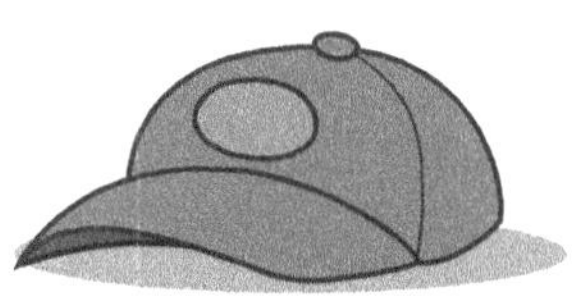

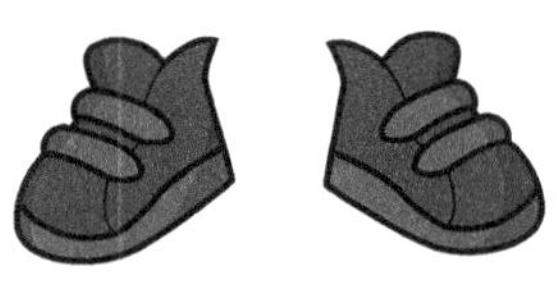

1	2	3	4

Activity Sheet 5

Things I can do	Things my friend can do

Activity Sheet 6

My favorite fruits	____________'s favorite fruits
My favorite vegetables	____________'s favorite vegetables

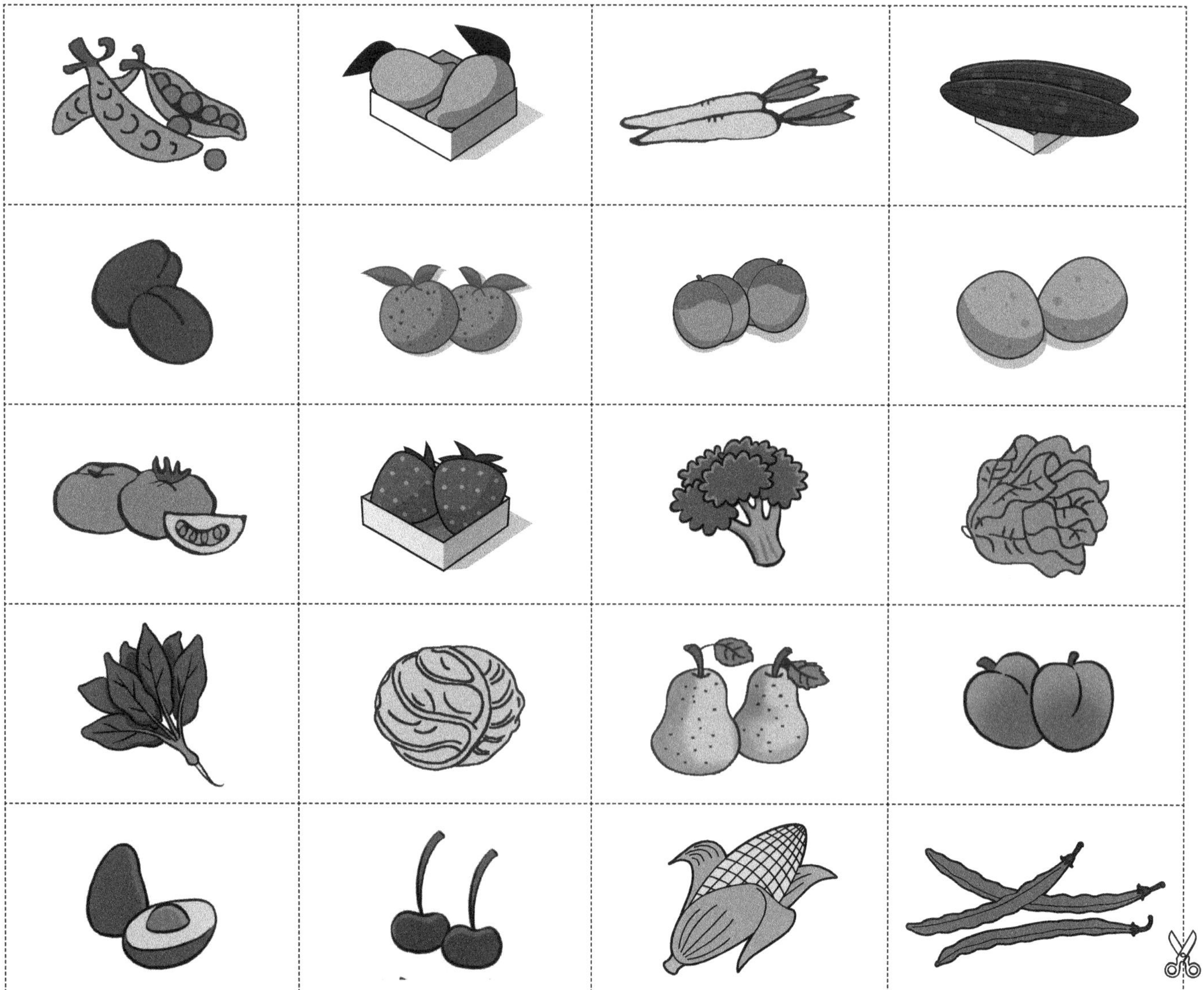

Activity Sheet 7

 ______ [giaredn]	 ______ [aigetn]	 ______ [nggiins]
 ______ [kignalw]	 ______ [inncgad]	 playing the ______ [ltufe]
 playing the ______ [iapon]	 playing the ______ [nlivoli]	 playing the ______ [umrtpte]
 ______ [ieutylq]	 ______ [ydolul]	 ______ [lcuqiky]
 ______ [lswoyl]	 ______ [reirtlby]	

Workbook Script

Welcome

3 Listen and write.

1 Thirty-eight
2 Fifty
3 Forty-six
4 Twenty-one
5 Ninety-nine
6 Seventy-two
7 Sixty-five
8 Eighty-four
9 Twenty-three
10 Thirty-seven

4 Listen and write.

1 There are thirty-three birds in the tree.
2 There are eighty-five flowers in the yard.
3 There are forty tables in the classroom.
4 There are twenty-nine teachers in the school.
5 There are sixty-one children at the party.

6 Listen and write. Then match.

1 Hi, I'm Boris. Today's my favorite day. It's Wednesday. It's cold and snowy today. I'm wearing my coat.
2 My name's Billy. My favorite day's Friday. I like Fridays because I can swim.
3 My name's Marie. Today's my favorite day. It's Saturday. I'm in the yard. Look at the flowers.
4 I'm Andy. My favorite day's Thursday. We have burgers on Thursday.
5 My name's Judy. My favorite day's Sunday. I have eggs and toast for breakfast.

Unit 1

2 Listen, draw, and color.

Draw two blue birds. There are brown rocks. There are pink insects. There is a gray cloud.
There are green trees. Draw a pond. Color it blue. Draw three flowers. Color them yellow. There are two mushrooms. Color them blue and yellow. Draw the sun and color.

6 Listen and read. Then draw and color.

There's a big blue pond. There are three green trees. There are some pink insects. There are six yellow birds. There's a rainbow. There aren't any butterflies. There isn't any wind.

7 Listen and check.

1 There's a tree. There are some flowers.
2 There's a cloud. There are five birds.
3 There's a mushroom. There are some insects.
4 There's a horse. There are two cats.

11 Listen and write.

Hello. My name's Linda. I love to play outside. I always play safe. I play in the playground. I don't play on the streets. I don't play at night, and I don't play by myself. I play with my friends. I don't play in the hot sun.

18 Listen and connect the letters. Then write.

1 t a p tap
2 r i ch rich
3 s a t sat
4 sh e l shell

19 Listen and write the words.

1 fair
2 year
3 near
4 hear

Unit 2

1 Listen and color. Then match.

Grandpa has a short beard and a white mustache. He has green eyes and small glasses.
He has gray hair. Mom has blonde hair and blue eyes.
Peter has red hair and blue eyes.

5 Listen and number.

1 Do you have a black beard? Yes, I do. I have a beard and a mustache.
2 Do you have long eyelashes? Yes, I do.
3 Do you have a beard? No, I don't, but I have a big mouth and a red nose.
4 Do you have a big chin? Yes, I do.

6 Listen again and circle or write.

1 Do you have a black beard? Yes, I do. I have a beard and a mustache.
2 Do you have long eyelashes? Yes, I do.
3 Do you have a beard? No, I don't, but I have a big mouth and a red nose.
4 Do you have a big chin? Yes, I do.

8 Listen and check. Then write.

He has curly hair. He doesn't have teeth. He has long eyelashes.

9 Listen and read. Then write.

My name is Meesoo. I'm 10 years old. I have long black hair, and dark eyebrows. I have brown eyes. I don't have glasses.

16 Listen and match.

I'm Amy. I wash my hands before and after eating. I'm Kim. I take a shower every day. I'm Mark. I brush my teeth every day.

20 Listen and connect the letters. Then write.

1 d a d ad
2 s i t sit
3 p a th path
4 th i s this

21 Listen and write the words.

1 day
2 way
3 hammer
4 summer

Unit 3

5 Listen and draw. Then write.

1 The turtle has a hard shell.
2 The cat is cute. It has a long tail.
3 The bird is scary. It has sharp claws.
4 Our dog is cute. It has white paws.

7 Listen and circle. Then write.

I have a pet. It's a rabbit. Its name's Lily. It's 3 years old. It's white, and it has soft fur. It has four legs, but you can't see them. There's a lot of fur! It likes fruit.

17 Listen and connect the letters. Then write.

1 k a p cap
2 d i g dig
3 r i ng ring
4 i n k ink

18 Listen and write the words.

1 peach
2 oil
3 foil
4 join

Unit 4

6 Listen and write.

1 Is the turtle in the tub?
2 Are the hamsters above the bird?
3 Is the rabbit under the hat?
4 Is the frog on the bed?
5 Is the snake above the chair?
6 Is the parrot next to the lamp?

8 Look at Activity 7. Listen and write the number.

a The hamster is in front of the sofa.
b The hamster is above the chair.
c The hamster is in the bathroom.
d The hamster is under the bed.
e The hamster is next to the computer.
f The hamster is behind the plant.

17 Listen and connect the letters. Then write.

1 k i k kick
2 t ai l tail
3 k i d kid
4 f ee t feet

18 Listen and write the words.

1 wave
2 shape
3 dive
4 like
5 note

21 Listen and draw. Then write.

a There's a bed in the bedroom. There are two pictures on the wall.
b There's a trash can next to the sink. There are towels on the wall.
c There are blankets in front of the sofa. There's a plant next to the TV.

Unit 5

3 Listen and draw. Then color.

What's Harry wearing? He's wearing a baseball cap. He's wearing a polo shirt. He's wearing shorts. He's wearing sandals.

5 Write. Then listen and color.

He's wearing a colorful wool sweater. He's wearing brown hiking boots. He's wearing a plain green beanie.
She's wearing a fancy pink ski jacket. She's wearing a red scarf. She's wearing black shoes.
She's wearing blue and red tights.

7 Check. Then listen, read, and circle.

1 Is she wearing a belt?
2 Is she wearing a plain baseball cap?
3 Is she wearing fancy glasses?
4 Is she wearing plain sneakers?

16 Listen and connect the letters. Then write.

1 h a t hat
2 k u p cup
3 l igh t light
4 k oa t coat

17 Listen and write the words.

1 smell
2 snip
3 squid
4 swim

Unit 6

3 Listen and check for *can* or cross for *can't*.

Hi, I'm Max. Can you play soccer? Yes, I can. My name's Jake. Hi, Jake. Over there in the field are my friends Paul, Beth, and Gina. Paul can climb, but he can't play baseball. What about Beth? Beth can play tennis, but she can't play soccer. Wow! I can't play tennis! What about Gina? She can run, but she can't climb. What about you, Max? Well, I can play soccer, but I can't ride a bike. Great! Let's play soccer.

6 Listen and check.

1 He was at the stadium.
2 She was at the gym.
3 He was at the ski slope.

13 Listen and number. Then write.

My name's Jane. I like exercise a lot. I play sports with my friend Sally. I also do taekwondo. At night, I go for a walk or ride my bike with my mother. Sometimes I run at the beach with my brother. And, oh, yes! I do push-ups, too! I want to be very strong.

15 Listen and number.

1 Stretch your arms up.
2 Bend your knees.
3 Twist your body to the right.
4 Twist your body to the left.
5 Turn around.

19 Listen and connect the letters. Then write.

1 p u f puff
2 b e l bell
3 f oo d food
4 b oo k book

20 Listen and write the words.

1 black
2 plum
3 float
4 plate

Unit 7

3 Listen and check for *likes* or cross for *doesn't like*.

She likes strawberries. She doesn't like plums. She doesn't like peas. He likes cucumbers. He doesn't like tomatoes.

7 Listen and draw a happy face or a sad face.

This is my son, Adam. For breakfast, he likes cereal. He doesn't like strawberries. But he likes eggs and toast. He doesn't like peaches. He doesn't really like fruit. I heard that, Mom. I do like fruit. I like bananas. What about avocados? Ugh. I don't like avocados!

12 Listen and read. Then underline the unhealthy food items.

My name's Millie. I eat healthy food every day. For breakfast, I have fruit juice and cereal. For lunch, I have a sandwich. I don't like burgers. I like rice, green vegetables, and carrots. For dinner, I eat chicken and salad, but sometimes I have pizza and fries. I eat fruit every day, but I like candy, too!

19 Listen and connect the letters. Then write.

1 k i s kiss
2 w e b web
3 sh ar k shark
4 g ir l girl

20 Listen and write the words.

1 brown
2 drop
3 green
4 press

Unit 8

1 Listen and number.

1 I'm eating an orange.
2 I'm drinking juice.
3 I'm sleeping on the chair.
4 I'm reading.
5 I'm cleaning.
6 I'm listening to music.
7 I'm doing homework.
8 I'm walking.
9 We're dancing.

3 Listen and match.

Look! Kim's reading a book. What's Katy doing? She's listening to music. And the PRODs?
What're they doing? They're drinking juice. And Captain Conrad's cleaning his shoes. What's the trickster doing? He's climbing a tree.

5 Listen and check.

1 Are you playing the flute? Yes, I am. I love it!
2 Is he playing the violin? No, he isn't. He's playing the piano. He's very good. Yes, he is.
3 Is he playing the violin terribly? Yes, he is. Oh, no!
4 Is she playing the trumpet quickly? No, she isn't. She's playing the trumpet slowly. It sounds sad! Yes, but it's beautiful.
5 Is he singing quietly? No, he isn't. He's singing loudly.

7 Listen and write.

Hi, Jason! I'm in Thailand, and it's very hot! I'm eating ice cream by the swimming pool. My sister's swimming slowly, and Mom's reading quietly. My dad's listening to music and singing loudly, but he's funny. I'm having fun! See you soon! Adam

13 Listen, draw, and color.

This is a hot-air balloon. It's very big and very colorful. It's yellow, and it has red spots. A pilot and his dog are flying the balloon. It can fly very slowly. This is a rocket. It's gray. It has three wings and two windows. It can fly very quickly.

16 Listen and connect the letters. Then write.

1 kw i z quiz
2 y e s yes
3 b u z buzz
4 d ow n down

17 Listen and write the words.

1 ask
2 left
3 nest
4 wisp

Goodbye

5 Listen and check. Then write.

This is my pet parrot. Its name is Pauli. It has colorful feathers and a sharp beak. It has two strong wings. It has sharp claws. Be careful!

Workbook Answer Key

Welcome

page 4, Activity 1

1 b **2** d **3** a **4** f **5** c **6** e

page 5, Activity 3

1 38 **2** 50 **3** 46 **4** 21 **5** 99 **6** 72 **7** 65
8 84 **9** 23 **10** 37

page 5, Activity 4

1 thirty-three **2** eighty-five **3** forty
4 twenty-nine **5** sixty-one

page 5, Activity 5

a 33 **b** 39 **c** 25, 30 **d** 40, 50
e 29, 34 **f** 22, 24

page 6, Activity 6

1 Wednesday, c **2** Friday, d **3** Saturday, a
4 Thursday, e **5** Sunday, b

page 6, Activity 7

What's your, favorite day (suggested answer: Friday)

page 7, Activity 8

1 March **2** September **3** November **4** June
5 January

page 7, Activity 9

1 September **2** I wasn't, was born in March

page 7, Activity 10

(Suggested answers: Ben July He 10)

Unit 1, Nature

page 9, Activity 2

blue birds, brown rock, pink insects, gray cloud, brown and green trees, blue pond, three yellow flowers, five brown mushrooms, sun

page 9, Activity 3

1 one blue pond **2** three yellow flowers
3 There is one; rock **4** There are two; birds
5 There are four pink insects. **6** There is one gray cloud.
7 There is one blue mushroom and one yellow mushroom.

page 10, Activity 4

1 wind **2** sky **3** rainbow **4** butterflies **5** roses
6 spiders **7** worms **8** ants

page 10, Activity 5

1 are six **2** is one **3** are five **4** are three
5 There are six roses. **6** There are four trees.
7 There are six spiders.

page 11, Activity 6

colored drawing of scene described in audio

page 11, Activity 7

1 b **2** a **3** b **4** a

page 11, Activity 8

1 How many spiders are there?
2 There are seven spiders. **3** Are there any ants?
4 No, there aren't.

page 12, Activity 9

2 Yes **3** Yes **4** No **5** No **6** No

page 12, Activity 10

a 2 **b** 1 **c** 4 **d** 6 **e** 3 **f** 5

page 13, Activity 11

1 Yes, she does. **2** No, she doesn't.
3 No, she doesn't. **4** No, she doesn't.
5 Yes, she does. **6** No, she doesn't.

page 13, Activity 12

1 ✗ **2** ✓ **3** ✗ **4** ✓ **5** ✗ **6** ✗

page 13, Activity 13

1 not safe, streets **2** safe, friends
3 not safe, hot sun **4** safe, playground
5 not safe, night **6** not safe, yourself

page 14, Activity 14

2 three mushrooms **3** three clouds **4** four flowers

page 14, Activity 15

1 butterfly **2** 20

page 14, Activity 16

a 2 **b** 7 **c** 1 **d** 5

page 15, Activity 17

Circle: chair, hair, pair of socks, tear

page 15, Activity 18

1 tap **2** rich **3** sat **4** shell

page 15, Activity 19

1 fair **2** year **3** near **4** hear

page 16, Activity 21

1 trees **2** clouds **3** flowers **4** birds
5 insects **6** mushrooms **7** rock **8** pond

page 16, Activity 22

(Suggested answers) **1** There is a tree. **2** There is a sun. **3** There is a rock. **4** There are some flowers. **5** There are some birds. **6** There are some insects.

page 17, Activity 23

Student's own answers

Unit 2, Me

page 18, Activity 1

Match the following:
Grandfather – white mustache – small glasses – short beard – green eyes – gray hair
Mom – blond hair – blue eyes
Peter – blue eyes – red hair

page 18, Activity 2

1 beard, white **2** hair **3** has, red
4 has, eyes **5** eyes

page 19, Activity 3

Student's own answers

page 19, Activity 4

David: **1** He has **2** He has **3** He has
4 He doesn't have
Nina: **1** She doesn't have **2** She has
3 She doesn't have **4** She has

page 20, Activity 5

a 4 b 3 c 2 d 1

page 20, Activity 6

1 she, black beard, Yes, she does. **2** she, long eyelashes, Yes, she does. **3** he, beard, No, he doesn't. **4** he, a big chin, Yes, he does.

page 20, Activity 7

Student's own answers

page 21, Activity 8

Picture 2: curly, eyelashes, teeth

page 21, Activity 9

1 No, she doesn't. **2** No, she doesn't.
3 Yes, she does. **4** No, she doesn't.
5 No, she doesn't.

page 21, Activity 10

Student's own answers

page 22, Activity 11

a 4 b 1 c 2 d 3

page 22, Activity 12

a 4 b 1 c 3 d 6 e 5 f 2

page 22, Activity 13

1 glasses **2** dark hair **3** She has spots.
4 She doesn't have a beard. **5** She has long hair.
6 She has blond hair.

page 23, Activity 14

1 ✓ **2** ✓ **3** ✗ **4** ✓ **5** ✗ **6** ✓

page 23, Activity 15

a 3 b 5 c 4 d 1 e 2 f 6

page 23, Activity 16

1 c **2** a **3** b

page 24, Activity 17

1 big ears, big feet, long tail **2** long eyelashes, long neck, wings **3** long body, small eyes, small head

page 24, Activity 18

Student's own answers

page 25, Activity 19

Circle: dinner, letter, girl playing, speech bubble

page 25, Activity 20

(words) **1** dad **2** sit **3** path **4** this

page 25, Activity 21

1 day **2** way **3** hammer **4** summer

page 26, Activity 23

Circle: **1** hair **2** eyebrows **3** teeth **4** glasses
5 nose **6** beard **7** mustache **8** neck

page 26, Activity 24

1 beard, mustache; **2** She has, curly, lips;
3 He has, chin, teeth; **4** He has, nose, hair, mouth

page 27, Activity 25

1 Yes, she does. **2** Yes, he does. **3** No, he doesn't.
4 Yes, she does. **5** No, she doesn't. **6** No, he doesn't.

Unit 3, Pets

page 28, Activity 1

1 feathers **2** paws **3** beak **4** fins **5** claws
6 wings **7** fur **8** tail

page 28, Activity 2

1 rabbit **2** whiskers **3** snake **4** skin **5** dog
6 paws **7** parrot **8** wing

page 29, Activity 3

1 It has, It doesn't have **2** It has, It doesn't have
3 They have, They don't have

page 29, Activity 4

(Suggested answers) **1** tail, fur **2** wings, beak
3 feathers **4** fur **5** legs **6** skin, a tail **7** fins

page 30, Activity 5

1 hard shell **2** a long tail **3** sharp claws
4 white paws

page 30, Activity 6

1 c **2** d **3** a **4** b

page 31, Activity 7

Circle: rabbit, Lily, three years old, four legs, fruit
1 rabbit **2** Lily **3** three **4** four **5** fruit

page 31, Activity 8

1 does it **2** No **3** doesn't **4** Does it have
5 No **6** doesn't **7** fur **8** Yes
9 does **10** What **11** rabbit

page 32, Activity 9

1 Yes, No, Yes, No **2** Yes, Yes, Yes, No
3 Yes, Yes, Yes, Yes

page 32, Activity 10

1 fur, tail, teeth, isn't **2** big, spots, isn't
3 fur, long, It is

page 33, Activity 11

1 turtle **2** feed **3** water **4** clean **5** exercise
6 vet

page 33, Activity 12

1 S **2** D **3** D **4** W **5** W **6** D

page 34, Activity 13

a 3 **b** 1 **c** 2 **d** 4
1 eggs **2** are caterpillars **3** there are cocoons
4 there are butterflies

page 34, Activity 14

1 eggs **2** small tadpoles **3** big tadpoles **4** frogs

page 34, Activity 15

1 Yes, they do. **2** Yes, they do. **3** No, they don't.
4 Yes, they do.

page 35, Activity 16

Circle: coin, eat, leaf, tea

page 35, Activity 17

(words) **1** cap **2** dig **3** ring **4** ink

page 35, Activity 18

1 peach **2** oil **3** foil **4** join

page 36, Activity 20

1 whiskers **2** wings **3** fur **4** tail **5** claws
6 skin **7** fins **8** feathers **9** paws **10** beak

page 36, Activity 21

Check the following: 1 hamster: fast, soft fur
2 turtle: slow, hard shell **3** frog: fast, green skin

page 36, Activity 22

1 fast, soft fur **2** slow, It has a hard shell.
3 is fast, It has green skin.

page 37, Activity 23–25

Student's own answers

Unit 4, Home

page 38, Activity 2

1 below **2** behind **3** in front of **4** above
5 next to

page 39, Activity 3

1 Yes **2** No **3** No **4** Yes **5** No **6** Yes
7 Yes

page 39, Activity 4

Items drawn in to match description

page 40, Activity 5

1 pot **2** pans **3** stove **4** table
5 blankets **6** computer

page 40, Activity 6

1 Yes, it is. **2** No, they aren't. **3** Yes, it is.
4 Yes, it is. **5** No, it isn't. **6** No, it isn't.

page 41, Activity 7

1 Yes, it is. **2** No, it isn't. It's under the bed.
3 No, it isn't. It's in front of the sofa.
4 Is the hamster, plant **5** Is the hamster, chair
6 No, it isn't. It's next to the computer.

page 41, Activity 8

a 3 **b** 5 **c** 1 **d** 2 **e** 6 **f** 4

page 42, Activity 9

a plant **b** kitchen **c** have **d** has
a 3 **b** 4 **c** 1 **d** 2

page 42, Activity 10

1 on **2** above **3** in front of **4** below

page 43, Activity 11

Student's own answers

page 43, Activity 12

Student's own answers

page 44, Activity 13

Color to show the frog

page 44, Activity 14

1 square **2** rectangle **3** circle **4** triangle

page 44, Activity 15

tiles stones glass

page 45, Activity 16

Circle: bone, cake, home, clock

page 45, Activity 17

(words) **1** kick **2** tail **3** kid **4** feet

page 45, Activity 18

1 wave **2** shape **3** dive **4** like **5** note

page 46, Activity 20

1 computer **2** closet **3** window **4** shelf
5 comb **6** toothbrush **7** plates **8** towels
9 blankets **10** pans

page 46, Activity 21

Draw: ***a*** 2 pictures above the bed ***b*** trash can next to the sink ***c*** plant next to the TV

Write: **1** towels, next to **2** pictures
3 No, there isn't. **4** No, there isn't.
5 blankets, in front of **6** Yes, there is.

page 47, Activity 22

Student's own answers

page 47, Activity 23

Student's own answers

page 47, Activity 24

Student's own answers

Unit 5, Clothes

page 48, Activity 1

1 g **2** i **3** e **4** b **5** d **6** f **7** c **8** h **9** a
10 j **11** k **12** l **13** m

page 48, Activity 2

1 sandals, belt **2** sweatshirt, baseball cap

page 49, Activity 3

Students draw: baseball cap, polo shirt, shorts, sandals

page 49, Activity 4

1 baseball cap, polo shirt, shorts, sandals **2** No, isn't
3 Yes, is

page 50, Activity 5

1 beanie (green) **2** wool sweater (colorful)
3 hiking boots (brown) **4** scarf (red)
5 ski jacket (pink) **6** tights (blue and red)
7 shoes (black)

page 50, Activity 6

1 he, colorful, he is **2** She, fancy **3** He, plain

page 51, Activity 7

Check: sneakers, shirt, glasses, baseball cap, belt, jeans
1 Yes, she is. **2** No, she isn't. **3** No, she isn't.
4 Yes, she is.

page 51, Activity 8

1 love **2** my favorite **3** These are **4** This is

page 51, Activity 9

Student's own answers

page 52, Activity 10

1 He has the tifftiff plant. **2** Look at the red shirt!
3 There! Behind the jeans! **4** PROD 2 is wearing a dress.

page 52, Activity 11

2 Yes, he is. **3** Yes, she is **4** No, he isn't

page 53, Activity 12

1 Excuse me **2** Please **3** Thank you., You're welcome. **4** I'm sorry **5** Have a nice day!

page 54, Activity 13

1 set the table **2** wash the dishes/car **3** make the bed **4** wash the car/dishes **5** clean my bedroom

page 54, Activity 14

a 2 or 4 **b** 5 **c** 3 **d** 2 or 4 **e** 1

page 55, Activity 15

Circle: scarf, skate, spoon, star

page 55, Activity 16

(words) **1** hat **2** cup **3** light **4** coat

page 55, Activity 17

1 smell **2** snip **3** squid **4** swim

page 56, Activity 19

Circle: shorts, sweatsuit, baseball cap, belt, sweatshirt, uniform, polo shirt, sandals, flip flops, scarf, beanie, ski jacket, wool sweater, tights

page 56, Activity 20

1 No, he isn't. He's wearing hiking boots. **2** Is he wearing a T-shirt? **3** No, he isn't. He's wearing shorts. **4** Is he wearing a baseball cap?

page 57, Activity 21–23

Student's own answers

Unit 6, Sports

page 58, Activity 1

a 7 **b** 6 **c** 4 **d** 2 **e** 3 **f** 5 **g** 8 **h** 1

page 58, Activity 2

Student's own answers

page 59, Activity 3

Jake: ✗ tennis, ✓ soccer
Beth: ✓ tennis, ✗ soccer
Max: ✗ bike, ✓ soccer
Paul: ✗ baseball, ✓ climb
Gina: ✓ run, ✗ climb

page 59, Activity 4

1 play soccer, ride a bike **2** play tennis, play soccer **3** He can climb, play baseball **4** play tennis, he can't **5** Can she run, she can

page 60, Activity 5

1 b **2** e **3** c **4** a **5** f **6** d

page 60, Activity 6

Check: 1 stadium; **2** gym; **3** ski slope

page 60, Activity 7

1 wasn't, was **2** was, wasn't **3** was, wasn't

page 61, Activity 8

1 ✓ **2** ✓ **3** ✗ **4** ✓ **5** ✓ **6** ✗ **7** ✓ **8** ✗

page 61, Activity 9

1 and **2** but **3** and **4** but **5** but

page 61, Activity 10

1 was, running track **2** wasn't, was, baseball field **3** wasn't at the, was at the beach **4** He wasn't at the, He was at the gym **5** He wasn't at the, He was at the soccer field

page 62, Activity 11

PROD 1: can play basketball, can swim, can't run fast, can't fly
PROD 2: can play tennis, can ride a bike, can catch

page 62, Activity 12

Student's own answers

page 63, Activity 13

6 – play sports **3** – do taekwondo; **1** – go for a walk **5** – ride my bike **4** – run **2** – do push-ups

page 63, Activity 14

Student's own answers

page 64, Activity 15

a 3 **b** 2 **c** 5 **d** 4 **e** 1

page 64, Activity 16–17

Student's own answers

page 65, Activity 18

Circle: flag, glass, sleep, slip

page 65, Activity 19
Answer Key

(words) **1** puff **2** bell **3** food **4** book

page 65, Activity 20

1 black **2** plum **3** float **4** plate

page 66, Activity 22

1 ✗, ✓ **2** ✓, ✗ **3** ✓, ✗ **4** ✗, ✓

page 66, Activity 23

2 She can play tennis, but she can't play basketball. **3** do taekwondo, climb a tree, He can do taekwondo, but he can't climb a tree. **4** catch a ball and play soccer, She can't catch a ball, but she can play soccer.

page 67, Activity 24–26

Student's own answers

Unit 7, Food

page 68, Activity 1

1 d **2** f **3** e **4** a **5** c **6** b **7** j **8** i **9** h **10** g

page 68, Activity 2

Student's own answers

page 69, Activity 3

1 ✓ **2** ✗ **3** ✗ **4** ✓ **5** ✗

page 69, Activity 4

2 like, Yes, she does. **3** Does, like, No, she doesn't. **4** Does, like **5** Does he like, No, he doesn't

page 70, Activity 5

Tim's house: N, N, Y, Y, Y, Y, Y, Y, N, Y, Y, Y, Y, N
Liz's house: Y, N, N, N, Y, N, N, Y, Y, Y, N, Y, Y, Y

page 70, Activity 6

Tim's house: **1** No, there aren't. **2** Yes, there are. **3** Yes, there is. **4** Yes, there is.
Liz's house: **1** Yes, there are. **2** No, there aren't. **3** Yes, there is. **4** Yes, there is.

page 71, Activity 7

1 happy **2** sad **3** happy **4** sad **5** happy **6** sad

page 71, Activity 8

2 No, he doesn't. **3** Yes, he does. **4** No, he doesn't. **5** Does he like **6** Does he like

page 71, Activity 9

Student's own answers

page 72, Activity 10

1 strawberries **2** don't **3** love **4** doesn't

page 72, Activity 11

Student's own answer

page 73, Activity 12

underline: burgers, pizza, fries, candy

page 73, Activity 13–14

Student's own answers

page 74, Activity 15

a 5, 7 **b** 1, 8 **c** 2, 9 **d** 3, 6, 10 **e** 4

page 74, Activity 16

Student's own answers

page 74, Activity 17

Student's own answers

page 75, Activity 18

Circle: crab, frog, string, train

page 75, Activity 19

(words) **1** kiss **2** web **3** shark **4** girl

page 75, Activity 20

1 brown **2** drop **3** green **4** press

page 76, Activity 22

1 tomatoes **2** plums **3** cabbage **4** lettuce **5** potatoes **6** carrots **7** peas **8** pears

page 76, Activity 23

1 Yes, he does. **2** Does he like, No, he doesn't. **3** No, she doesn't. **4** Does she like, Yes, she does.

page 77, Activity 24–25

Student's own answers

Unit 8, Things we do

page 78, Activity 1

1 e **2** h **3** d **4** c **5** a **6** g **7** f **8** i **9** b

page 78, Activity 2

a He's cleaning. **b** They're dancing. **d** He's sleeping. **f** She's doing homework. **h** She's drinking. **i** He's walking.

page 79, Activity 3

1 reading a book, b **2** listening to music, c
3 drinking juice, a **4** cleaning his shoes, e
5 climbing a tree, d

page 79, Activity 4

1 cleaning my shoes **2** He's reading a book.
3 What are you doing **4** They're drinking juice.
5 climbing a tree

page 80, Activity 5

1 Jenny **2** Ken **3** John **4** Kelly **5** Pete

page 80, Activity 6

1 playing the piano **2** playing the violin **3** playing the violin **4** No, I'm not. I'm playing the trumpet quickly. **5** No, he isn't. He's singing loudly.

page 81, Activity 7

1 eating **2** slowly **3** quietly **4** listening
5 loudly

page 81, Activity 8

1 Is he, he isn't, He's reading. **2** he playing the piano, he is **3** she walking, she isn't, She's walking quickly.

page 82, Activity 9

1 doing, She's **2** he doing, quickly **3** are they

page 82, Activity 10

1 flying **2** going **3** reading **4** listening **5** are

page 83, Activity 11

1 sing **2** teacher **3** favorite **4** cookies
5 cleaning **6** violin **7** birthday

page 83, Activity 12

Student's own answers

page 84, Activity 13

hot-air balloon: big, yellow, red spots, a dog
rocket: gray, three wings, two windows

page 84, Activity 14

1 flying **2** quickly **3** wings **4** pilot
5 windows **6** airplane

page 85, Activity 15

Circle: bump hand paint wind

page 85, Activity 16

(words) **1** quiz **2** yes **3** buzz **4** down

page 85, Activity 17

1 ask **2** left **3** nest **4** wisp

page 86, Activity 19

2 reading **3** eating **4** drinking
5 cleaning (secret word) sleeping

page 86, Activity 20

2 I'm singing. **3** I'm doing homework.
4 I'm listening to music.

page 87, Activity 21

1 He's playing the trumpet. **2** They're dancing.
3 She's playing the flute. **4** They're singing.
5 He's playing the violin. **6** She's playing the piano.

Goodbye

page 88, Activity 1

1 in **2** next to **3** behind **4** on **5** below
6 behind **7** above **8** in front of

page 89, Activity 2

a 3 **b** 1 **c** 2 **d** 5 **e** 4 **f** 6

page 89, Activity 3

Student's own answers

page 90, Activity 4

(Possible answers) a pond. There's a rainbow. There's some wind. birds, and animals. There are some clouds and butterflies. There are three mushrooms. There are two trees. There are some ants on the tree. There are some worms on the roses.

page 90, Activity 5

Check the parrot.
1 parrot **2** feathers **3** beak **4** wings **5** claws

page 90, Activity 6

Student's own answers

page 91, Activity 7

Student's own answers

page 91, Activity 8

1 drinking **2** sleeping **3** cleaning **4** climbing

page 91, Activity 9

Student's own answers

Assessment

Two types of assessment

1 Assessment *for* learning
2 Assessment *of* learning
There are many activities and techniques throughout the *Poptropica English* Teacher's Edition which will help you assess where your students are in their learning.
There is a wide range of tests to be used after each unit, to review multiple units, and at the end of the level. However, any test can be used either as an **assessment *for* learning** or **assessment *of* learning**. Using tests as an **assessment *of* learning**, usually takes place after the learning, and this provides information about what the student is achieving by giving a grade. You can also use tests as an **assessment *for* learning**, providing specific feedback on students' strengths and weaknesses as part of the continuing learning process. It is a combination of both types of assessment which can provide powerful tools for helping students on their learning adventure.

Placement Tests

There are two *Poptropica English* Placement Tests. These will help you grade students and place them into the appropriate level of *Poptropica English*.
Placement Test A can be found in Teacher's Editions 1–3. It covers the language from Levels 1–3.
Placement Test B can be found in Teacher's Editions 4–6. It covers the language from Levels 4–6.

Choosing the appropriate test

When choosing a test, try to find out if the student has studied English before, and to what level. Use this information to decide whether the student would fit better into a lower-level class or upper-level class. Give Placement Test A to students better suited to a lower-level class, and Placement Test B to students better suited to an upper-level class. If in doubt, have the student start with Placement Test A, and if necessary continue the assessment with Placement Test B.

Procedure

- Make a copy of the test pages, and complete the student's name and the date at the top of the page.
- Begin with the speaking part. Prepare the relevant Picture Cards.
- Give the rest of the Placement Test to the student. Play the audio for the student to complete the listening part.
- Allow student 20 minutes to complete the test.
- Check the answers against the Answer Key on page 179 for Placement Test A.

Placement Test A
10 points or below: Place in a Level 1 class.
11–40 points: Place in a Level 2 class.
41–80 points: Place in a Level 3 class.
81 points or above: Give Placement Test B.
Placement Test B
10 points or below: Give Placement Test A.
11–40 points: Place in a Level 4 class.
41–80 points: Place in a Level 5 class.
81 points or above: Assign to a Level 6 class.

Unit Tests

There are eight Unit Tests in each level of *Poptropica English*. These test the learning objectives from each unit. Have students take the Unit Test after studying each of the eight core units.

Review Tests

There are four Review Tests in each level of *Poptropica English*, covering Units 1–2, 3–4, 5–6, and 7–8. These can be given after completion of every two units in the Student Book.

End of Level Test

There is an End of Level Test in each level of *Poptropica English*, covering Units 1–8. This should be used in combination with ongoing assessment in class.

Exam preparation

For students taking the Cambridge Young Learner Exams, there are some exam-style activities in the Review Tests.

Procedure

- Copy the test for students, and have them write their name.
- Play the audio, and have students complete the listening activities. Then set students a time limit within which to complete the remainder of the test.
- When handing tests back to students, go through the answers and explain any errors.

Tests Script

Placement Test A

B C:29 **Listen and number.**

1 Hello. What's your name? My name's Tina. How old are you? I'm eleven.
2 Hello. What's your name? My name's Gary. How old are you? I'm nine.
3 Hello. What's your name? Don. I'm Don. How old are you, Don? I'm seven.
4 What's your name? It's David. My name's David. How old are you? I'm eight.
5 Hello. What's your name? It's Kelly. How old are you? I'm twelve.

C C:30 **Listen and circle.**

1 How old is your dog, Ben? He's one. Is he a puppy? Yes, he is.
2 Where's Andy? Erm. I don't know. Is he in the kitchen? No, he isn't. Ah! He's in the dining room.
3 Is this your dog, Joe? Yes, it is. He has a long tail. Yes, he does.
4 Where are my books, Dad? Are they on your bed? No, they're not. Look, they're under the bed! Mary! Sorry, Dad.
5 What a nice parrot, Sam! He is nice. He has red and blue wings, and a tail. That's nice. He's very colorful. Yes, he is.
6 What do you have in your bedroom, Kim? There's a bed, a desk, and a chair. What's on the desk? There's a lamp.
7 Do you have a snake, Jenny? Yes, I do. He's brown and yellow. Brown and white? No, brown and yellow.
8 Where are the kittens, Paul? I think they're on the sofa. No, they aren't. They're under the sofa. Oh!

D C:31 **Listen and match.**

1 What are you wearing today? Today I'm wearing a red skirt.
2 Is that man wearing a blue hat? No, it isn't blue. It's black. He's wearing a black hat.
3 I love the clothes that woman is wearing. She looks really good! Which woman? Oh, the one over there in the pink pants.
4 Are you wearing jeans and a t-shirt today? Yes, it's a bit cold, so I'm wearing my purple sweater on top of my Tshirt.

E C:32 **Listen and check.**

1 Do you want chicken for dinner, Sue? No, I don't like chicken. Burgers for me, please. Not pizza? No, burgers please.
2 Are you looking at the bat, Charlie? No, I'm not. And I'm not looking at the owl. Then you can see the fox! Yes! I can see the fox!
3 Frank do you like toast for breakfast? No, I don't, and I don't like rice. Ah! So do you like coconut for breakfast? Yes, I do!
4 Dad, what's your favorite farm animal? Hmm, well I like cows. Do you like sheep? Not really. No, I think my favorite farm animals are chickens. OK, chickens.
5 Mom, can I have some milk? No I'm sorry, we don't have any milk. Oh. Can I have some raisins? No. I don't have any raisins. But we're having corn for lunch. You like corn. It's your favorite!

F C:33 **Listen. Choose A, B, or C to complete the sentences.**

1 Hi. I'm Helen, and I have a pet. It has two fins and purple spots. It's a fish, and its name is Fishy!
2 In my bedroom there's a bed, and next to it there's a closet. I also have a big mirror. It's in front of the bed, above a plant.
3 Where's my toothbrush? Next to the mirror. There. No, it isn't. Below the towel? Yes! Found it!
4 Why is the broom in your bedroom? I'm cleaning it. I found my comb. Where was it? Inside my closet.
5 I'm drawing a picture of a bird. It's big and it flies very fast. It isn't cute, but it isn't scary either. It has very big wings.
6 My name's Paul, and I have a pet. It has a hard shell. It doesn't have fins or whiskers. Do you know what animal it is?
7 Our dog is quite big and very friendly. He is brown, with black ears and a long, black tail.
8 I can't find my book. It isn't in my bag. I was reading it last night. I think it's on the table next to my bed.

Unit Tests

Unit 1

1 C:34 **Listen. Then circle.**

1 Hi, John. Is Thursday your favorite day? No, it isn't. It's Wednesday. Oh. My favorite day is Friday!
2 Hi, Liz. When were you born? I was born in November. Excuse me? September? No, November. Oh, OK.
3 Look! There are some mushrooms over there! There are five big mushrooms! And...two small mushrooms. Five plus two equals seven mushrooms!
4 Are there any butterflies in the tree? No, there aren't. But there are some worms, and some spiders. Ewww!

2 C:35 Listen and number.

1 There are six butterflies, and a spider in my yard.
2 There are some ants, three spiders, and a long worm in my yard.
3 In my yard, there are some flowers, two black birds, and a pond.
4 In my yard, there's a pond, and a rock. There aren't any flowers.
5 There aren't any flowers. I have two tall trees, and a pond in my yard. There are two big spiders, and a bird.

Unit 2

1 C:36 Listen. Then match.

1 Hi there! I'm Maggie. I have short blonde hair. I have a long neck, and I have glasses.
2 Hi. I'm Bob. I have short black hair, and a mustache. I have glasses too!
3 Hi. I'm Jenny. I have long blonde hair, and a long neck. I don't have glasses.
4 Hi. I'm Pete. I have short hair, and a small nose. I don't have a mustache or a beard.

2 C:37 Listen and circle.

Hello. I'm Hugo. I'm Pete's dad. I have short brown hair. I have green eyes, and long eyelashes. I have a brown mustache. I don't have a beard. I have red and purple glasses.
Hello. I'm Stella. I'm Pete's mom. I have long blonde hair. I have brown eyes, and long eyelashes. I have pink lips, and a small nose. I don't have a big chin.

Unit 3

1 C:38 Listen. Then circle.

1 I have a big dog. She has a long tail, and big soft paws.
2 My pet's called Bip. He has thick skin, and soft fur.
3 Hi. My pet's a black bird. It has black wings and a black beak.
4 I have a pet mouse. It's small, and it has a long tail. It has white whiskers and... Ouch!! Sharp claws!!
5 It lives in the sea. It doesn't have stripes or spots. It has fins, and sharp teeth!
6 I'm Cindy, and I have a parrot. I really like its feathers because they are soft with lots of colors. It doesn't have a long tail, and its beak isn't sharp.

2 C:39 Listen and circle T for True or F for False.

What's your favorite pet, Andy? My favorite pet is my pet parrot. What does it look like? It has different colored feathers – green and yellow; blue and red; orange and purple. Wow! That's amazing. And it has a big yellow beak, and sharp claws. Its claws are yellow. Does it have long wings? Yes, it does, but it can't fly. Its wings are yellow and green. Can it climb? Yes, it can. It can climb trees and on me!! And it can hop, and walk very fast. What's its name? It's called Joey.

Unit 4

1 C:40 Read and circle. Then listen and check.

1 Look! This is my living room. Can you color it for me? Yes, I can. OK. Color the blanket green. All right.
2 Right. Can you see the trash can? Yes. OK. Write "trash" on it, please. Excuse me? Write "trash" on it. I'm writing it now.
3 Now, do you see the plants? Yes. There are two below the window. Can you color one of the plants? OK. I'll color it blue. Great!
4 Can you see the comb? Yes, I can. Can you color it? OK. What color? You choose. Erm ...I'll color it brown.
5 Now, do you want to draw something? Sure! Can you draw a shelf? A shelf, OK. Where? Draw it above the desk. OK. Finished! Well done!

2 C:41 Listen. Then circle.

1 In my living room, there is a picture next to the table.
2 The piano is next to the sofa.
3 There is a trash can in front of the chair.
4 The broom is in the kitchen. It's opposite the cupboard.
5 There's a towel below the sink.

Unit 5

1 C:42 Listen. Then circle.

What are you wearing, Jan? I'm wearing my new brown hiking boots. Do you like them? And look! I'm also wearing my red and white socks. Do you like them? Yes. I like them. But... what are you wearing on your head? Oh, that? That's my new hat. Do you like it? Ummmmm. It's my favorite hat. It's blue and green. And...your shorts? Ah, yes. These are my new colorful shorts. They're red, and purple, and orange. You look like a rainbow!! Thanks, Carol! And this is my new red polo shirt. Oh...I like that. Do you have two? Thank you! No, I don't have two!

2 C:43 Listen. Then write T for True or F for False.

Hi. I'm Rob. I have a soccer match today. I'm wearing my favorite blue soccer shorts, and my favorite green hat. I'm wearing my soccer socks. They're blue and yellow.
Hi. I'm Becky. It's my birthday. I'm wearing my new colorful hat. I have my new pink dress on. It's my favorite dress. And I'm wearing my pink shoes.
It's sports day at school today. I'm wearing a plain green shirt. I have my blue and white shorts in my backpack. They aren't my favorite shorts, but Mom likes them. And I'm wearing my new white sneakers.
It's cold today. I want to play in the snow. I'm wearing a woolly jumper. I have my red scarf and hat. They're in my bag. And I'm wearing my new leather boots. They're great!

Unit 6

1 C:44 Listen. Then check.

1 He wasn't at the baseball field. He was at the basketball court.
2 He wasn't at the ski slope. He was at the gym.
3 She wasn't at the running track. She was at the stadium.
4 She wasn't at the soccer field. She was at the swimming pool.

2 C:45 Listen. Then circle.

1 I can play tennis. My friend, Sue, can't.
2 I can't climb trees, but Sue can. She's very fast.
3 I can't catch a ball. Sue can't catch a ball.
4 Sue can jump. I can't jump.
5 I can't play basketball. Sue can't play basketball. But we play tennis.

Unit 7

1 C:46 Read. Listen and circle T = True or F = False.

Good morning, Jack. What's that? Yogurt with strawberries and a pear. It's my breakfast. That's very healthy. Yes! I like fruit and vegetables. What's your favorite vegetable? That's a difficult question! I like peas, lettuce, and spinach. And your favorite fruit? I really like cherries and plums. I like cherries too, but I don't like plums. So, what do you eat for lunch? I have bread and cheese. Sometimes I have pizza or fries! Yum! For dinner, I eat a salad and an egg. I'm not very hungry at night. OK, Jack.

2 C:47 Listen. Then match.

1 How many oranges do you want? I want five oranges, please. Here you are.
2 How many apricots do you want? I want six, please. Yes. Here you are.
3 Are there any plums? Yes, there are. And is there any broccoli? Yes, there is.
4 What do you want Jenny? Are there any mangoes? Yes, there are lots of mangoes. How many do you want? I want six mangoes, please. Yes. Here you are.

Unit 8

1 C:48 Listen. Then check.

1 What are you doing? I'm sleeping.
2 What are they doing? They are eating pizza.
3 What are you doing? I'm playing the piano.
4 What is she doing? She's washing the car.
5 What are you doing? I'm dancing to the music.
6 What is he doing? He's playing on his computer.

2 C:49 Listen. Then write.

1 Ben is late! He is walking to school quickly.
2 Sam is singing his favorite song. He's singing loudly.
3 Sue is playing the flute. She is playing slowly.
4 Kate is doing her homework slowly. It's difficult.

Review Tests

Review Test 1

1 C:50 Listen. Then color and draw.

1 Can you see the boy and his grandpa? Yes, I can. They're walking home from school. The grandpa has a mustache. It's big! Color it gray. OK.
2 Now, can you see the mushroom? Which one? There are two. The mushroom on the rock. Color it red. I can't color all of it! Yes, you can. Do it quickly. All right.
3 Would you like to draw something now? Yes, OK. Draw a spider. A spider! OK. Where? Put it on the rock, next to the mushroom. OK.
4 Right. Now can you see the boy's lips? Yes, I can. Can you color them? OK. What color? You choose. OK. I'll color them pink. Good idea.
5 One last thing now. Can you color one of the butterflies? OK. I'll color the small one. Great! Color it purple. All right. There. I'm done. That's a really nice picture. Well done!

2 Listen. Then circle.

C:51

1 What are you looking at? I'm looking at some insects. Look! They're going up the tree! Are they worms? No. They're ants. Oh, yes! They're very small.
2 Hi! Who's that? He's my son, Jim. He has beautiful eyelashes. They're so long! Yes. He doesn't have curly hair – like you do. No, he doesn't.
3 Look at the butterflies! Yes, there are three butterflies. They're pretty! No, there are four. Look, there's one here. You're right!
4 Is that man over there the English teacher? Yes, it is. He has a short beard and long curly hair. And a mustache! That's right. His name is Mr Bonson.
5 Here. These roses are for you. Thank you! They're so beautiful – two red roses and five pink ones. And an orange rose, here. Oh, yes! They smell really nice.

3 Listen and check.

C:52

1 Where is Mr Brown? I don't know. What does he look like? He has curly hair, a big nose and a small chin. Oh. He is in the library. Thank you!
2 Helen has nice hair. It's long and blond. You have nice hair too. I have short and dark hair. I don't like it. Don't be silly!
3 Look! I have some insects in this box. Can I see? Wow! Two big spiders. Yes. And four ants here. I don't have any worms. Eww...
4 I want to go to the beach! Me too, but it's so cloudy! It's going to rain. Yes, it's so dark outside.
5 Here. These flowers are for you. Thank you! They're so beautiful – and so many colors! Purple, red, pink, orange. But no yellow flowers. You don't like them. That's right!

Review Test 2

1 Listen. Draw lines from the names to the children. There are two names you don't need.

C:53

1 The children are playing. It's a nice picture. Do you know them? Yes, I do. This is Mary. She has a comb. Oh, yes. She's combing her doll's hair. That's right.
2 Who's this boy? He's holding a toy animal. The toy animal with the stripes? No, with the spots. Oh, that's Ben. He loves animals. OK.
3 This is Harry. He's holding some pots and pans. Where? Over there. He's putting them on the shelf. Oh yes. I see him. Is Harry tidy? Yes, very tidy!
4 And who's that girl sitting next to the plant? That's Anna. She has a computer. Is it a real computer? No, it's a toy.

2 Listen. Then circle.

C:54

1 Hi. I'm Helen and I have a pet. It has two fins and purple spots. It's a fish and its name is Fishy!
2 In my bedroom there's a bed and next to it there's a closet. I also have a big mirror. It's in front of the bed, above a plant.
3 Where's my toothbrush? Next to the mirror. There. No, it isn't. Below the towel? Yes! Found it!
4 Why is the broom in your bedroom? I'm cleaning it. I found my comb. Where was it? Inside my closet.
5 I'm drawing a picture of a bird. It's big and it flies very fast. It isn't cute but it isn't scary either. It has very big wings.
6 My name's Paul and I have a pet. It has a hard shell. It doesn't have fins or whiskers. Do you know what animal it is?

Review Test 3

1 Listen. Then match. There's one extra picture.

C:55

1 Monday. Why are you wearing your sweatsuit? Oh. I was at the running track. Can you run fast? Yes, I can.
2 Tuesday. I was at the tennis court. Great! I can play tennis, too. I'm very good. Really? I'm not that good.
3 Wednesday. Hi, Charlie. How are you? Tired! I was at the swimming pool. Oh...can you swim fast? Yes, I can!
4 Thursday. Are you OK, Charlie? You look thirsty. Yes. I'd like some water, please. I was at the beach. Did you swim? No, I went running. Great!
5 Friday. You're late! Sorry, I was at the gym. Really? You exercise every day? Yes, I do. You're really fit, Charlie. Well done!

2 Listen. Then color and draw.

C:56

1 Look. This is my student, Jack. I like his clothes! Can I color them? OK. Can you color his sweatshirt? Yes. Is it plain or colorful? Colorful. It's green, white and purple. Great! There it is. Fantastic!
2 What would you like to color now? His hiking boots. I'll color them gray. Good idea. That's nice.
3 Can I draw something now? Sure. What? I'd like to draw a scarf. Great. Make it green. OK.
4 Now. Color his pants. They're plain. All right. I'll color them orange. I like orange pants. Me too!
5 Can I draw something else? Yes, of course. Draw a bike. A bike?! Yes. Jack rides his bike to school. It's red. OK. Here it is. That's really nice. Well done!

Review Test 4

1 C:57 **Listen. Check the six food items Fred and Sarah need to buy.**

Let's go to the supermarket today, Sarah. We need to buy some food. OK, Fred. Let's look at what we have. We have oranges but there aren't any peaches. Write that down. OK. There aren't any tomatoes or cucumbers. Let's buy some for salad. Good idea. We have eggs but there isn't any bread. OK. Bread. Is there any spinach in the refrigerator? Yes, there is. But there isn't any cabbage or any peas. Good. Let's buy some. I think we're ready. Let's go!

2 C:58 **Listen and check.**

1 Hi, Anna. What are you doing? I'm dancing! But you're not listening to any music. I know. I can dance without music. You're funny!
2 I'm hungry. Let's make some cheese and tomato sandwiches. I'm sorry but there aren't any tomatoes or any bread. Oh, no! Let's have some fruit. Are there any cherries? Yes, there are.
3 Look! That's Sarah and her sister Emma. Are they playing the trumpet? No, they aren't. They're playing the flute. I can play the flute too! Great! I can play the violin. Let's go talk to them.
4 Hello, Peter. Where are the children? They're sleeping. So early? What about dinner? They had dinner – chicken, peas, and juice. OK. I'll talk quietly then.
5 So what shall we put in the salad – lettuce and cucumber? We don't have any lettuce. Can we use spinach? Oh no! Dad hates spinach. We can't use spinach. No, Dad hates broccoli. He loves spinach. Well, I don't like spinach and I don't want to put it in the salad. OK.

3 C:59 **Listen and circle.**

1 Hello, John. What are you doing? Are you playing the piano? No, I'm not because my brother is sleeping. So what are you doing? I'm cleaning my bedroom. It's very dirty.
2 Hi, Mary. I'm drinking orange juice and reading a book. That's nice! What are you doing? I'm playing the violin loudly! Listen! That is loud!
3 Let's make a fruit salad! OK. Are there any strawberries? Yes, there are. And there are oranges and mangoes. There aren't any pears. It's OK. We don't need pears.
4 Fred, do you like carrots? Yes, I do. I like spinach too, but I don't like lettuce. Really? Lettuce is really healthy. It's good for you. I know...but I just don't like it.

End of Level Test

1 C:60 **Listen. Then match.**

1 Are Jane and Jack your cousins? Yes, they are. What do they look like? Well, Jack has big blue eyes, and blond hair. His eyebrows are really dark. And Jane? She has red hair, and brown eyes, and long eyelashes.
2 What food do they like? Does Jack like vegetables? No, he doesn't. Does he like fruit? Yes. He likes mangoes and strawberries. Does Jane like fruit? Yes, she does. She likes peaches and plums.
3 What are they doing? Jane is playing the trumpet. Ah, yes! She's playing the trumpet very loudly! That's Jane! And Jack is playing the flute.
4 Do they like sports? Yes, they do. Jack can run, and kick a ball. He likes soccer. He was at the stadium yesterday. And Jane – does she like sport? Yes, she does. Jane can't run fast, but she can ride her bike fast.

2 C:61 **Listen. Then check.**

1 Do you like potatoes, Sally? Yes, I do. Do you like vegetables? Well, I like broccoli. And what about fruit? Do you like fruit? I like oranges and plums.
2 Does Ian like mangoes? No, he doesn't. Does he like avocado? Yes, he does. Does he like pears and apricots? He likes pears, but he doesn't like apricots.
3 Is Mom setting the table? No, she isn't. She's washing the car.
4 Look! What? Under the window. There's a big spider! Arghh! It's running fast! Look over there... above the roses. Where? Above the roses. There's a beautiful red and brown butterfly.

3 C:62 **Listen. Then write T for True or F for False.**

1 I'm walking in my yard. There's a pond in the yard. It's next to the roses. The roses are beautiful – red, pink, orange, and white.
2 Under the tree there are some mushrooms. You can't eat them. And there are some more flowers behind the tree.
3 Oh, look. There's a beautiful butterfly sitting on a leaf. It's brown and red with black spots. Shhh. I'm walking very slowly and quietly!
4 My mom and dad like gardening. They have spinach, and lettuce, and cabbages. In front of the lettuce they have carrots and potatoes. This is my little vegetable garden. I have some tomatoes and peas.

Tests Answer Key

Placement Test A

B

1 e **2** a **3** b **4** c **5** d

C

1 young **2** dining room **3** long **4** under
5 red and blue **6** lamp **7** red and blue **8** under

D

1 a red skirt **2** a black hat **3** pink pants
4 a purple sweater

E

1 c **2** a **3** b **4** c **5** a

F

1 B **2** A **3** C **4** A **5** C **6** B **7** C **8** B

G

1 F **2** T **3** F **4** T **5** T **6** F **7** T **8** T

H

1 mouse with a long tail **2** three lamps
3 cat under a table **4** black and white rabbit
5 girl reading on a bed **6** tub in a bathroom

I

1 c **2** d **3** g **4** b **5** e **6** a **7** f

Unit Tests

Unit 1

Reading and writing

1 1 is **2** six **3** aren't **4** there **5** Is
2 1 c **2** b **3** e **4** a **5** d
3 1 pond **2** spider **3** ants **4** roses **5** ten
6 rainbow
4 Student's own answers

Listening and speaking

1 1 b **2** c **3** b **4** a
2 1 d **2** e **3** a **4** c **5** b
3 Student's own answers

Unit 2

Reading and writing

1 1 My friend has a small nose. **2** She has curly hair.
3 Does he have a short beard? **4** She doesn't have long eyelashes. **5** Do they have white teeth?
6 We don't have dark eyebrows.
2 Student's own answers
3 1 mustache **2** eyebrows **3** doesn't have
4 curly **5** glasses **6** nose
4 Student's own answers

Listening and speaking

1 1 c **2** d **3** a **4** b
2 1 short **2** green **3** eyelashes **4** brown
5 doesn't have **6** has **7** blond **8** doesn't have
9 pink **10** has
3 Student's own answers

Unit 3

Reading and writing

1 ***rabbit:*** paws, claws, whiskers, fur
bird: feathers, wings, beak, claws
fish: fins
2 1 c **2** b **3** d **4** a
3 1 hard **2** scary **3** smooth **4** soft **5** sharp
6 cute
4 Student's own answers

Listening and speaking

1 **1** c **2** a **3** c **4** b **5** b **6** a
2 **1** T **2** F **3** T **4** F **5** T **6** T
3 Student's own answers

Unit 4

Reading and writing

1 (pictures)
2 **1** No, it isn't. It's below the sink. **2** No, they aren't. They're on the bed. **3** Yes, it is. **4** Yes, it is. **5** No, it isn't. It's above the bed / bathroom sink. **6** Yes, they are.
3 ***bathroom:*** toothbrush, toothpaste, shower, comb
kitchen: cooker, refrigerator, pans, pots, plates
4 Student's own answers

Listening and speaking

1 **1** blanket: green **2** draw a trash can and write "trash" on it **3** one of the plants: blue **4** comb: brown **5** a shelf above the desk
2 **1** next to **2** next to **3** in front of **4** opposite **5** below
3 Student's own answers

Unit 5

Reading and writing

1 ***Summer:*** shorts, flip-flops, sandals, T-shirt
Summer / Winter: belt, school uniform, shoes
Winter: wool sweater, ski jacket, woolly scarf
2 **1** scarf **2** hiking boots **3** tights **4** baseball cap **5** uniform
3 **1** e **2** d **3** g **4** f **5** b **6** a **7** c
4 Student's own answers

Listening and speaking

1 **1** brown **2** red and white **3** hat **4** colorful **5** polo shirt
2 **1** F, T **2** T, F **3** F, F **4** T, T
3 Student's own answers

Unit 6

Reading and writing

1 **1** fast **2** rope **3** baseball **4** ball **5** taekwondo
2 ***Kate:*** ✗, ✗, ✓, ✓, ✓
Ben: ✓, ✗, ✓, ✓, ✗
3 **1** court **2** track **3** field **4** field **5** pool **6** slope
4 Student's own answers

Listening and speaking

1 **1** a **2** b **3** b **4** a
2 **1** can **2** can **3** can't **4** can **5** can't
3 Student's own answers

Unit 7

Reading and writing

1 **1** broccoli **2** avocados **3** lettuce **4** spinach **5** cherries **6** cabbage
2 **1** Do you like plums? **2** Do you like cucumbers? **3** Does your friend like mangoes? **4** Does your teacher like pears?
Student's own answers
3 **1** Is there any cabbage? **2** Yes, there is. **3** Is there a lot of yogurt? **4** No, there isn't. **5** Are there any potatoes? **6** No, there aren't.
4 Student's own answers

Listening and speaking

1 **1** T **2** T **3** F **4** F **5** T
2 **1** b **2** c **3** a **4** d
3 Student's own answers

Unit 8

Reading and writing

1 **1** d **2** a **3** c **4** b **5** e **6** f
2 **1** are, doing, I'm **2** 's / is, doing, He's **3** What are, doing, They're **4** What is / What's, doing, She's
3 **1** homework **2** eat **3** bedroom **4** flute **5** music **6** drink
4 Student's own answers

Listening and speaking

1 **1** sleeping **2** eating pizza **3** playing the piano **4** washing the car **5** dancing to music **6** playing on the computer
2 **1** quickly **2** singing **3** slowly **4** doing her homework
3 Student's own answers

Review Tests

Review Test 1

Reading and writing

1 **1** b **2** e **3** f **4** d **5** a **6** c
2 **1** grow **2** but **3** eat **4** are **5** is **6** has
3 **1** ants **2** wind **3** sky **4** tree **5** hair
6 mustache
4 **Adjectives:** short, dark, curly, big
Nature: worms, pond, sun, roses
Body parts: teeth, eyelashes, eyebrows, mouth
5 Student's own answers
6 Student's own answers

Listening and speaking

1 **1** mustache: gray **2** mushroom on the rock: red
3 a spider on the rock **4** boy's lips: pink
5 small butterfly: purple
2 **1** ants **2** eyelashes **3** four **4** short hair
5 red
3 **1** A **2** A **3** C **4** B **5** B
4 Student's own answers
5 Student's own answers

Review Test 2

Reading and writing

1 **1** c **2** a/d **3** g **4** b **5** e **6** a/d **7** f
2 **1** favorite animals **2** cute **3** fur **4** (soft) fur
3 Student's own drawings
4 **1** No, it isn't. **2** Yes, there are. **3** Students' own answer. **4** Yes, they do. **5** No, it doesn't.
5 Student's own answers
6 Student's own answers

Listening and speaking

1 **1** boy with toy tiger: Ben
2 girl combing doll's hair: Mary
3 boy putting toys on the shelf: Harry
4 girl with toy computer: Anna
2 **1** B **2** A **3** C **4** A **5** C **6** B
3 Student's own answers
4 Student's own answers

Review Test 3

Reading and writing

1 **1** f **2** a **3** e **4** b **5** d **6** c
2 **1** no **2** yes **3** yes **4** no
3 **1** jacket **2** field **3** rides **4** fit
4 **1** sweatsuit **2** uniform **3** sandals **4** belt
5 baseball cap **6** polo shirt
5 Student's own answers
6 Student's own answers

Listening and speaking

1 **1** b **2** f **3** e **4** a **5** c
2 **1** sweatshirt: green, white, purple
2 hiking boots: gray **3** draw a scarf: green
4 pants: orange **5** draw a bike: red
3 Student's own answers
4 Student's own answers

Review Test 4

Reading and writing

1 **1** c **2** f **3** b **4** d **5** e
2 **1** no **2** no **3** yes **4** no
3 **1** broccoli **2** cherries **3** cucumber **4** oranges
5 potatoes **6** plums
4 Student's own answers
5 Student's own answers

Listening and speaking

1 **1** peaches **2** tomatoes **3** cucumbers **4** bread
5 cabbage **6** peas
2 **1** a **2** b **3** b **4** c **5** a
3 **1** cleaning **2** playing the violin **3** pears
4 lettuce
4 Student's own answers
5 Student's own answers

End of Level Test

Reading

1 Student's own drawings
2 **1** c **2** b **3** c **4** a **5** b **6** c

Writing

1 **1** track **2** beanie **3** ski **4** eyelashes **5** hair **6** wash **7** ants **8** like
2 Student's own answers

Listening

1 Jack: blue eyes and blond hair, dark eyebrows, mangoes and strawberries, playing the flute, can run, likes soccer Jane: red hair and brown eyes, long eyelashes, peaches and plums, playing the trumpet, can't run fast, can ride a bike fast
2 **1** potatoes, broccoli, oranges, plums **2** avocados, pears **3** washing the car **4** spider, butterfly
3 **1** T, F **2** F, F **3** T, F **4** T, F

Speaking

1 Students say five things about the pictures and find the five differences.
Five differences in picture two: glass now under the table, now two dogs, girl's dress now black, pen deleted from girl's hand, all rocks deleted.

Placement Test A

Name: ______________________

Score: ___ / 110

A Ask students. (50 marks)

<table>
<tr><th>Questions</th><th>Marks</th><th>Material</th></tr>
<tr><td>1 Is it a...?
Yes, it is. / No, it isn't.</td><td>5 questions –
score out of 5</td><td>Picture Cards of classroom objects from Level 1, or use objects in your classroom</td></tr>
<tr><td>2 What's this?
It's a...</td><td>5 questions –
score out of 5</td><td>Picture Cards of classroom objects from Level 1, or use objects in your classroom</td></tr>
<tr><td>3 How many...are there?
(There's/There are...)</td><td>5 questions –
score out of 5</td><td>Use objects in your classroom – show, or draw three pencils, four desks, etc.</td></tr>
<tr><td colspan="3">Vocabulary for 1–3: book, pen, pencil, ruler, eraser, pencil sharpener, pencil case, backpack, board, desk, classroom, school, numbers (1–10)</td></tr>
<tr><td>4 Who is it?
What's your (mom's/dad's/ friend's) name?</td><td>5 questions –
score out of 5</td><td>Picture Cards of family members from Level 1 or 2, or draw a family tree on the board</td></tr>
<tr><td colspan="3">Vocabulary: mom, dad, brother, sister, grandmother, grandfather, friend, boy, girl, student, teacher</td></tr>
<tr><td>5 Do you like...?
Yes (, I do). / No (, I don't).</td><td>5 questions –
score out of 5</td><td>Picture Cards of food from Level 1–3, or draw food items on the board</td></tr>
<tr><td colspan="3">Vocabulary: salad, cheese, bread, meat, vegetables, milk, juice, fish, honey, soda, yogurt, water, chocolate, jello, cake, ice cream, carrots, oranges, apples, tomatoes, eggs, etc.</td></tr>
<tr><td>6 Do you have...?
Yes (, I do). / No (, I don't).</td><td>5 questions –
score out of 5</td><td>Picture Cards of animals from Level 1–3, or draw animals on the board</td></tr>
<tr><td colspan="3">Vocabulary: dog, cat, fish, bird, cow, sheep, horse, pig, duck, rabbit, mouse, snake, owl, fox, etc.</td></tr>
<tr><td>7 Does he/she have...?
Yes (, he/she does). /
No (, he she doesn't).</td><td>5 questions –
score out of 5</td><td>Picture Cards of parts of the body from Level 1–3, or draw figures on the board</td></tr>
<tr><td colspan="3">Vocabulary: head, hands, arms, feet, legs, fingers, toes, neck, knee eyes, ears, nose, mouth, hair; curly, straight, dark, blond, neat, messy, red, etc.</td></tr>
<tr><td>8 What's he/she wearing?
What are you wearing?
I'm/He's/She's wearing...</td><td>5 questions –
score out of 5</td><td>Picture Cards of clothes from Level 1–3, draw food items on the board</td></tr>
<tr><td colspan="3">Vocabulary: skirt, shirt, pants, sneakers, socks, sweater, hat, coat, belt, boots, t-shirt, jacket</td></tr>
<tr><td>9 Where's/What's this?
It's a/the...</td><td>5 questions –
score out of 5</td><td>Picture Cards of house items from Level 1–3, or draw food items on the board</td></tr>
<tr><td colspan="3">Vocabulary: house, yard, living room, kitchen, bedroom, bathroom, dining room, window, door; bed, stove, refrigerator, TV, sofa, lamp, tub, sink</td></tr>
<tr><td>10 Can you/he/she...?
Yes (, I/he/she can). /
No (, I/he/she can't)
What are/is you/he/she doing?</td><td>5 questions –
score out of 5</td><td>Picture Cards of activities from Level 1–3, or draw figures on the board</td></tr>
<tr><td colspan="3">Vocabulary: clap, stamp, snap, wiggle, touch your..., stand on your head, sit down, jump, swim, dance, climb, swing, read, write, play</td></tr>
</table>

Placement Test A

B Listen and number. (10 marks)

C:29

a

Gary – nine ☐

b

Don – seven ☐

c

David – eight ☐

d

Kelly – twelve ☐

e

Tina – eleven ☐

C Listen and circle. (8 marks)

C:30

1 Ben has (an old / a young) dog.

2 Andy is in the (kitchen / dining room).

3 Joe has a dog with a (long / short) tail.

4 Mary's books are (on / under) the bed.

5 Sam's parrot is (red and blue / red and green).

6 There's a (lamp / picture) on the desk.

7 Jenny's snake is (brown and yellow / brown and white).

8 The two kittens are (on / under) the sofa.

Placement Test A

D C:31 **Listen. Then match. (8 marks)**

1		blue	dress.	**2**		black	T-shirt.
	She has a	red	T-shirt.		He has a	yellow	sweater.
		brown	skirt.			white	hat.
3		green	pants.	**4**		purple	shoe.
	She has	pink	socks.		He has a	black	dress.
		red	shoes.			orange	sweater.

E C:32 **Listen and check (✓). (5 marks)**

1 What does Sue like for dinner?

2 What animal can Charlie see?

a

☐

b

☐

c

☐

3 What is Frank eating for breakfast?

a

☐

b

☐

c

☐

4 What is Dad's favorite animal?

a

☐

b

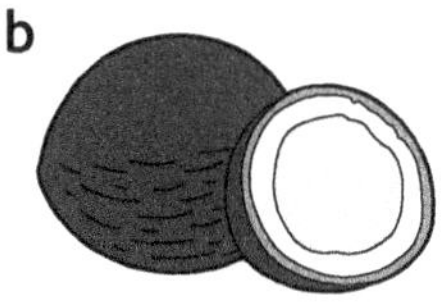

☐

c

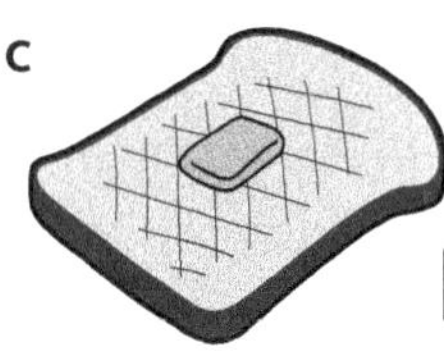

☐

5 What's for lunch?

a

☐

b

☐

c

☐

a

☐

b

☐

c

☐

Placement Test A

F Listen. Choose A, B, or C to complete the sentences. (8 marks)

C:33

1 Helen's pet doesn't have any ______________.

A spots B whiskers C fins

2 There's a big mirror ______________ the bed.

A in front of B next to C above

3 The toothbrush is below the ______________.

A mirror B blanket C towel

4 Inside the closet, there's a ______________.

A comb B broom C picture

5 The bird is ______________.

A scary B cute C fast

6 Paul's pet is a ______________.

A cat B turtle C fish

7 Our dog is ______________.

A black and white B white and brown C black and brown

8 My book is ______________.

A on the kitchen table B next to my bed C under the table

G Read. Then write T = True or F = False. (8 marks)

Hi. I'm Tony. This is my family. This is my mom. She's an artist. Her name's Fiona. This is my dad. He's a pilot. His name's John. This is my sister. She's thirteen. Her name's Sally. This is my grandmother. Her name's Lily. This is my grandfather. His name's Harry. They have a dog. Its name is Fred.

1 Fred has two sisters. ☐

2 Sally is thirteen. ☐

3 Tony's mom is a dancer. ☐

4 Tony's dad is a pilot. ☐

5 Sally is Tom's sister. ☐

6 John is Harry's dad. ☐

7 Lily is Tony's grandmother. ☐

8 Tony's grandparents have a dog. ☐

Placement Test A

H **Read. Then draw. (6 marks)**

1 What's that?

It's a small mouse. It has a long tail.

2 What are those?

They're lamps. There are three lamps.

3 Where is the cat?

It's under the table.

4 Is your favorite animal a hamster?

No, it's my black and white rabbit.

5 Where's Anne?

She's lying on her bed reading.

6 What's that?

It's a tub. It's in the bathroom.

I **Read. Then match. (7 marks)**

1 Is the computer on the table?
2 Are the plates under the table?
3 Do you and Jack have a dog?
4 What does the cat look like?
5 Does the bird have big claws?
6 Are the bird's wings green?
7 Where are the towels?

a Yes, they are.
b It's very cute.
c No, it isn't.
d No, they aren't.
e No, it doesn't.
f In the closet.
g No, we don't.

1 Nature

Reading and writing

1 Read. Then write. (5 marks)

Is aren't is there six

1 In my garden there ______ a pond.

2 There are ______ rocks.

3 There ______ any spiders.

4 Are ______ any trees?
Yes, there are.

5 ______ there a mushroom?
No, there isn't.

2 Read. Then match. (5 marks)

1 How many rocks are there in the park?
2 Are there any flowers?
3 Is there a pond in the park?
4 Where is the girl?
5 How many animals are there?

a At the museum.
b Yes, there are.
c There are twenty.
d There's one animal.
e Yes, there is.

3 Read. Then write. (6 marks)

roses ants spider rainbow pond ten

I'm in the park. It's very beautiful. There's a blue [1] ______, and some trees. There's also a big rock. On the rock there's a [2] ______. It has eight legs.There are also some [3] ______ on the rock. There are flowers in the park too. My favorite flowers are the [4] ______. There are [5] ______ roses. In the sky there's a beautiful [6] ______. I like it here.

4 Draw an island. Then write. (6 marks)

On my island there's ______
______.
There are ______
and ______
There isn't ______
______.
There aren't ______
______.

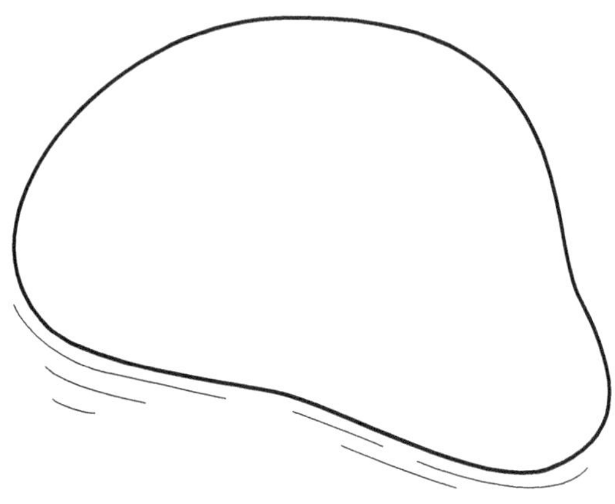

Score: ___ / 22

1 Listen. Then circle. (8 marks)

1 John's favorite day is
  - a Tuesday.
  - b Wednesday.
  - c Thursday.

2 Liz was born in
  - a September.
  - b October.
  - c November.

3 There are ... mushrooms in the park.
  - a five.
  - b seven.
  - c twelve.

4 There aren't any ... in the tree.
  - a butterflies.
  - b spiders.
  - c worms.

2 Listen and number. (5 marks)

a  ☐

b 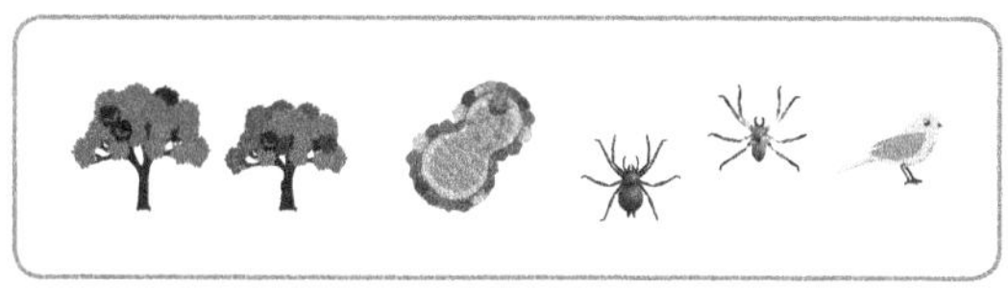 ☐

c 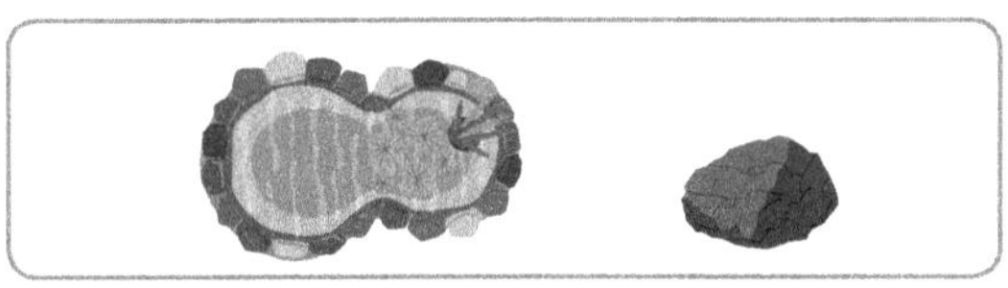 ☐

d  ☐

e 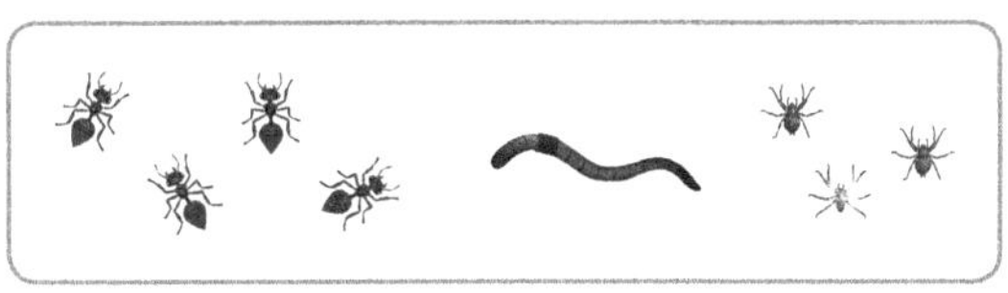 ☐

3 Draw a yard. Then ask and answer. (6 marks)

Where is / are the...?

Is / Are there a(n) / any...?

There is / are...

Score: ___ / 19

Whole test score: ___ / 41

1 Unscramble and write the sentences. (6 marks)

1 friend / nose. / has / small / a / My ____________________

2 has / She / hair. / curly ____________________

3 a / Does / beard? / he / short / have ____________________

4 eyelashes. / have / doesn't / long / She ____________________

5 have / Do / teeth? / they / white ____________________

6 eyebrows. / have / dark / We / don't ____________________

2 Read. Then answer. (5 marks)

1 Do you have long eyelashes? ____________________

2 Does your teacher have glasses? ____________________

3 Do you have brown eyes? ____________________

4 Do you have pink lips? ____________________

5 Does your friend have a beard? ____________________

3 Read. Then circle. (6 marks)

This is my grandfather. His name is Tim. He has a long, white 1 (mustache / beard), and big, white 2 (eyelashes / eyebrows). He 3 (has / doesn't have) much hair, but it's 4 (curly / long). He has small 5 (glasses / eyes) because he can't see very well. He also has a big 6 (nose / mouth).

4 Write about someone in your family. (6 marks)

nose hair eyebrows eyes eyelashes lips chin glasses teeth

My __________ has __________ and ____________________ ____________________.

He/She doesn't have ____________________ ____________________ ____________________.

Score: ___ / 23

1 Listen. Then match. (4 marks)

1 Maggie **2** Bob **3** Jenny **4** Pete

2 Listen and circle. (10 marks)

1 Hugo has (long / short) brown hair.
2 He has (blue / green) eyes.
3 He has long (eyebrows / eyelashes).
4 He has a (brown / black) mustache.
5 He (has / doesn't have) a beard.
6 He (has / doesn't have) glasses.
7 Stella has long (brown / blond) hair.
8 She (has / doesn't have) blue eyes.
9 She has (pink / red) lips.
10 She (has / doesn't have) a small chin.

3 Draw a person. Then talk. (6 marks)

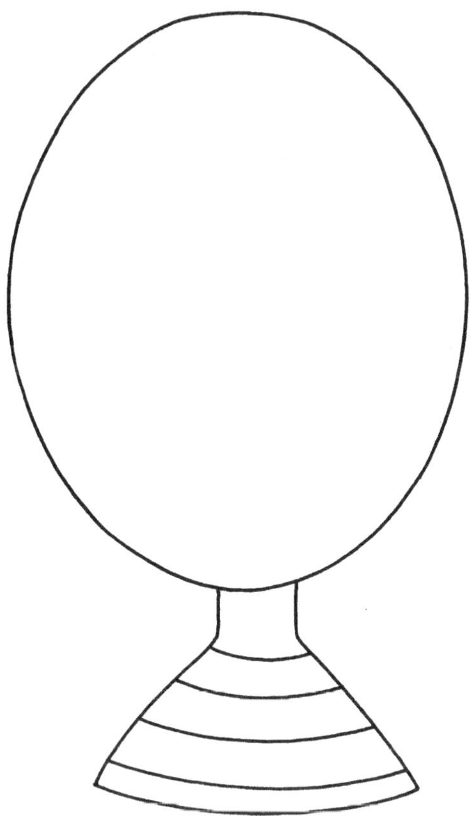

This is...

He / She has...

He / She doesn't have...

Score: ___ / 20

Whole test score: ___ / 43

3 Pets

Reading and writing

1 **Read. Then match. (9 marks)**

paws | fur

beak | whiskers

rabbit | **bird** | **fish**

claws | wings

fins | feathers

2 **Read. Then match. (4 marks)**

1 What does the dog look like?
2 Does it have big paws?
3 What do the rabbits look like?
4 Do they have long claws?

a No, they don't.
b Yes, it does.
c It's big and cute.
d They're cute and they have soft fur.

3 **Read. Then circle. (6 marks)**

1 My turtle has a (hard / slow) shell.
2 Tarantulas are very (scary / sharp).
3 Frogs have (fast / smooth) skin.
4 My rabbit has (hard / soft) black fur.
5 Her bird has (fast / sharp) claws.
6 I like your hamster. He's (scary / cute).

4 **Write about an animal. (6 marks)**

skin fur whiskers feathers claws paws fins wings beak scary fast slow hard soft

This animal has ______________, ______________ and ______________.

It doesn't have ______________ or ______________.

What is it? It's ______________.

Score: ___ / 25

1 Listen. Then circle. (6 marks)

C:38

1 The dog has
   a sharp claws.
   b long claws.
   c soft paws.

2 Bip has
   a soft fur.
   b hard skin.
   c white fur.

3 The bird has
   a different colored wings.
   b hard wings.
   c black wings.

4 The mouse has
   a a short tail.
   b sharp claws.
   c black whiskers.

5 The animal has
   a wings.
   b fins.
   c claws.

6 Cindy likes her parrot's
   a feathers.
   b tail.
   c beak.

2 Listen and circle T = True or F = False. (6 marks)

C:39

1 Andy's favorite pet is a parrot. T / F

2 It has black feathers. T / F

3 It has a big beak. T / F

4 Its claws are green. T / F

5 Its wings are yellow and green. T / F

6 It's called Joey. T / F

3 Choose a pet and make notes. Ask and answer. (8 marks)

Do you have a pet?

What's its name?

What does your pet look like?

Does it have...?

Can it...?

Score: ___ / 20

Whole test score: ___ / 45

1 Read. Then draw. (8 marks)

1 There are two towels in the bathroom.
2 There's a closet in the bedroom.
3 There's a shelf above the tub.
4 There's a broom next to the stove.
5 There's a mirror in the bedroom.
6 There's a trash can in the bathroom. It's below the sink.
7 There are three pictures above the sofa.
8 There are two blankets on the bed.

2 Look at Activity 1 and answer. (5 marks)

1 Is the trash can next to the sink? No, it isn't. It's below the sink.
2 Are the blankets below the bed? __________
3 Is the shelf in the bathroom? __________
4 Is the closet in the bedroom? __________
5 Is the mirror above the sofa? __________
6 Are the pictures in the living room? __________

3 Read. Then match. (9 marks)

plates comb toothbrush pans pots cooker mirror shower refrigerator

bathroom **kitchen**

4 Draw your kitchen. Then write. (6 marks)

above below next to
stove sink table chairs

In my kitchen there's a __________.

____

____

____

Score: ___ / 28

4 Home

Listening and speaking

1 C:40 **Listen. Color, draw, and write. (5 marks)**

2 C:41 **Listen. Then circle. (5 marks)**

1 The picture is (next to / above) the table.

2 The piano is (opposite / next to) the sofa.

3 The trash can is (behind / in front of) the chair.

4 The broom is (next to / opposite) the cupboard.

5 There's a towel (above / below) the sink.

3 **Draw your bedroom. Then ask and answer. (8 marks)**

What's in your bedroom?

Where is / are the...?

Is / Are the...?

What color is...?

Score: ___ / 18

Whole test score: ___ / 46

5 Clothes

1 Read. Then write. (10 marks)

wool sweater tights flip-flops belt school uniform
sandals a polo shirt ski jacket shoes woolly scarf

Summer	Summer / Winter	Winter
______	______	______
______	______	______
______	______	______

2 Read and circle. (5 marks)

1 You wear this around your neck. (scarf / belt / beanie)

2 You don't need these shoes at the beach. (sandals / flip-flops / hiking boots)

3 Girls wear them with dresses when it's cold. (tights / polo shirts / sweatsuits)

4 You wear this when it's very sunny. (beanie / baseball cap / wool sweater)

5 You wear this every day at school. (ski jacket / uniform / blouse)

3 Read. Then match. (7 marks)

1 I'm	a you wearing?
2 I love my new blue	b is wearing her favorite beanie.
3 This is	c colorful socks!
4 These are	d jeans.
5 My sister	e wearing my favorite clothes.
6 What are	f my soccer boots.
7 What	g my favorite sweater.

4 Write about what you are wearing. (6 marks)

fancy plain colorful wool favorite new

I'm ______________________________.

____

I love ______________________________.

Score: ___ / 28

5 Clothes

Listening and speaking

1 **Listen. Then circle. (5 marks)** C:42

1 Jan is wearing (brown / black) hiking boots.

2 Her socks are (red and white / red and orange).

3 Jan's favorite (shirt / hat) is blue and green.

4 Her shorts are (cotton / colorful).

5 Jan is wearing a red (polo shirt / sweatshirt).

2 **Listen. Then write T = True or F = False. (8 marks)** C:43

1 Rob's favorite shorts are green. ________

His soccer socks are blue and yellow. ________

2 Becky is wearing a hat. ________

Her favorite dress is purple. ________

3 Lynda is wearing a yellow shirt. ________

She has her favorite shorts. ________

4 Richard is wearing a red scarf. ________

He isn't wearing his new sandals. ________

3 **Draw clothes on the person. Then talk. (6 marks)**

What's he / she wearing...?

He's / She's wearing...

Is he / she wearing...?

This is / These are...

Score: ___ / 19

Whole test score: ___ / 47

1 Read. Then write. (5 marks)

ball baseball fast rope taekwondo

1 run ______________________
2 jump ______________________
3 play ______________________
4 catch a ______________________
5 do ______________________

2 Read. Then check (✓) or cross (✗). (6 marks)

Kate					
Ben					

1 Kate can run, but she can't ride a bike.
2 Ben can run, and ride a bike.
3 Kate can't play tennis.
4 Ben can't climb trees.
5 Kate can play soccer, and she can climb trees.
6 Ben can play soccer, but he can't play tennis.

3 Read. Then write. (6 marks)

court slope track field pool field

1 I can play basketball at the basketball ______________________.
2 I can run at the running ______________________.
3 I can play soccer at the soccer ______________________.
4 I can bowl at the baseball ______________________.
5 I can swim at the swimming ______________________.
6 I can ski at the ski ______________________.

4 Write about your weekend. (6 marks)

was wasn't gym stadium beach school park

On Friday night, I ______________________. On Saturday ______________________.

On ______________________ I ______________________.

Score: ___ / 23

6 Sports

1 Listen. Then check (✓). (4 marks)

C:44

1 a
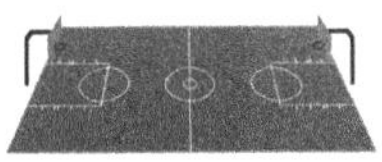
☐

b

☐

2 a

☐

b

☐

3 a

☐

b

☐

4 a

☐

b

☐

2 Listen. Then circle. (6 marks)

C:45

1 Ben (can / can't) play tennis.

2 Sue (can / can't) climb trees.

3 Ben (can / can't) catch a ball.

4 Sue (can / can't) jump.

5 Ben (can / can't) play basketball.

3 Draw pictures of what you can and can't do. Then talk. (6 marks)

Can	Can't

What can / can't you do?

Where can you...?

When do you...?

Score: ___ / 16

Whole test score: ___ / 39

7 Food

Reading and writing

1 **Unscramble and write. (6 marks)**

1 rlioocbc ______ 2 oadocavs ______

3 luetcte ______ 4 sparcoti ______

5 crerihes ______ 6 cbagabe ______

2 **Write questions. Then write your answers. (8 marks)**

1 (you / like / plums) ______? ______

2 (you / like / cucumbers) ______? ______

3 (your friend / like / mangoes) ______? ______

4 (your teacher / like / pears) ______? ______

3 **Unscramble. Write the questions and answers. (6 marks)**

1 there / is / cabbage / any ______

2 is / there / yes, ______

3 lot / there / of / a / yogurt / is ______

4 isn't / no, / there ______

5 potatoes / there / any / are ______

6 aren't / there / no, ______

4 **Draw some foods you and your friend like and don't like. Then write sentences. (6 marks)**

I like/don't like He/She likes/doesn't like

Me	My friend

______ ______

______ ______

______ ______

______ ______

Score: ___ / 26

1 Read. Listen and circle T = True or F = False. (5 marks)

C:46

1 Jack has fruit and yogurt for breakfast. T / F

2 Jack's favorite vegetables are green. T / F

3 Jack doesn't like plums. T / F

4 Jack eats healthy food for lunch. T / F

5 Jack doesn't eat a lot for dinner. T / F

2 Listen. Then match. (5 marks)

C:47

a

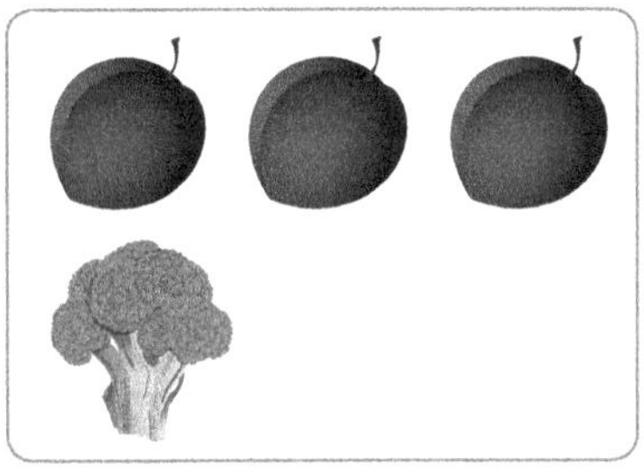

1

2

b

c

3

4

d

3 Draw your favorite lunch. Then talk. (6 marks)

What's in your lunch?

Is / Are there any...?

Do you like...?

Score: ___ / 16

Whole test score: ___ / 42

8 Things We Do

Reading and writing

1 Read. Then match. (6 marks)

a 

b 

c 

d 

e 

f 

1 drinking   2 cleaning

3 reading   4 listening

5 playing soccer   6 doing homework

2 Read. Then write. (8 marks)

1 What ______ you ______________? ____________________ washing the car.

2 What ______ he ______________? ____________________ walking to school.

3 __________ they ______________? ____________________ sleeping.

4 __________ she ______________? ____________________ eating a plum.

3 Read. Then write. (6 marks)

drink music eat bedroom homework flute

Please do your 1 ____________________. Then, 2 ____________________ lunch – it's in the kitchen – and clean your 3 ____________________. Then you can play the 4 ____________________ or listen to 5 ____________________, but do it quietly, please. Oh...and please 6 ____________________ some orange juice.

4 Draw yourself doing things at home and at school. Then write. (6 marks)

reading sleeping playing cleaning walking dancing
quietly loudly quickly slowly terribly

At home	At school

____________________   ____________________

____________________   ____________________

____________________   ____________________

____________________   ____________________

Score: ___ / 26

8 Things We Do

Listening and speaking

1 **Listen. Then check (✓). (6 marks)** C:48

1	singing	☐	sleeping	☐
2	eating pizza	☐	making pizza	☐
3	playing the flute	☐	playing the piano	☐
4	washing the car	☐	washing the dishes	☐
5	dancing to music	☐	listening to music	☐
6	playing soccer	☐	playing on the computer	☐

2 **Listen. Then write. (4 marks)** C:49

1 Ben is walking to school ______________________.

2 Sam is ______________________ loudly.

3 Sue is playing the flute. She's playing ______________________.

4 Kate is ______________________ slowly.

3 **Draw you and a friend. Then talk about what you are doing in the picture. (6 marks)**

Where are you?

What are you doing?

Are you...?

Is he / she...?

Score: ___ / 16

Whole test score: ___ / 42

Review Test 1

(Units 1 and 2) Reading and writing

1 **Read. Then match. (6 marks)**

1 What's your favorite day?
2 When were you born?
3 How many insects are there?
4 Does she have glasses?
5 Does he have dark eyebrows?
6 Do Tom and Sarah have a pet rabbit?

a Yes, he does.
b It's Wednesday.
c Yes, they do.
d No, she doesn't.
e In February.
f There are twenty-four.

2 **Read. Then write. (6 marks)**

Mushrooms [1] ________________ in forests and mountains. Flowers and plants need the sun to grow, [2] ________________ mushrooms don't. A lot of people [3] ________________ mushrooms. Some people go to the mountains and look for mushrooms. There [4] ______________ different types of mushrooms: small, big, red, brown, white. In this picture, there [5] ______________ a small red mushroom. It [6] ______________ white spots! It's pretty!

1	**a** grow	**b** growing	**c** grows	**2**	**a** and	**b** because	**c** but
3	**a** eats	**b** eat	**c** eating	**4**	**a** is	**b** are	**c** aren't
5	**a** have	**b** is	**c** are	**6**	**a** have	**b** hasn't	**c** has

3 **Read. Then write. There are two words you don't need. (6 marks)**

tree rock wind hair sky ants lips mustache

My name is Tom. I like insects like [1] ________________, but my favorite insect is the butterfly. On Saturday, I went to the park with my dad. We wanted to fly a kite but there wasn't any [2] ________________. There were clouds in the [3] ________________ and it started to rain. We sat under a [4] ________________ and waited. Then we saw a man. He was running in the rain. He came under our tree. He had long dark [5] ________________ and a big [6] ________________. He had a jar full of butterflies. When the rain stopped, he opened the jar and the butterflies flew away. It was great!

Review Test 1

(Units 1 and 2)
Reading and writing

4 **Read. Then sort. (12 marks)**

teeth short worms dark eyelashes pond
eyebrows sun roses curly mouth big

Adjectives	Nature	Body parts

5 **Read. Then write. (4 marks)**

1 What's the first day of the week? ____________________

2 Do you have short blond hair? ____________________

3 Are there any flowers in this room? ____________________

4 What does a spider look like? ____________________

6 **Write about a family member. (8 marks)**

My ...'s name is... He's/She's... He/She has... hair
He/She has... eyes He/She doesn't have...

____

____

____

____

Score: ____ / 42

Review Test 1

(Units 1 and 2) Listening and speaking

1 C:50 **Listen. Then color and draw. (5 marks)**

2 C:51 **Listen. Then circle. (5 marks)**

1 Vicky can see some (ants / worms) in the yard.

2 Jim has long (hair / eyelashes).

3 There are (three / four) beautiful butterflies.

4 The English teacher doesn't have (short hair / a short beard).

5 She has two (red / pink) roses.

3 C:52 **Listen and check (✓). (5 marks)**

1 Mr Brown has

a ☐ curly hair and a big nose.

b ☐ straight hair and small chin.

c ☐ curly hair and a small nose.

2 Helen *doesn't* have

a ☐ short, dark hair.

b ☐ long, blond hair.

c ☐ nice hair.

3 In the box, there aren't any

a ☐ ants.

b ☐ spiders.

c ☐ worms.

4 The weather is

a ☐ rainy.

b ☐ cloudy.

c ☐ sunny.

5 She doesn't have any

a ☐ purple flowers.

b ☐ yellow flowers.

c ☐ purple and yellow flowers.

4 Color five things in the picture. Then point and say. (10 marks)

This is a...

It's red/blue/ green...

It's big/small/ pretty/ugly...

I like/don't like...

5 Choose two people and describe them. (8 marks)

Score: ___ / 33

Whole test score: ___ / 75

Review Test 2

(Units 3 and 4)
Reading and writing

1 Read. Then match. (7 marks)

1	Is the computer on the table?	a	Yes, they are.
2	Are the plates on the shelf?	b	It's very cute.
3	Do you and Jack have a dog?	c	No, it isn't.
4	What does the cat look like?	d	Yes, they are.
5	Does the bird have big claws?	e	No, it doesn't.
6	Are the bird's wings green?	f	In the closet.
7	Where are the towels?	g	No, we don't.

2 Read the story. Then write 1 or 2 words to complete the sentences. (4 marks)

Peter likes animals but he doesn't have a pet. Today, Peter is very happy because he's at the zoo with Uncle Tim. They are looking at the lions and the tigers. They are Peter's favorite animals. They look scary, but Peter thinks they are cute.

There's a big tiger inside the cage. It has sharp claws, and long whiskers just like the other tigers, but it's different. "This is a White Tiger," said Uncle Tim. "Does it have soft fur? Can I touch it?" asks Peter. "No, you can't. Sorry," says the zookeeper. Peter is sad. When they leave, Uncle Tim has a present for Peter – a toy tiger! It's a white tiger, just like the real tiger in the cage.

1 Peter's ________________ ________________ are lions and tigers.

2 Peter thinks lions and tigers are ________________.

3 The big tiger's ________________ is white.

4 Peter wants to touch the tiger's ________________.

Review Test 2

(Units 3 and 4)
Reading and writing

3 **Read. Then draw and color. (8 marks)**

1 There's a bed. On the bed there's a green blanket. A closet is next to the bed. There's a blue comb under the bed.

2 This is my pet. It's a big bird. It has a long beak, and a big tail. It doesn't have claws. It has purple feathers on its head.

4 **Read. Then write. (5 marks)**

Are there any classrooms in your school? Yes, there are.

1 Is your bed in the classroom? ____________________

2 Are there any pots in your kitchen? ____________________

3 What does a parrot look like? ____________________

4 Do lions have paws and fur? ____________________

5 Does a rabbit have a hard shell? ____________________

5 **Draw an animal and write about it. (8 marks)**

tail beak claws fins whiskers
skin fur claws fast cute

____

____

____

____

Score: ___ / 32

Review Test 2

(Units 3 and 4)
Listening and speaking

1 C:53 **Listen. Draw lines from the names to the children. There are two names you don't need. (4 marks)**

Ben
Mary
Harry

Anna
Jane
Sally

2 C:54 **Listen. Then circle. (6 marks)**

1 Helen's pet doesn't have any ________________.

a spots **b** whiskers **c** fins

2 There's a big mirror ________________ the bed.

a in front of **b** next to **c** above

3 The toothbrush is below the ________________.

a mirror **b** blanket **c** towel.

4 Inside the closet, there's a ________________.

a comb **b** broom **c** picture

5 The bird is ________________.

a scary **b** cute **c** fast

6 Paul's pet is a ________________.

a cat **b** turtle **c** fish

Review Test 2

3 **Choose two animals and describe them. (10 marks)**

Is it big or small?

How many legs/wings/ fins does it have?

What color is it?

Does it have fur/claws/ a beak/whiskers?

Does it have a long/curly tail?

Do you like this animal?

4 **Choose a room and describe it. (5 marks)**

This is the ...

There's...

In this room, people...

Next to the...there's...

There are...

Score: ___ / 25

Whole test score: ___ / 57

Review Test 3

(Units 5 and 6) Reading and writing

1 Read. Then match. (6 marks)

1 What are you wearing?
2 Is your dress colorful?
3 Can Tom ride a bike?
4 Why are you wearing hiking boots?
5 These are my favorite sandals.
6 Are these your favorite sneakers?

a No, it's plain.
b I was in the mountains.
c No, they're not.
d They're really nice.
e Yes, he can.
f My school uniform.

2 Read. Then circle *Yes* or *No*. (4 marks)

I'm Lucy. It's summer and I'm wearing a red T-shirt, a white skirt, and brown sandals. I have many T-shirts, but this is my favorite. I also love colorful belts. At school, I wear a uniform. It isn't fancy, but it's comfortable. When we play soccer at school, I wear a sweatsuit. I can play soccer very well!

1 Lucy is wearing a uniform. Yes / No
2 She's wearing a white skirt. Yes / No
3 At school, Lucy wears a sweatsuit for sport. Yes / No
4 Lucy doesn't play soccer very well. Yes / No

3 Read. Then write. (4 marks)

This is Scott. He's wearing his school uniform: a shirt, pants, a [1] ____________________, and shoes. Scott can play soccer very well. He goes to the soccer [2] ____________________ every day! He also [3] ____________________ his bike to school. He's a very [4] ____________________ boy. Scott can't swim fast, but he can run fast.

1 a scarf b jacket c beanie
2 a field b court c track
3 a catches b runs c rides
4 a sick b fit c bored

4 Look and read. Then write. (6 marks)

polo shirt

sweatsuit

sandals

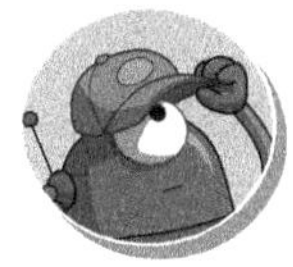
baseball cap

belt

uniform

1 You wear it when you climb, run or do sport. ______________
2 You wear this at school. It's always the same. ______________
3 You put them on your feet when you go the beach. ______________
4 You wear this around your pants or jeans. ______________
5 You put this on your head. It's a type of hat. ______________
6 It looks like a T-shirt. Girls and boys wear it. ______________

5 Read. Then write. (8 marks)

1 What are you wearing? ______________
2 Do you like colorful clothes? ______________
3 What's your favorite sport? ______________
4 Where do you play your favorite sport? ______________

6 Draw a friend. What is he/she wearing? What can he/she do? (8 marks)

Me	My friend

I'm wearing... ______________

____

I can... ______________

____

She / He is wearing... ______________

____

She / He can... ______________

____

Score: ___ / 36

Review Test 3

(Units 5 and 6)
Listening and speaking

1 C:55 **Listen. Then match. There's one extra picture. (5 marks)**

a 

b 

c 

1 Monday

2 Tuesday

3 Wednesday

4 Thursday

5 Friday

d 

f 

e 

2 C:56 **Listen. Then color and draw. (5 marks)**

Review Test 3

(Units 5 and 6)
Listening and speaking

3 **Work with a friend. Look at the pictures. Then ask and answer. (10 marks)**

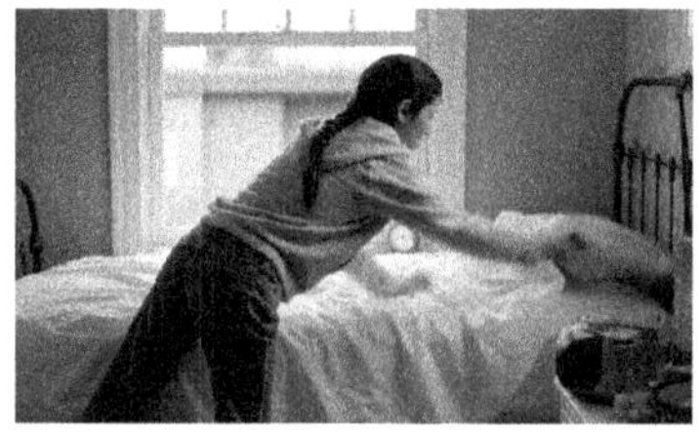

Do you wash the dishes?

What do you do to help your mom?

4 **Look at the pictures. Ask and answer about what you can/can't do. (10 marks)**

Can you...?

I can/can't...

I can..., but I can't...

Score: ___ / 30

Whole test score: ___ / 66

Review Test 4

(Units 7 and 8) Reading and writing

1 Read. Then match. There's one extra answer. (5 marks)

1 Mom: Hello, John. What are you doing?
  John: ______________________.
2 Mom: Is your sister sleeping?
  John: ______________________.
3 Mom: Oh. She's tired. Is there lettuce in the refrigerator?
  John: ______________________.
4 Mom: Do you like broccoli?
  John: ______________________.
5 Mom: OK. Can you look in the refrigerator? Are there any potatoes?
  John: ______________________.

a She's dancing and singing.
b No, there isn't, but there are cucumbers.
c I'm reading and dad is cleaning the kitchen.
d Yes, I do. Can we have some for dinner?
e No, there aren't.
f Yes, she is. On the sofa.

2 Read. Then circle *Yes* or *No*. (5 marks)

My name is Henry. On Saturdays, I wake up early. I have an orange, and a sandwich with cheese and tomato for breakfast. I have some milk too! Then, I clean my bedroom, and I play the trumpet for a bit. My sister's playing the flute now. My dad is sleeping, so she's playing quietly.

1 Henry has cereal for breakfast. Yes / No
2 He drinks orange juice on Saturday mornings. Yes / No
3 After breakfast, Henry plays music in his room. Yes / No
4 Henry's sister is playing music loudly. Yes / No

Review Test 4

(Units 7 and 8) Reading and writing

3 **Look and read. Then write. (6 marks)**

1 It's a vegetable and it's green. It looks like a small tree. ________________
2 They're small and round. They're red and sweet. ________________
3 It's green and it's long. It's good for salads. ________________
4 They're round and orange. You can make juice. ________________
5 They're brown outside. You can make French fries. ________________
6 They're purple. They're a fruit. They're good for you. ________________

4 **Read. Then write. (5 marks)**

1 What's your favorite fruit? ________________
2 What do you have for dinner? ________________
3 Do you like healthy food? ________________
4 Imagine your dad is home. What is he doing? ________________
5 Imagine it's Sunday morning. What are you doing? ________________

5 **It's Saturday night. You and your family are home. Draw a picture and write. (8 marks)**

eating reading sleeping dancing listening to music
doing homework singing playing the (piano)

Score: ___ / 29

Review Test 4

(Units 7 and 8) Listening and speaking

1 C:57 **Listen. Check (✓) the six food items Fred and Sarah need to buy. (6 marks)**

 ☐

 ☐

 ☐

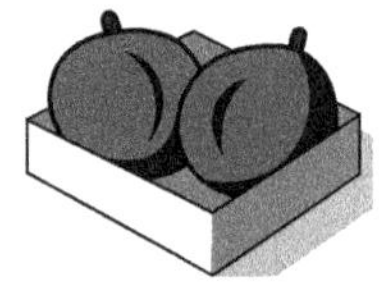 ☐

 ☐

 ☐

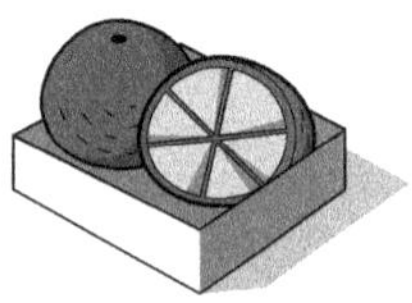 ☐

 ☐

 ☐

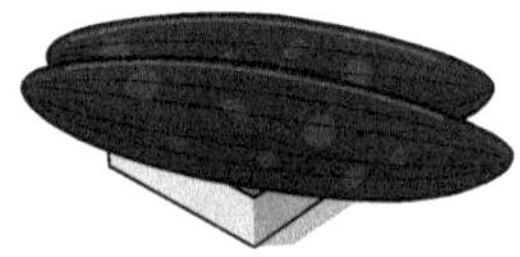 ☐

2 C:58 **Listen and check (✓). (5 marks)**

1 Anna is
- **a** ☐ dancing.
- **b** ☐ listening to music.
- **c** ☐ singing.

2 There are some
- **a** ☐ sandwiches.
- **b** ☐ cherries.
- **c** ☐ tomatoes.

3 Sarah and Emma are playing
- **a** ☐ the violin.
- **b** ☐ the flute.
- **c** ☐ trumpet.

4 The children are
- **a** ☐ drinking juice.
- **b** ☐ eating dinner.
- **c** ☐ sleeping.

5 Dad hates
- **a** ☐ broccoli.
- **b** ☐ spinach.
- **c** ☐ lettuce.

3 C:59 **Listen and circle. (4 marks)**

1 John is (sleeping / cleaning / playing the piano).

2 Mary is (playing the violin / drinking / reading).

3 There aren't any (mangoes / strawberries / pears) for the fruit salad.

4 Fred doesn't like (carrots / lettuce / spinach).

Review Test 4

(Units 7 and 8)
Listening and speaking

4 Look at the picture. Then ask and answer. (8 marks)

What's this?

Is it a...?

What are these?

Do you like...?

Are they...?

I love...

5 Look at the pictures. Then ask and answer. (8 marks)

What's he/she doing?

What are they doing?

He/She's ...ing.

They're ...ing.

Score: ___ / 31

Whole test score: ___ / 60

1 **Read. Then draw and color. (8 marks)**

Do you like my parrot? He's on a table. He's in front of a plant and next to my computer. His feathers are green, red, and blue. He has a long tail. He has a black beak and yellow claws. He's eating cherries and plums! I love my parrot!

2 **Read. Then circle. (6 marks)**

Hi, I'm Brett. I like unhealthy food like sweets and cakes, but I eat healthy food. I like all kinds of fruit except plums. I don't like them.

I'm walking to school now, and my lunch is in my backpack. There are some apricots. There's a chicken sandwich with lettuce, and some orange juice. It's a very healthy lunch!

Yesterday I was at the gym after school. I love the gym. There's a tennis court, a soccer field, and a swimming pool. I like swimming. I can swim quickly. I can play soccer too.

1 Brett doesn't like

a sweets.

b cakes.

c plums.

2 Brett is

a at the gym.

b walking to school.

c at the tennis court.

3 Brett has got

a a soccer ball.

b an unhealthy lunch.

c a backpack.

4 In his lunch there is

a a sandwich.

b an orange.

c sweets.

5 Brett likes

a reading.

b swimming.

c school.

6 Brett

a can't swim.

b can't walk.

c can play soccer.

Score: ___ / 14

End of Level Test

3 Read. Then write. (8 marks)

wash	hair	like	track	eyelashes	ants	beanie	ski

1 I was at the running ______________________ yesterday.

2 I'm wearing a ______________________, pants, and a sweatshirt.

3 Yesterday we were at a ______________________ slope. It was very cold.

4 She's got long ______________________ and green eyes.

5 He's got big brown eyes and blond ______________________.

6 I can ______________________ the dishes.

7 There are insects on the rock – spiders and ______________________.

8 What does your brother look ______________________? He's tall with black hair.

4 Write about someone in your family. (10 marks)

What's his/her name?	How old is he/she?
What does he/she look like?	What's he/she wearing?
What's his/her favorite sport?	What food does he/she like?

A person in my family

____

____

____

____

____

____

____

____

____

____

____

____

Score: ___ / 18

End of Level Test

1 C:60 **Listen. Then match. (6 marks)**

blue eyes and blond hair		red hair and brown eyes
long eyelashes	**Jack**	dark eyebrows
peaches and plums		mangoes and strawberries
playing the flute		playing the trumpet
likes soccer	**Jane**	can run
can't run fast		can ride a bike fast

2 C:61 **Listen. Then check (✓). (8 marks)**

1 broccoli ☐ potatoes ☐
oranges ☐ plums ☐

2 avocados ☐ mangoes ☐
apricots ☐ pears ☐

3 washing the dishes ☐ setting the table ☐
making the beds ☐ washing the car ☐

4 worms ☐ spider ☐
ants ☐ butterfly ☐

3 C:62 **Listen. Then write T = True or F = False. (8 marks)**

1 She's walking in her yard. ______
The pond is behind the roses. ______

2 There are mushrooms under a rock. ______
You can eat the mushrooms. ______

3 The butterfly is brown and red with black spots. ______
She's walking quickly. ______

4 Her parents have spinach and cabbages. ______
Her yard has broccoli and peas. ______

Score: ___ / 22

End of Level Test

1 Look. Talk to a friend. Find five differences. (10 marks)

above	below	next to	behind	in front of

dog table girl boy rock wearing eating writing

1

2

In my picture there is/are...

Is/Are there...?

I can/can't see...

He/She is/isn't ... ing.

Score: ___ / 10

Whole test score: ___ / 64